Ox _re_

HENRY V

edited by
Roma Gill, OBE
M.A. *Cantab.*, B. Litt. *Oxon*

OXFORD
UNIVERSITY PRESS

OXFORD
UNIVERSITY PRESS

Great Clarendon Street, Oxford, OX2 6DP, United Kingdom

Oxford University Press is a department of the University of Oxford.
It furthers the University's objective of excellence in research,
scholarship, and education by publishing worldwide. Oxford is a
registered trade mark of Oxford University Press in the UK and in
certain other countries

British Library Cataloguing in Publication Data

Data available

ISBN 978-0-19-835903-6

10 9 8 7 6 5 4 3 2 1

Printed by Bell and Bain Ltd., Glasgow

MIX
Paper from
responsible sources
FSC® C007785
www.fsc.org

Illustrations by Victor Ambrus

Cover artwork by
Katharine Asher

All photographs by Donald Cooper
(Photostage) with the exception of p150

For Cyril

Oxford School Shakespeare
edited by Roma Gill

A Midsummer Night's Dream
The Taming of the Shrew
Romeo and Juliet
Othello
As You Like It
Hamlet
Macbeth
King Lear
Julius Caesar
Henry V
The Merchant of Venice
The Winter's Tale
Henry IV Part I
Antony and Cleopatra
Twelfth Night
The Tempest
Much Ado About Nothing
Richard II
Measure for Measure
Coriolanus
Love's Labour's Lost

Contents

Introduction

About the Play

Mention *Henry V* nowadays and most people will think of a *film*—either Laurence Olivier's gallant attempt in 1944 to rally a nation exhausted by war but still intensely patriotic; or the more recent (1989) version made for a very different audience by Kenneth Branagh. In both films a distinguished actor-director with great personal charisma (and very sharp cutting-scissors) drove the action at full speed from the city of London to the walls of Harfleur and the plains of Agincourt, thence to the council-chamber of Troyes. But neither of these is Shakespeare's *play*!

Henry V was the last in a group of four related plays (a 'tetralogy') showing the fortunes of the English monarchy between 1398 and 1420. The first of these, *Richard II*, dealt with the downfall of one king and the rise of his successor. Richard II banished Henry Bullingbrook and confiscated his lands. Bullingbrook returned to England, led a rebellion against Richard (who was forced to abdicate), and was himself crowned Henry IV. His reign was restless: he was threatened constantly by insurrection, and greatly distressed by the conduct of the Prince of Wales, his only son and heir. The second part of the tetralogy, *Henry IV Part 1*, is most memorable for the royal tearaway, Prince Hal, who begins to redeem his riotous youth at the end of the play when he fights valiantly in his father's cause against the rebels. The relationship of father and son is further explored (still with the background of civil strife) in *Henry IV Part 2*. Prince Hal distances himself from his old mates, discarding the ringleader of their riots, Sir John Falstaff, and assuming the royal personality. At last he is crowned as King Henry V.

This is the second of Shakespeare's historical tetralogies; the first, mentioned by the Chorus in the closing speech of *Henry V*, consisted of *Henry VI*—in three parts—and *Richard III*. Such plays were very popular in Elizabethan England. As well as themes of perennial interest—greed, envy, lust, the struggle for power and the clash of ideologies—they were able to reveal some aspect of its past to a nation which was searching for its own identity. Henry VIII had severed all links with the Church of Rome when he declared himself head of the Church in England, and now his country was trying to find its own individuality, distinct from Europe, by learning about its history. 'What is my nation?' (3, 3, 62). Official historians, such as Raphael Holinshed, had been appointed to research the archives and to chronicle events of the past in vast tomes—but these were largely inaccessible to the multitudes (most of whom were illiterate anyway). The popular writers—ballad-makers, pamphleteers, and, above all, dramatists— found themselves with avid audiences and a plentiful supply of source material. A character in one of Ben Jonson's plays, commended for his knowledge of history, disclaimed any academic study and confessed 'I ha't from the *play-books*, And think they are more authentic' (*The Devil is an Ass*, II, iv, 13–14).

Once again, at the beginning of a new millennium, we are at a cultural crossroads. England, together with Wales, Scotland, and Northern Ireland, is a full member of the European Community. Sharing a common future, but possessed of an individual past, we should be one in spirit but distinct in character. And however this ideal may be realized, it is certain that the theatre, with dramatists past and present, will have a very large part to play.

Leading Characters in the Play

Henry V is a play with, unusually for Shakespeare, very few 'in-depth' characters. Mostly they are 'cameo' parts, where one or two pointers are given to direct the actor in his performance, but the actor himself must supply the internal motivation for what he does.

The Chorus however, seems to be more fully characterized than one might expect! The part is traditionally played by a male actor wearing a large cloak—although productions in recent years have 'modernized' him with jeans and sweater, overalls, and rehearsal clothes. His speeches show him to be excited and excitable, very enthusiastic about the events he is describing, and intensely patriotic. He would seem to be a 'gentleman' rather than a 'player': his words are addressed to the 'gentles' and to those who '*sit* and see' (Chorus 4, line 52) rather than to the groundlings who stood around the stage.

King Henry V is the character about whom we know the most. There are no secrets about his past life (as Shakespeare's Prince Hal), and we are given full details of the outward manifestation of his conversion. He is a man with a great mission—called by God (he feels) to confirm the Plantagenet dynasty on the throne of England, and to unite the kingdoms of France and England. He prays for God's guidance in all his actions; and his triumphs are always ascribed to the wonderful power of God's strength. Until the night before Agincourt (*Act 4*, Scene 1) we do not see Henry alone, and his motives might be open to misconstruction, but his soliloquy at the end of this scene leaves no room for doubt as to his personal sincerity. For the Elizabethans, Henry V was the ideal monarch, deserving of comparison only with Alexander the Great, and he featured in many other writings before Shakespeare's play. But by the turn of the century (when this play was written) the mood of the times was changing—and Shakespeare himself was becoming increasingly sceptical. As a result, the character of his Henry is capable of many interpretations.

The two churchmen are also somewhat ambiguous figures. Their respect and admiration for their new king in his conversion *seems* to be from the heart—but how much is their concern for their own Church property? Should the men of God advocate warfare? Is the Bishop of Ely any more than a 'yes-man' to the machiavellian Archbishop of Canterbury?

The English nobility are barely differentiated. Exeter, the older man, is given most responsibility in Henry's campaigns—and consequently the most lines to his part. The men closest to the king, his counsellors, are also related to him in blood: it is indeed a 'band of brothers'. They are all—except the three conspirators—honourable, trustworthy, and loyal.

The army Shakespeare's introduction of the four captains is unhistorical—but it may have been politically diplomatic and prophetic, anticipating the formation of the United Kingdom. He uses the captains to provide light comic relief with their squabbling, but the issues they raise are quickly abandoned. The English captain is characterized by his quiet reserve; the Scot is taciturn; and the Irish captain is impetuous. Only Llewellyn is developed into a full personality, staunchly defending his nation and his king—whom he greets as a fellow Welshman. He is old-fashioned, strict on the subject of military etiquette—and romantically sentimental. Early editions of the play spell his name phonetically as 'Fluellen'.

The private soldiers, weary of fighting with danger and trudging through the mud of France, are critical of their leader but mindful of their duty. By giving them personal names (rather than referring simply to '1 Soldier' etc.), Shakespeare insists that they are all individuals.

The Eastcheap mob are fairly static characters who have changed little since their first appearance as the companions of Prince Hal. Bardolph's red nose is as spectacular as it ever was, and his end—he is hanged for pilfering—was predicted in *Henry IV Part 1*. Pistol 'swaggers' as much as he did in *Henry IV Part 2*, strong in words and threats but empty of deeds. He sees himself as an epic warrior, but comes at last to a bleak reality of destitution, losing even the ransom money promised by his French captive when the prisoners' throats are cut. Mistress Quickly makes a brief appearance with her elegiac account of the death of Falstaff—but she is needed in this play only as a reporter and not for her character. Falstaff's Boy—the page given to him by Prince Hal in *Henry IV Part 2*—is streetwise, and sees his companions for what they really are.

The French monarchy Contrary to his sources (which suggest that Charles VI was incompetent and even insane) Shakespeare presents the French king as a judicious monarch who takes the English threat very seriously, controlling his son, the scornful Dauphin, with a firm hand. The part of Katherine, his daughter, is a tricky one for the actress—just as it was indeed for the real princess! Knowing that it is her destiny to marry the English king, Katherine must act out the wooing scene as though she were free to choose or reject her lover, and make a personal relationship out of a political alliance.

The French nobility are shown collectively as being frivolous and boastful—although they are perhaps a little more distinguishable than their English counterparts. Bourbon is the one who excels in silliness on the night before Agincourt (*Act 3*, Scene 8). In the Folio text the lines here assigned to Bourbon are spoken by the Dauphin, and they certainly seem more appropriate for the sender of the tennis balls; but in historical fact the Dauphin was not present at the battle of Agincourt, and in *Act 3*, Scene 6 of the play Shakespeare's character is expressly ordered to remain in Rouen. Burgundy stands out from the rest in honour and dignity, partly because he was historically not of the French king's party but the ruler of an independent power—and therefore best able to act as a go-between at the Council of Troyes.

Montjoy the French herald, is given unusual opportunities to develop a relationship with King Henry. His manner changes from armed neutrality to an almost affectionate respect.

Family Tree : *French and English Royal Families*

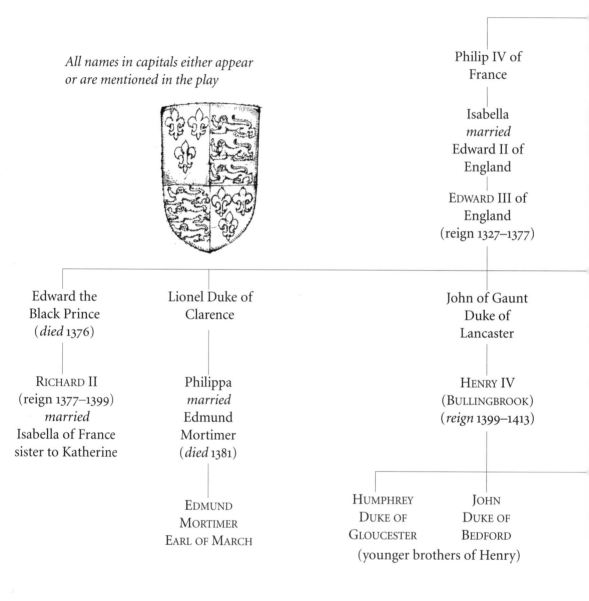

*All names in capitals either appear
or are mentioned in the play*

Philip IV of
France

Isabella
married
Edward II of
England

EDWARD III of
England
(reign 1327–1377)

Edward the
Black Prince
(*died* 1376)

Lionel Duke of
Clarence

John of Gaunt
Duke of
Lancaster

RICHARD II
(reign 1377–1399)
married
Isabella of France
sister to Katherine

Philippa
married
Edmund
Mortimer
(*died* 1381)

HENRY IV
(BULLINGBROOK)
(*reign* 1399–1413)

EDMUND
MORTIMER
EARL OF MARCH

HUMPHREY
DUKE OF
GLOUCESTER

JOHN
DUKE OF
BEDFORD
(younger brothers of Henry)

Philip III of
France

Philip VI
(*reign* 1328–1350)

John II

Edmund
Duke of York

Charles V

RICHARD
EARL OF
CAMBRIDGE
(*died* 1415)

CHARLES VI
(*reign* 1380–1422)

HENRY V ——————— *married* ——————— PRINCESS
(*reign* 1413–1422)   KATHERINE

HENRY VI
(*reign* 1422–1471)

Synopsis

Henry V: commentary

Act 1

Prologue   The 'Chorus' (a part traditionally played by a single male actor, wearing a large cloak) begins a tale of epic dimensions, using language in the 'grand style' appropriate for such an exalted theme. But his tone soon changes as he reminds the audience where they really are, in the little 'wooden O' made by the circular walls of the playhouse. Yet these can be transcended if the audience will only put their imaginations to work!

The Chorus manipulates audience response through the words and rhythms of his speech, contrasting the simple 'cockpit' with the 'vasty fields of France' and the poor 'crooked figure' with 'a million'. In the first eight lines the verse builds up to the horrific vision of a conqueror who can bring total devastation with 'famine, sword, and fire'; and then, with a strongly marked pause (a 'caesura') in the middle of one line, drops down to a humble confession of the actors' unworthiness: 'pardon, gentles all'.

And now, like the 'warm-up man' in a modern television studio, he begins to stir up his hearers to participate in the action, with himself as their guide.

Scene 1   Having prepared ourselves mentally for the excitement of a battle, it is rather disconcerting to find that we are now eavesdropping on a private and highly confidential conversation between two eminent churchmen. They are discussing the perennial problem of money! Church property before the Reformation was enormous, and much of it (having been bequeathed by legacy) was exempt from tax. Successive governments tried to wrest some of this wealth for themselves, to pay for national debts—and now these efforts are being renewed. The Archbishop of Canterbury, head of the Church in England, is acutely aware of the situation, but he has also got hopes of the new king. With awe and wonder he describes the change that has come over the wild Prince Hal since he ascended the throne of England after his father's death. Canterbury's language comes from the Bible and the Prayer Book, presenting the king's reformation as a religious conversion. Henry has become a model of learning, wisdom, temperance, and prudence—the ideal monarch.

Although it is undramatic, the speech, which has the approval of the Bishop of Ely, serves to prepare the audience to receive his gracious majesty, King Henry V. Regular theatre-goers would remember, and Shakespeare intends that they *should* remember, the impact made by Prince Hal and his unruly comrades in the two *Henry IV* plays; but they must now believe in the transformation that has been accomplished.

As well as accepting, reverencing, and applauding the change that has come over the new king, the Archbishop of Canterbury has also found a means of solving the royal economic difficulties—without damaging the Church's own finances!

Scene 2   In the previous scene the archbishop spoke of some property in France—perhaps even extending as far as the French throne—which the English king might rightfully claim as his own. Now Canterbury comes into the royal presence to explain himself. King Henry is conscious of the seriousness of the enterprise, and the probable cost in human lives if he were to pursue his claim. Is the warfare justified? The archbishop must examine his conscience before he gives the king an answer, and speak with all religious sincerity.

The king speaks in measured terms, in a regular formal blank verse; and the archbishop replies in the same manner. His researches have been thorough, and the results are presented in meticulous detail as he expounds the Salic law and the fallacy that has deprived the English crown of territory that properly belongs to it. He points out that the Salic land is not in France at all, but is a French possession in Germany (between the rivers Elbe and Sala). He argues, moreover, that three French kings have themselves asserted their rights to the crown by claiming descent through a female line—which is precisely what is now being *denied* to Henry.

It is reassuring to know that Henry's claims can be thus validated—but for the reader the archbishop's speech seems tedious and long-winded, whilst in performance the director must decide how to keep his audience entertained.

In Olivier's film the scene was played as comedy, where a flustered archbishop was encumbered with massive volumes of untidy manuscripts and impeded by scurrying clerics. But this is surely wrong! Shakespeare's character may be verbose, but he is by no means stupid. And although he is being a little devious in turning the king's attention towards France (and consequently away from Church financial affairs), he is a sincere and loyal churchman.

Kenneth Branagh's recent film was, I think, closer to Shakespeare's intentions. This shows a well-briefed archbishop expounding his case, in all its precise legalistic details, to a bewildered audience until eventually the king, no less confused than are his peers, cuts through the verbiage with a curt question:

> May I with right and conscience make this claim?

The question is answered in the affirmative. Canterbury brings the authority of Holy Writ (the Book of Numbers) to endorse his thesis, and urges a precedent in the battle of Crécy (1346), when Edward III and his son, the Black Prince, conquered the French and captured Calais. The other nobles, as if brought to life by a magic touch, join the churchmen in urging the king to fight. Henry still demurs, mindful now of the threat posed by the Scots, who, as they have always done, will maraud into England as soon as the country's defences are removed. His counsellors answer all Henry's objections until at last the Archbishop of Canterbury, taking up a remark from the Duke of Exeter, delivers a speech that is almost a sermon on the subject of the well-ordered state.

Exeter compares the state to a piece of music: the high and the low—both notes in music or human beings in their social ranks—combine to form one perfect harmony. The archbishop develops this notion, using the analogy (first proposed by the Roman poet Virgil) of a beehive, where each individual cheerfully performs the allotted task to the benefit of the whole colony. This leads to the conclusion that it is the king's *duty* to go to war, a moral obligation upon him for the good of his country, 'your happy England'.

Whether or not this poetic argument (commonplace in the sixteenth century) has any force on him, Henry at the end of the oration is fully resolved on action, and he declares his mind with bravura; 'France being ours, we'll bend it to our awe, Or break it all to pieces'.

Calling in the French ambassadors, he listens to the Dauphin's contemptuous message which taunts him by recalling his licentious past. Even the messengers are embarrassed, but Henry, unruffled, replies with a dangerously icy calm that returns the 'tennis ball' image back to the server. Henry's anger, like his other passions, is 'fetter'd' (line 243)—but his spirit is now aroused. Hitherto in this play he has been a man of few words, but here the kingly lion is stretching his limbs and showing what he is made of. He admits the 'barbarous licence' of his 'wilder days', his neglect and under-valuation of 'this poor seat of England', but he promises henceforth to be 'like a king' and show a 'sail of greatness'. The humility of his confession makes us—and the French ambassadors—take his threats very seriously. The man means what he says!

Shakespeare has here made a significant alteration to the history as it was reported by Holinshed, who says that the 'tennis balls' incident occurred *before* the king had determined to fight for his rights and pursue his claim as far as the throne of France. By making this change Shakespeare ensures that there can be no suspicion that Henry's decision was in any way affected by the personal insult, which is only a spur to urge him forward. The incident also prepares us—audience and readers—to greet the French with hostility. The Dauphin is the immediate target.

After the departure, in silence, of the ambassadors, the tense atmosphere is eased by Exeter's wry comment: 'This was a merry message'. Henry is now businesslike, calling for action—'with reasonable swiftness'. But he does not forget the vocational aspect of his expedition:

> God before,
> We'll chide this Dauphin at his father's door.

With God helping them, the mission will be divinely sanctioned and will indeed be a *fair* action. Rhyming couplets bring the episode, the scene, and the whole first movement of the play to a neat conclusion.

ACT 2

Chorus   The Chorus returns, eager to tell us of the intense wave of patriotic fervour that is sweeping England. But not all men are loyal. We hear of treachery which must be foiled—or else all will be lost! Carried away by the magnitude of the events he is relating—and by his own importance and cleverness as narrator—the Chorus becomes melodramatic, with a rhetorical question addressed to 'O England'. His word-play ('kind and natural', 'hollow bosoms', 'gilt'/'guilt') gets increasingly self-conscious, and he almost giggles as he assures the audience that in the imaginary sea-crossings between England and France the play will not 'offend one stomach'.

Scene 1   Although, as we learned from the Chorus, 'The king is set from London', the setting of this scene is still within the city—in one of London's most seedy areas, a 'red light' district, where street-violence was common.

Henry IV Part 1 showed this as one of the favourite haunts of Prince Hal, before he became Henry V, and the characters who now assemble belong to the past he has so decisively rejected. By turns squabbling, threatening, joking, and grumbling, they speak a language which is all their own, made up of thieves' cant, bawdy innuendo, vulgarisms, and clichés, and enlightened with snatches of popular songs. Their words—those of Nym especially—often have no precise meanings. Intonation says it all.

Absent from the company is the man who was once the ringleader in mischief, Sir John Falstaff, but his presence is strongly felt. He was the personification of lawlessness, disorder, and misrule—but in another aspect he also represented carefree pleasure, comradeship, and, in a word, fun. All that is past. Now Falstaff is dying, and a few shabby ruffians are all that remain of the life he embodied.

When Henry was newly crowned, he refused to acknowledge Falstaff and publicly rejected his claim for friendship—and also the association with his former mates. We must agree that these are most undesirable companions for a king of England; a knowing audience—those familiar with Prince Hal from *Henry IV Parts 1* and *2*—should feel glad that he is no longer part of such a low-life fraternity. They should rejoice, like the bishops and the nobles, in the reformation (which he had always promised), and look forward to seeing 'what use' he has made of his 'wilder days' (1, 2, 267–8) and yet . . . These characters seem to have a warmth that has so far been lacking in the play. They care about each other, and their quick, unruly passions are a welcome contrast to the deliberate calculations of the politicians.

The news of Falstaff's sickness is sobering, and the Hostess's accusation, coming so suddenly, casts a different light on King Henry's much praised reformation. Falstaff is very ill: 'The king has killed his heart'. At the end of the scene Nym's criticism, though imperfectly articulated, cannot pass unnoticed: 'The king is a good king, but it must be as it may. He passes some humours and careers'.

Scene 2 Time has passed whilst we lingered in Eastcheap—long enough for the king to have journeyed as far as Southampton. Before he himself appears, we are given some preparation for the scene that will take place. Although Bedford and Westmorland seem apprehensive, Exeter is confident that the king is fully in control of the situation.

Trumpets sound, and Henry enters with three men who seem to be his very close friends. Apparently he sets great store by their judgements and their loyalty, and each of them, in turn, affirms his devotion to the king and his cause. Reassured, Henry turns his attention to a minor misdemeanour—verbal abuse from a drunken man. The king is ready to pardon the man, but Scroop, Cambridge, and Gray counsel against such clemency and recommend 'much correction' for the offender, 'lest example Breed by his sufferance more of such a kind'. Henry thanks them for their advice, but for the moment he ignores it and the drunkard is set free. The king turns to more weighty business.

Cambridge, Scroop, and Gray are to rule the kingdom during the king's absence in France, and they are now given the official documents which should—or so they expect—detail the extent of their powers and responsibilities. But when they read the papers they find themselves indicted of the most heinous treachery. They have taken bribes from the French to murder King Henry, and (although little is made of this in the play) they are hoping by Henry's death to secure the throne for the Earl of March and then, since March has no children, for the descendants of the Earl of Cambridge (see 'Family Tree', p. x). In fact the Earl of March himself was loyal to the king—and it was he who revealed the plot to Henry.

The guilty traitors confess their crimes and beg for mercy—but they stand condemned out of their own mouths: the king metes out their punishment with the same strict justice that they themselves recommended for the abusive drunkard. The treachery of Cambridge and Gray angered the king, but he is most cruelly hurt by Lord Scroop's betrayal of his friendship. He denounces Scroop with a passion such as we have never heard from this otherwise self-controlled king: repeated rhetorical questions build to a climax of emotion which dissolves into tears.

With a few words of cold prose, Exeter makes a formal arrest to which all the traitors react with signs of relief, appearing glad that they have been prevented from acting out their own evil schemes. Henry, once more in full possession of himself, briefly points out what would have been the consequences of their crime, not for himself alone, but for his entire kingdom. Sentences of death are pronounced, and the king moves off to war. Surely, he argues, this timely discovery of the conspiracy must be a sign that God is in favour of the expedition.

The director of a production, the actor playing the part of Henry V, or the solitary reader, must determine the extent to which the king is in control of this scene. He instructed the three traitors to expect that their 'commissions' would be given to them now (see line 61), and clearly he introduced the subject of the drunkard to allow them to sentence themselves. But in the denunciation of Lord Scroop—how much of his passion is performance?

Scene 3   Whilst the king's party sets sail boldly from Southampton, a less heroic bunch of warriors in Eastcheap is preparing to follow him. They are leaving behind them a past life that has died with Sir John Falstaff, and they listen in silence to the Hostess's account of the knight's death. They must have heard her words many times already. She speaks a poetic elegy in which her simple grief is emphasized by those idiosyncrasies of her language which, at other times, are so amusing—the homely wisdom ('at turning of the tide'), the mistaken allusions ('Arthur' for 'Abraham') and the 'malapropisms' (verbal misapprehensions—such as 'in carnation' for 'incarnate', 'rheumatic' when she intends 'lunatic'). At last, after brief words of parting, the men begin their trudge to Southampton.

Scene 4   Across the channel the French are preparing to resist the threatened invasion. The French king is taking all precautions, being mindful of previous Anglo-French engagements, but the Dauphin makes light of his fears. He scoffs at the English king, seeing only the wild Prince Hal (whom he insulted with his gift of tennis balls in *Act 1, Scene 2*) and refusing to recognize the reformed King Henry.

In the Dauphin's mind is a picture of the parody king of English folk-festivals, but the French king and the Constable, older and wiser men, are thinking of distinguished precedents—the early Roman Brutus, and the almost legendary Black Prince of England, who was Henry's ancestor. To the French king the English seem as fighting-dogs, bred from a 'bloody (= bloodthirsty) strain' and trained ('flesh'd') on the meat they are to kill. To the Dauphin they are merely 'coward dogs' who make a lot of noise but who will turn tail and run as soon as they meet any resistance.

Exeter comes as the English ambassador—the situation is grave enough to warrant a member of the royal family to perform this function. He makes his demands in formal language, invoking all laws, divine as well as human and international, to sanction Henry's claim to the French throne. And if the king of France will not yield? In calm, measured tones Exeter declares the full horrors of war, and his almost matter-of-fact description makes the threat sound very, very real.

ACT 3

Chorus   The Chorus now has the immediacy of a 'live' outside-broadcast on television news: we see through his eyes as through a video-camera. First we focus on the royal party as the king embarks at Southampton Pier, all flags flying. Henry is showing himself in all his glorious majesty—and the rising sun is a most fitting comparison. We watch the ship-boys who swarm up the rigging to unfurl the great sails, and we can even hear the bo'sun's pipe which gives the orders. The sails billow out and the huge galleons move off. This is (as the Chorus presents it) truly heroic action, and it is impossible to resist the exhortation to become part of it and join the expedition—especially when we look back at sleepy old England!

Before we know it, we are in France and laying siege to Harfleur. The graphic details of cannon pointing at the city speak their threats as eloquently to a twentieth-century mind as ever they could to Shakespeare's audience.

A 'news-flash' of information comes to let us know the official response to the demands made by Exeter in the previous scene. Understandably, the French king is refusing to surrender his crown—but he is willing to compromise with Henry, offering his daughter's hand in marriage (which would secure the throne of France for Henry's descendants) and, as a dowry for her, certain 'dukedoms' (which were described as 'almost kingly' in 1, 2, 227 but which are now despised as 'petty and unprofitable'). The offer has been rejected, and war is declared. As the Chorus is speaking, we hear the sound of cannonfire.

The speech sounds urgent and impassioned; strong, active verbs and frequent alliterations hurry the lines along at a great pace.

Scene 1   The stage should be alive with frenzied activity (or the impression of this) as soldiers with weapons and ladders charge the breach the artillery has made in the city wall at Harfleur. But their first assault has failed, and they are now in retreat.

Henry rallies his troops, speaking first to the commanders of the campaign (and perhaps meaning particularly the three lords who accompany him). His 'dear friends' now, they must adopt the monstrous appearance of fighting machines. The 'noble English' (the knights and cavalry officers) are reminded of their forefathers, war heroes who must not be betrayed by their descendants: don't let the side down—and set a good example to the men who are (both socially and in military terms) beneath you! The common soldiers, 'men of grosser blood', are not forgotten. Henry speaks to the 'yeomen of England' in the language of farmstock—the language that they, as countrymen, ought to appreciate. The exhortations are effective, and the king leads a fresh assault on Harfleur.

The scene—merely an oration spoken against a background of activity—shows us yet another aspect of this new Henry. Here he is the military leader, the inspiration of his soldiers, who must be able at once to persuade, flatter, and stir up to action. With one of the most famous of opening lines, the speech is by no means easy to deliver!

Scene 2   Once again, the earlier heroics of the flag-waving Chorus and the militaristic king seem to be deflated by the baser realities. Although Bardolph has caught something of the spirit of Henry's fervour, Nym and Pistol are resistant. Nym is frightened and Pistol is too much of a coward to go anywhere near the fighting. The Welsh captain Llewellyn, making his first appearance in the play, rounds them up and drives them to where the action is. The Boy remains behind, alone on the stage. He knows and despises all three—braggarts, cowards, and petty thieves. Any sympathy the audience might remember for these former companions of Sir John Falstaff (and associates of Prince Hal) is quickly being dispersed.

Scene 3   There is still another aspect of war that has not yet been touched upon—the point of view of the professionals. The trio that comes before us now—the Welshman, the Irishman, and the Scotsman—are all of them experienced soldiers.

These three nations were all represented in Henry's French campaigns, and in the Folio text the characters are identified simply as 'Welch', 'Irish', and 'Scot'. Shakespeare has used the national speech-habits to give each man a separate voice—and they all have different ideas about the proper way to do things. Shakespeare does not find the Welsh accent difficult to imitate: a single phrase ('look you'), a few unusual grammatical forms ('is' for 'are', 'is digged' for 'has dug'), and the fairly regular *p/b* substitution are all that is necessary. Llewellyn is formal and old-fashioned, as his language ('beseech', 'vouchsafe') shows; and he works strictly by the book—perhaps even using Thomas Digges's *Stratioticos*, a volume which describes the classical battles of the ancient Romans and their 'disciplines of war'.[1] Llewellyn has no regard for the Irish captain who, he suspects, 'will plow up all, if there is not better directions'.

Macmorris himself is near to panic and throws up his hands in despair: 'there ish nothing done, so Christ sa' me law'. For 'the Scots captain', however, Llewellyn has nothing but praise: 'Captain Jamy is a marvellous falorous gentleman . . . and of great expedition and knowledge in th'ancient wars'. Jamy is a man of few words, but his

---

[1] This book was re-issued in 1590 by a Stratford man, Richard Field, who subsequently published Shakespeare's poems.

resolution is certain: 'I'll dee guid service, or I'll lig i'the grund for it'. A quarrel is being threatened, but the trumpet-call sounds a truce: for the present, all hostilities will be postponed.

The little episode has served to introduce to the audience three new characters—who will take the places of Bardolph, Nym, and Pistol in providing some prose entertainment and light relief from the epic seriousness.

Scene 4   Henry seems now to have become the bloody-minded fighting monster that he himself described. His threat of the horrors of war is terrible, depicting brutal soldiers who rape and massacre, uncontrolled in their destructive rage which spares no one: old men and infants alike, both mothers and daughters. Thanks to Henry's gracious restraint, the air is clear now; but in a moment, unless the French will yield, it will be dark and thick with gunsmoke and the screams of the victims. Once again, the twenty-first-century audience/reader—educated by television—knows even better than Shakespeare's first audiences that what Henry describes is all too possible. It is frightening to think that one man can unleash such forces!

From the walls of Harfleur (or, in theatre terms, the balcony at the back of the stage), the Governor concedes defeat: the Dauphin has disappointed them, and now the city is at the mercy of the English king. Shakespeare's King Henry is more generous than his historical counterpart. Setting Exeter in command, he orders 'Use mercy to them all': Holinshed reports that in reality the town was ransacked. No victory was more easily won!

The English, when they are rested, will retire to Calais—which at this time was an English possession.

Scene 5   A complete and most welcome change. From the outdoor, very 'masculine', atmosphere of the previous scenes we go inside to the enclosed and 'feminine' world of the French court where the princess (already conscious of her destiny) is learning about the English language from her lady-in-waiting—whose own knowledge is rather uncertain! The parts of speech for the parts of the body meet with girlish giggles. By learning the new language, the princess is preparing to begin a new life.

Scene 6   At the French king's court, things are beginning to look serious. The king himself speaks little, allowing his nobles to give their opinions. The French lords are proud, despising the English as a 'barbarous people' who live in a 'nook-shotten isle' with a disgusting climate, 'foggy, raw and dull'! Even their national drink, 'sodden [boiled] water' making 'barley-broth', is not fit to be compared with the wine which gives spirit to the blood in France. Honour demands that the French lords must demonstrate their superiority in birth, breeding, and manhood. Occasional phrases such as '*O Dieu vivant*', '*Mort de ma vie*' are enough to sketch in the foreign language.

Having heard the counsel of the lords, who are shamed into unanimity, the king responds with an impressive roll-call of French nobility—and a complicated image that likens his forces to an avalanche that will quite overwhelm the English invaders. Confident of victory, the French prepare to fight—but the Dauphin is forbidden to join in the fun.

Scene 7   There has been a skirmish on the road to Calais where the French were trying to block the English retreat by breaking down a bridge over the river Ternoise. The fighting is now over; the French are defeated; and the Duke of Exeter is in command (although according to Holinshed he did not re-join the king until the action reached Agincourt).

Llewellyn speaks highly of the duke, and singles out for high praise 'an ancient lieutenant' who has done 'gallant service'. But when we hear his name, we recognize the man (who comes on to the stage) as the loud-mouthed braggart from Eastcheap—all word and no deed. But Pistol has a heart, and he pleads now for Bardolph. That incurable thief—no more than a petty pilferer (we remember the Boy's observation in Scene 2)—has stolen again. Military rules are strict and must be obeyed: Bardolph must die. Pistol, with a rude gesture, quits the scene.

The incident is based on Holinshed's Chronicles, which describe how

> in this great necessity, the poor people of the country were not spoiled, nor any thing taken of them without payment, nor any outrage or offence done by the Englishmen, except one, which was, that a soldier took a pix out of a church, for which he was apprehended, and the king not once removed [from the place] till the box was restored, and the offender strangled.

Shakespeare, identifying the soldier with his fictional character Bardolph, has changed the 'pix', a box holding communion wafers, to a 'pax', a plate—less valuable and less sacred—kissed by the communicants. With a quick stroke he dismisses another part of the king's youth. When Henry is told of Bardolph's crime and punishment, he is apparently unmoved: 'We would have all such offenders so cut off'.

As though to allow Henry to demonstrate afresh his new personality, the French herald brings another challenge. Its wording is contemptuous, but it is spoken 'fairly', and the king answers with dignity and courage: the English are in no fit state to fight, but they will not refuse the French challenge. Everything is in God's hand.

Scene 8   The French lords are restive, eager to join battle with the English. Time passes slowly for them, enlivened only by Bourbon's rhapsody on his horse, which is almost a formal rhetorical exercise. His companions tease him—and when he has gone out they scoff at Bourbon's empty boasting. But they are confident of victory.

Act 4

Like the previous one, this act is made up of cross-cutting scenes that move the audience into different parts of the field and show contrasting attitudes to warfare in general and to the battle of Agincourt in particular.

Chorus   Now the Chorus beckons us conspiratorially to come to the battlefield. We must create darkness in our imaginations (in the Elizabethan theatre all performances took place in the afternoon), and peer through the night, lit by the occasional campfire, to see the army preparing for the next day's fighting. All is still—but we become aware of a hum of activity. Noises sound louder at night—the neighing of war-horses, the clunk of hammers, the rasp of metal against metal. The sound of the words echoes their sense: 'creeping murmur', 'hum . . . stilly sounds', 'high . . . neighs Piercing'. Every word in this speech adds to the picture in sight and sound.

The Chorus seems to speak louder now, contrasting the two armies who wait, with such different expectations, for morning. Although the night, personified as 'a foul and ugly witch', fills all his men with foreboding, the English king appears unaffected. His presence amongst them gives comfort, light, and life: the royal sun shines on all alike.

Scene 1   Henry is fully aware of the danger of the situation, but although he can admit this to his nobles he must show no signs of panic. He moralizes on the subject, 'gather[ing] honey from the weed' to 'make a moral of the devil himself'. Gloucester and Erpingham listen dutifully and then Henry, disguised under Erpingham's cloak, embarks on a 'walkabout'.

His first encounter is with Pistol, who attempts to 'pull rank' as an 'ancient' or standard-bearer (= second lieutenant). Pistol's hostility to Llewellyn is re-introduced, but there is no doubt where our sympathies should lie—especially after Henry's comment:

> Though it appear a little out of fashion,
> There is much care and valour in this Welshman.

So far there has been nothing to worry the king. But three common soldiers (who, unusually for Shakespeare, are given individual names) raise serious problems. How far is a king responsible to and for his subjects? What are the subject's duties to the king, to his own family, to his own soul, and to God? Disobedience to the king is disobedience to God—because the king is God's deputy on earth. But if the king's cause is not just ...?

Henry tries to make the soldiers understand that the king is a man just the same as they are, but they are unconvinced. Accepting a challenge from Williams, Henry watches the soldiers depart and, alone on the stage, meditates on the lonely burden that a king must bear and the inadequacy of empty ceremonious formalities to compensate.

This is the central scene of the play: all the issues seem to come to a head here, and for the moment they are resolved—insofar as they are capable of resolution—in Henry's final prayer. We can now appreciate what has been always at the back of his mind—and which is perhaps the real reason for this entire campaign: Henry's insecurity on the throne! Again we are reminded that Henry, guiltless himself, owes his crown to the murder by Henry Bullingbrook (Henry IV) of Richard II.

Scene 2   In the opposing camp the French are excitedly waiting for the battle to commence. They are fresh, in tiptop condition, and scornful of the pathetic band of British soldiers. Sickness—dysentery—had taken its toll of Henry's army even before the siege of Harfleur; and the march to Calais had taken twice as long as expected. By the time they reached Agincourt the men were exhausted—cold, wet, hungry, and ill—and their horses were in no better state. The French gloat over their expected victims.

Scene 3   The English nobles reckon up the odds against them. The actual numbers are in dispute, but it is certain that the English were heavily outnumbered (perhaps by as many as 30,000 French against 7,000 English). The king enters just in time to hear Westmorland longing for reinforcements. The great speech that follows is one of the finest dramatic expressions of military patriotism, and celebrates the achievements—as yet unaccomplished—of the 'few': 'We few, we happy few, we band of brothers'. Henry anticipates the festive celebrations that will annually commemorate the glorious victory. Those who fought at Agincourt will be united in a blood brotherhood that will transcend all the social barriers that divide 'high and low and lower' (1, 2, 180).

Westmorland is convinced. Now the English are ready to fight—but the French herald interrupts with yet another insulting demand for the king's ransom. Henry, enraged, sends back a proud retort which Montjoy, the herald, hears with respect and addresses him for the first time as 'King Harry'. The quickest of prayers, 'how Thou pleasest, God' ('Thy will be done'), and the battle is on.

Scene 4   The first sign of victory is a parody of conquest: Pistol has captured an unfortunate Frenchman—who is an even greater coward than Pistol and will plead and flatter and *pay* to save his life. The Boy scornfully translates Pistol's empty threats and, before he leaves the stage, makes the apparently irrelevant observation that the English camp is unprotected: 'there is none to guard it but boys'.

Scene 5   With disgust and shame the French nobles contemplate their overthrow, determining to re-join the battle and die with some honour rather than live with such disgrace. Their resolution, because it is expressed with such exaggerated language, is laughable rather than heroic.

Scene 6   The English take time for a moment's grief. Hearing a trumpet, Henry assumes that the French must be about to make a renewed onslaught and, contrary to all conventions of warfare, orders his soldiers to kill their prisoners.

Scene 7   Llewellyn has just heard of an outrage 'against the law of arms' committed by the French, who have murdered innocent civilians and looted the English tents (now we understand the Boy's comment in Scene 4). Lines of communication seem to have crossed—Gower believes that the king had ordered the killing of all prisoners as a form of retaliation, and he applauds the deed as 'most worthily' done by 'a gallant king'. Llewellyn joins in his praise of Henry, reiterating the comparison (see 1, 1, 46) with the classical model of conquering kings, Alexander the Great. Even the rejection of Falstaff by the newly-crowned King Henry V (see 2, 1, 76 note) is seen by Llewellyn to have its counterpart in the life of Alexander. But Henry was, as the Welshman himself recalls, 'in his right wits and his good judgements' when he 'turned away the fat knight with the great belly doublet'.

It is interesting that Shakespeare chooses this moment of Henry's greatest triumph to remind us of the price that had to be paid in personal relationships. Prince Hal could only become Henry V by sacrificing his friend—and renouncing all that Falstaff represented.

Another crossed line! The king has only just learned of the massacre of the boys in the camp. His claim to have his emotions well under control (see 1, 2, 242–3) is momentarily forgotten, and he is now very angry and threatens the French. His language is strong and confident: the alliteration—'skirr away as swift as stones'—makes the task sound easy. Again he orders (apparently for the first time) that the prisoners' throats are to be cut.

The English herald departs—but meets the returning French herald, who presents a very different appearance, 'His eyes are humbler than they used to be'. Henry, still angry, assumes that this is another ransom demand, but Montjoy is submissive now, asking permission for the French to rescue the bodies of their dead—who even in death must observe social distinctions. As though taken by surprise, Henry can only ask who has won the battle!

A kind of light relief is needed here to relax after the tensions of fighting. The king turns to Llewellyn, and they rejoice in their Welsh kinship. Henry, when he was Prince Hal, was fond of practical jokes, and he now sets up a duel (which was in fact prepared for earlier—in Scene 1—when he walked through the camp the previous night).

Scene 8   The joke continues, involving more people. The soldiers' loyalty is praiseworthy, and it seems hard that Henry should take such pleasure in the discomfiture of Williams and the embarrassment of the officers. Williams is dignified in his reproach to the king and in his refusal of the shilling offered by Llewellyn in imitation of the royal gesture. All's well that ends well—but class distinctions, abandoned before Agincourt, seem to be returning: Williams is now 'this fellow'.

The French and English casualty lists are compared. The French seem to have lost more noblemen than common soldiers—truly 'a royal fellowship of death'. The English, however, are almost unscathed: only five men 'of name', and no more than twenty-five 'other men' (the total is taken from Holinshed's reckoning—although the historian remarks that other estimates of the dead range between one hundred and six hundred). God's is the glory, and His must be the praise. Insisting on this, and claiming a victory won 'without stratagem', Shakespeare's king ignores the role of military tactics and the 'politic invention' described by Holinshed whereby Henry

> sent privily two hundred archers into a low meadow which was near to the vanguard of his enemies, but separated with a great ditch, commanding them there to keep themselves close till they had a token to them given, to let drive at their adversaries . . . [and] he caused stakes bound with iron sharp at both ends, of the length of five or six foot to be pitched before the archers, and of each side the footmen like an hedge, to the intent that if the barded horses ran rashly upon them, they might shortly be gored and destroyed . . . This device of fortifying an army was at this time first invented.

> Singing hymns of thankfulness, the army retires to Calais—and then home to England.

Act 5

Chorus The Chorus is now brisk and businesslike: his speech must cover a lot of ground, and account for several years of historical time, for the benefit of those in the audience who are not already familiar with the story of Henry V (from history books, ballads, and from earlier plays). Making the usual apologies for the theatre's inadequacies, he takes the king to Calais—and immediately across the Channel to a vociferous welcoming crowd, then quickly into London. A victorious conqueror should be honoured (as Julius Caesar was) with a triumphal procession, but Henry's religious modesty forbids this.

A sudden change of rhythm and line-length introduces a contemporary allusion—which also ties the date when the play was written to the period between April and September 1599, when the Earl of Essex was commanding the English forces in Ireland (see 'Source, Date, and Text', p. xxxix). After a short time at home—about five years, in fact—the king returns to France.

Scene 1 As so often in this play, the Chorus's formality is broken by a comedy scene. Fighting in France continued for some time after the Battle of Agincourt (25 October 1415). This scene would appear to take place on 2 March, the day after St David's day. The quarrel between Llewellyn and Pistol still goes on, but now there is leisure to settle it. Pistol is most ignominiously defeated, and the news from England—'my Doll is dead i'th'Spital of a malady of France'—demoralizes him further; he is also penniless (having lost even the promised ransom money when all prisoners were killed). But Pistol, the last of the Eastcheap mob, is irrepressible: punning on 'steal' and 'steal' he exits with characteristic bravado in a rhymed couplet and an allusion to Caesar's *Gallic Wars*.

Scene 2   This time we are really, as the Chorus promised us, with the king at a summit conference in Troyes. The two parties assemble on opposite sides of the stage, 'eyeballing' each other and speaking formal words of greeting.

In the centre of the stage stands Burgundy, lord of an independent French dukedom and, therefore, an ideal mediator between the two kings. He delivers a lecture to the warring factions on the beauties of peace, developing an analogy of the wasteland of a neglected countryside and the uncivilized savagery of a nation at war. The regular rhythms and rich language emphasize the content of his speech.

Delegates are appointed to negotiate terms of conciliation. King Henry ensures that he is represented by all his kinsmen—including the Earl of Huntington, who has not before appeared in the play (although in fact he fought at Harfleur). The French queen accompanies the negotiators to make sure that a woman's voice is heard.

Alone on the stage (apart from the interpreting Alice) are Henry and his 'capital demand', the Princess Katherine. Henry's demands have been considerably modified since he insisted (2, 2, 189) 'No king of England if not king of France'. Now he is asking only that his heirs should inherit the French crown through his marriage to the French princess.

The scene is a tricky one to play. Both characters must know their political roles, yet by teasing and joking they must act out a romantic comedy of love (whose outcome is preordained). Henry is content to make a fool of himself in pretending to be no lover, secure in the knowledge that he is 'the best king of good fellows' and Katherine—by extension of the proverb—'the queen of beggars'. Katherine's French nicety yields to English customs, and their contract is sealed with a kiss: 'nice customs curtsy to great kings'. The counsellors return, having made equally good progress in their negotiations. Burgundy tries to make a joke of the situation with some rather crude humour, and Henry joins in—showing more restraint and wit than the French lord. Finally, when all parties are in full agreement, the French queen speaks a blessing. The stage is left to the Chorus to wind up the history.

Chorus   Still apologizing for the theatre's inadequacies, the Chorus has a last word of praise for Henry V, 'This star of England', before pointing the audience towards Henry's son, Henry VI. In looking forward he also looks back—to the three *Henry VI* plays of Shakespeare's first tetralogy.

Hal to Henry:

From Prince of Wales to King of England

No one can forget Prince Hal! All the characters in *Henry V* remember the prince who was created by Shakespeare (with only a little help from historical sources) in the early scenes of *Henry IV Part 1*, and they make sure that we—the twenty-first-century audiences and readers—are not allowed to forget either. A royal prince, apparently an adolescent (his age is never ascertained), is led astray by a much older man (Sir John Falstaff), and joins with a bunch of hooligans and petty criminals ('unlettered, rude and shallow') in sessions of heavy drinking and practical joking ('riots, banquets, sports'—1, 1, 55–6). To the bystanders, it all seems fairly harmless, and even quite amusing—but to the prince's father, and to all representatives of law and order in the state, such misconduct appears dangerously subversive. The future of the English monarchy is threatened by it!

Those who *understand* Prince Hal, however, and who become intimate with his thoughts by listening to his soliloquies, know better what to expect. From his earliest appearance in the play, Hal shows a streak of determined calculation. As he parts from his drinking pals, he excuses and justifies his actions:

> I know you all, and will awhile uphold
> The unyok'd humour of your idleness.
> Yet herein will I imitate the sun,
> Who doth permit the base contagious clouds
> To smother up his beauty from the world,
> That, when he please again to be himself,
> Being wanted he may be more wonder'd at
> By breaking through the foul and ugly mists
> Of vapours that did seem to strangle him . . .

The effect, he promises, will be spectacular:

> . . . like bright metal on a sullen ground,
> My reformation, glitt'ring o'er my fault,
> Shall show more goodly, and attract more eyes
> Than that which hath no foil to set it off.

Henry IV Part 1, 1, 2, 197–205; 214–17.

Throughout *Henry IV Part 1* Prince Hal is contrasted with Henry Hotspur, son of the Earl of Northumberland. Hotspur, 'the theme of honour's tongue' (*1*, 1, 80), has earned the admiration of Henry IV, Hal's own father, even whilst he is fighting in rebellion against the king. At the battle of Shrewsbury, which ends the play, Hal overcomes Hotspur in physical combat. Their duel also, metaphorically, strikes a blow against Falstaff, who, like the allegorical Riot, misleader of Youth in the Morality Plays, seems to tempt Prince Hal away from the straight and narrow path of his royal calling. Much of *Henry IV Part 2* is taken up by the gradual undermining of Falstaff's influence. Shakespeare shows the fat knight in an increasingly unfavourable light—cowardly, unscrupulous, and diseased. At the end of the play Prince Hal, newly crowned Henry V, disclaims his former friend: 'I know thee not, old man' (5, 5, 47). Falstaff, and all that he represents, has to be sacrificed for the sake of the kingdom.

By the grace of God—or so it appears to the clerics in the opening scene of *Henry V*—a religious conversion has taken place: 'The king is full of grace and fair regard' (*1*, 1, 22). The Christian concept of 'grace' is important in this play. The word has many connotations, but it generally refers to the assistance given freely by God to any human being who will freely accept it, and particularly to those whose efforts (whether or not they understand what they are doing) ensure that the will of God is being carried out. Prince Hal was given the grace to recognize the error of his adolescent past, to repent and reform; he will now hope and pray for still further grace to accomplish the task for which—he believes—God has called him.

But in shaking off the burden of his own past, Henry has been compelled to recognize and shoulder the burdens which were his father's.

Henry IV attained the crown by rebellion against the rightful king, Richard II, and his reign was an uneasy one. He confesses this, shortly before he dies, to Prince Hal:

> God knows, my son,
> By what by-paths and indirect crook'd ways
> I met this crown, and I myself know well
> How troublesome it sat upon my head.
> To thee it shall descend with better quiet,
> Better opinion, better confirmation . . .

He gives his son a warning:

> ... though thou stand'st more sure than I could do,
> Thou art not firm enough, since griefs are green ... ;

and the advice:

> Therefore, my Harry,
> Be it thy course to busy giddy minds
> With foreign quarrels, that action hence borne out
> May waste the memory of the former days.
>
> *Henry IV Part 2*, 4, 5, 182–215

All this Henry V must bear in mind at the important crises of the play—when the Archbishop of Canterbury urges him to war with France; when he discovers the treachery of Cambridge, Scroop, and Gray; and when he prepares himself mentally and spiritually for the battle of Agincourt.

Shakespeare's Verse

Easily the best way to understand and appreciate Shakespeare's verse is to read it aloud—and don't worry if you don't understand everything! Try not to be captivated by the dominant rhythm, but decide which are the most important words in each line and use the regular metre to drive them forward to the listeners.

Shakespeare's plays are mainly written in 'blank verse', the form preferred by most dramatists in the sixteenth and early seventeenth centuries. Blank verse is a very flexible medium, which is capable—like the human speaking voice—of a wide range of tones. The lines, which are unrhymed, are ten syllables long and divide into five 'feet' with alternating stresses, just like normal English speech. The technical name for this is 'iambic pentameter'.

> **Canterbury**
> It múst be só, for míraclés are céas'd,
> And thérefore wé must néeds admít the meáns,
> How thíngs are pérfectéd.
> **Ely**
>   But mý good lórd,
> How nów for mítigátion óf this bíll
> Urg'd bý the Cómmons? Dóth his májestý
> Inclíne to ít or nó?
> **Canterbury**
>   He séems indífferént ... (1, 1, 67–72)

Here the two prelates, men of great seriousness and in complete agreement with each other, are speaking a verse which is fairly regular (there is an extra foot in the last line), and where the lines are divided between the speakers without losing the rhythm.

Sometimes the verse line contains the grammatical unit of meaning, thus allowing for a pause at the end of the line before a new idea is started—'It must be so, for miracles are ceas'd'. At other times the sense runs on from one line to the next—'we must needs admit the means / How things are perfected'. This makes for the natural fluidity of speech, avoiding monotony but still maintaining the basic iambic rhythm. On occasion Shakespeare deviates from the norm, writing lines that are longer or shorter than ten syllables, and varying the stress patterns for unusual emphasis. In the king's meditation the night before Agincourt there are two short lines whose 'missing' syllables speak more than words:

> What ínfiníte heart's eáse must kíngs negléct
> That prívate mén enjóy?   (4, 1, 224–5)

and

> Whereín thou árt less háppy béing féar'd
> Than théy in feáring?   (lines 236–7)

Again, in the Chorus's speech introducing *Act 5* (lines 28–31) there is a sudden change of rhythm and line-length when Shakespeare inserts a contemporary allusion: the citizens

> Go fórth and fétch their cónquering Cáesar ín —
> As, bý a lówer bút by lóving líkelihoód
> Were nów the géneral óf our grácious émpress,
> (As ín good tíme he máy) from Iŕeland cóming . . .

Much of *Henry V* is written in prose, which is the proper medium for comic scenes and those involving 'low-life' characters. King Henry sometimes speaks in prose—but only when he is adopting a persona different from his usual character—the 'man amongst men' on the night before Agincourt (*Act 4*, Scene 1), for instance, or the unskilled wooer of the French princess.

Source, Date, and Text

The initial inspiration for *Henry V* may well have been an anonymous play, *The Famous Victories of Henry the Fifth*, whose only surviving text, printed in 1598, seems to be a debased and abbreviated version of the lost original. Two history books gave further information, Raphael Holinshed's *Chronicles of England* (1587) and Edward Hall's *Union of the Two Noble Families* (1548); passages from the former are printed at the end of this edition.

The date of Shakespeare's play is fairly certainly established by a topical allusion in the Chorus's *Act 5* speech (lines 30–2). He compares Henry's reception in London to that which would be given

> Were now the general of our gracious empress,
> As in good time he may, from Ireland coming,
> Bringing rebellion broached on his sword . . .

The reference is to the Earl of Essex, whose campaign left England for Ireland on 27 March 1599, returning—unsuccessful—in September of that year.

There are two early editions of the play—the Quarto (Q) published in 1600 and reprinted, with some few corrections, in 1602 and 1619; and the Folio (F) of 1623. F seems to have been based on Shakespeare's own manuscript and, although much later, is more authoritative than Q, which could have originated from a reconstruction of the play by one or more actors working from memory. The present edition uses the text established by Professor Andrew Gurr (*The New Cambridge Shakespeare*, 1992). Significant variations and any omissions are remarked in the Notes.

People in the Play

ON THE FRENCH SIDE

Royalty	King Charles VI	
	Queen Isabel	*his wife*
	The Dauphin	*their eldest son*
	Princess Katherine	*their daughter*
The Nobility	Duke of Berri	
	Duke of Bourbon	
	Duke of Orléans	
	Duke of Burgundy	
	The Constable of France	
	Rambures	
	Grandpré	*Lords of France*
	Beaumont	
Citizens	Governor of the city of Harfleur	
	Montjoy	*the French Herald*
	Alice	*lady-in-waiting to* Princess Katherine
	Ambassadors	*to the English court*
	Monsieur Le Fer	*a French gentleman captured by* Pistol

Attendants at both courts, and soldiers in both armies
The action of the play takes place in England and in France

'O for a muse of fire, that would ascend The brightest heaven of invention', (*Prologue*, 1–2). Ian McDiarmid as Chorus, Royal Shakespeare Company, 1984.

PROLOGUE

Prologue

The Prologue to the play, which is spoken by a single actor known as the 'Chorus' (see p. vii), laments the inadequacies of the theatre, and urges the audience to use their own imaginations to supply the actors' deficiencies.

1 *muse*: In Greek mythology, the nine Muses were goddesses of inspiration; creative artists invoked the one they thought most appropriate for their purposes.
fire: the lightest of the four elements—earth, water, air, and fire— of which the world (according to Elizabethan cosmology) was composed. The astronomer Ptolemy taught that fire would always rise to the highest heaven, the empyrean.

2 *invention*: poetic creation.

3–4 *princes . . . behold*: See the description of the Battle of Crécy (*1*, 2, 105–10) in which the Black Prince 'played a tragedy', watched by his father, Edward III.

4 *swelling*: increasingly splendid.

5 *warlike*: skilled in military matters.
Harry: the familiar form of 'Henry'.
like himself: presented in an appropriate manner.

6 *port*: bearing (with a possible pun on 'part' = actor's role).
Mars: the Roman god of war.

7 *famine, sword, and fire*: the instruments of war, personified as hounds which, for hunting, were fastened in a 'leash' of three.

8 *gentles all*: ladies and gentlemen.

9 *flat unraised spirits*: unraisèd; dull and uninspired creatures—i.e. the author of this play, and the actors.
hath: Shakespeare often mixes singular and plural verbs and subjects.

PROLOGUE

London: the Globe Theatre. Enter Chorus

Chorus
O for a muse of fire, that would ascend
The brightest heaven of invention,
A kingdom for a stage, princes to act,
And monarchs to behold the swelling scene.
5 Then should the warlike Harry, like himself,
Assume the port of Mars, and at his heels
(Leash'd in, like hounds) should famine, sword, and
    fire
Crouch for employment. But pardon, gentles all,
The flat unraised spirits, that hath dar'd,

10 *scaffold*: platform, stage.
11 *cockpit*: pit for cock-fighting.
12 *vasty fields*: huge battlefields.
13 *wooden O*: small circular building made of wood—i.e. the theatre.
   the very casques: the actual helmets (*and* the men who wore them).
14 *affright*: frighten.
15 *a crooked figure*: i.e. the 0 of arithmetic: 0 added to 100,000 makes a million—1,000,000.
16 *Attest*: signify.
17 *us*: i.e. the actors.
   ciphers: nothings, nonentities.
   to: compared to.
18 *imaginary forces*: powers of imagination.
19 *Suppose*: imagine.
   girdle: surroundings.
21 *high upreared*: uprearèd. The image is of warhorses rearing to challenge each other: the reference is to the cliffs of Dover, standing opposite to the shores of France.
   abutting: adjacent.
   fronts: foreheads, frontiers.
22 *the . . . ocean*: the English Channel, which is particularly treacherous for shipping.
23 *Piece out*: augment.
25 *puissance*: power, forces (the word is pronounced with three syllables).

10 On this unworthy scaffold, to bring forth
   So great an object. Can this cockpit hold
   The vasty fields of France? Or may we cram
   Within this wooden O the very casques
   That did affright the air at Agincourt?
15 Oh, pardon: since a crooked figure may
   Attest in little place a million,
   And let us, ciphers to this great account,
   On your imaginary forces work.
   Suppose within the girdle of these walls
20 Are now confin'd two mighty monarchies,
   Whose high upreared and abutting fronts
   The perilous narrow ocean parts asunder.
   Piece out our imperfections with your thoughts.
   Into a thousand parts divide one man,
25 And make imaginary puissance.
   Think when we talk of horses that you see them

27 *proud*: spirited.
28 *deck*: equip.
30 *th'accomplishment . . . years*: that which took many years to achieve: the events of the play took place between 1414 and 1420.
31 *for the which supply*: to help you with this.
32 *Admit*: accept.
32–3 *Chorus . . . Prologue-like*: Although he appears as a 'Prologue' now, he will return from time to time to comment on the action as a 'Chorus' would do.

Printing their proud hooves i'th'receiving earth,
For 'tis your thoughts that now must deck our kings,
Carry them here and there, jumping o'er times,
30 Turning th'accomplishment of many years
Into an hour-glass. For the which supply
Admit me Chorus to this history,
Who, Prologue-like, your humble patience pray,
Gently to hear, kindly to judge our play.   [*Exit*

Act 1 Scene 1
The Archbishop of Canterbury and the
Bishop of Ely have a problem; a bill has
been presented in Parliament which, if it is
passed, will deprive the Church of much of
its great wealth. But there is a new king on
the throne, and the two churchmen are
encouraged by his amazing abilities. The
Archbishop of Canterbury has a scheme
which may solve their dilemma. This scene
is not present in Q.

1–19 These lines are particularly close
   to the wording of Shakespeare's
   source; see 'The sources of *Henry V*'
   p. 133.
1 *that . . . urg'd*: the very same bill is
   being presented. In 1410—
   'th'eleventh year of the last king's
   reign'—the House of Commons had
   tried to wrest from the Church some of
   its enormous, untaxable, property
   holdings. This problem was not a new
   one in 1410—and was still unsolved
   in 1599.
3 *Was . . . pass'd*: was likely to be, and
   would indeed have been passed.
4 *scambling*: violent, unruly.
5 *question*: debate.
8 *the better . . . possession*: more than
   half of what we own.
9 *temporal*: secular—i.e. land which
   had been bequeathed to the Church
   and was consequently exempt from
   taxation.
10 *By testament*: as a legacy.
15 *lazars*: lepers; the term came from the
   story of Lazarus (St Luke's Gospel,
   16:20), and was generally applied to
   all chronically sick persons.
16 *indigent*: needy, destitute.
   corporal: physical.
19 *by th'year*: annually.
   the bill: the bill before Parliament;
   and the cost.
20 *drink deep*: take a lot away from us.
22 *grace*: Christian goodness; see p. xxxiii.
   fair regard: highly respected and with
   great respect for [the Church].

SCENE 1

London: the Palace of Westminster. Enter the two
Bishops of Canterbury *and* Ely

Canterbury
My lord, I'll tell you, that self bill is urg'd
Which in th'eleventh year of the last king's reign
Was like, and had indeed against us pass'd
But that the scambling and unquiet time
5 Did push it out of farther question.
     Ely
But how, my lord, shall we resist it now?
     Canterbury
It must be thought on. If it pass against us
We lose the better half of our possession,
For all the temporal lands, which men devout
10 By testament have given to the Church
Would they strip from us, being valu'd thus:
As much as would maintain to the king's honour
Full fifteen earls and fifteen hundred knights,
Six thousand and two hundred good esquires,
15 And to relief of lazars and weak age
Of indigent faint souls, past corporal toil,
A hundred alms-houses, right well supplied;
And to the coffers of the king beside
A thousand pounds by th'year. Thus runs the bill.
     Ely
20 This would drink deep.
     Canterbury
                           'Twould drink the cup and all.
     Ely
But what prevention?
     Canterbury
The king is full of grace, and fair regard.

24 *courses of his youth*: undisciplined behaviour when he was a boy; see 'Hal to Henry', p. xxxiii.

26 *mortified*: put to death.

27 *Yea*: yes indeed.

28 *Consideration*: self-awareness.

29 *Adam*: the first man (according to the Book of Genesis), who was expelled from the Garden of Eden because he broke God's law.

30 *paradise*: the Garden of Eden, and *also* Heaven, the home of all divine spirits.

32 *was . . . made*: did anyone become a theologian so quickly.

33 *in a flood*: Here, and also in line 35, Shakespeare alludes to the twelve labours imposed on Hercules, the superman of classical mythology. The fifth of these was the cleansing of the Augean stables, which Hercules achieved by diverting a river through them.

34 *heady currance*: rush of flowing water. *scouring*: scrubbing out.

35 *Hydra-headed*: manifold and persistent—i.e. with as many heads as the Hydra. The monster (which was killed by Hercules as his second labour) had nine heads; when one was cut off, two more grew in its place.

36 *seat*: power.

38 *reason in*: discuss.

42 *all . . . study*: his special subject.

43 *List*: listen to. *discourse*: talking about.

44 *render'd you in music*: narrated with eloquence.

45 *cause of policy*: argument about politics.

46 *gordian knot*: The intricate knot tying the chariot of Gordius would only—according to ancient prophecy—be unloosed by the man who was to conquer Asia. Alexander the Great cut through the knot with his sword.

47 *Familiar*: i.e. as easily.

Ely
And a true lover of the holy Church.
   Canterbury
The courses of his youth promis'd it not.
25 The breath no sooner left his father's body
But that his wildness, mortified in him,
Seem'd to die too. Yea, at that very moment
Consideration like an angel came,
And whipp'd th'offending Adam out of him,
30 Leaving his body as a paradise
T'envelop and contain celestial spirits.
Never was such a sudden scholar made,
Never came reformation in a flood
With such a heady currance scouring faults,
35 Nor never Hydra-headed wilfulness
So soon did lose his seat, and all at once,
As in this king.
   Ely
                We are blessed in the change.
   Canterbury
Hear him but reason in divinity,
And all-admiring, with an inward wish,
40 You would desire the king were made a prelate.
Hear him debate of commonwealth affairs,
You would say it hath been all in all his study.
List his discourse of war, and you shall hear
A fearful battle render'd you in music.
45 Turn him to any cause of policy,
The gordian knot of it he will unloose,
Familiar as his garter, that when he speaks

48 *charter'd libertine*: licensed free-ranger.
49 *the mute wonder*: silent amazement.
50 *honey'd*: well-spoken.
   sentences: maxims.
51 *art and practic*: practical experience.
52 *mistress to*: controller: practice is more important than theory ('*theoric*').
53 *his grace*: his majesty; but see also line 22 and note.
   glean: pick up, learn.
54 *courses vain*: useless activities.
55 *companies*: companions.
   unletter'd: uneducated.
   rude: ignorant.
   shallow: frivolous.
58 *sequestration*: withdrawal into some privacy.
59 *open haunts*: public places.
   popularity: throngs of common people.
60 *strawberry*: The strawberry was used as an emblem of righteousness because it was untainted by neighbouring plants 'of baser quality' (such as onions or garlic). The strawberries of Ely House, the London home of the Bishop of Ely, were famous.

63 *obscur'd his contemplation*: hid the seriousness of his thinking.
66 *crescive in his faculty*: increasing because it was in its nature to increase.
67 *miracles are ceas'd*: The Protestant Church taught that the only miracles were those recorded in Holy Scripture. In the time of Henry V, England was still a Catholic country, but Shakespeare's audience would be unlikely to notice the anachronism.
68 *admit the means*: find a natural cause.
69 *perfected*: brought to spiritual perfection; the stress is on the first syllable.
72 *indifferent*: impartial.

The air, a charter'd libertine, is still,
And the mute wonder lurketh in men's ears
50 To steal his sweet and honey'd sentences,
So that the art and practic part of life
Must be the mistress to this theoric.
Which is a wonder how his grace should glean it,
Since his addiction was to courses vain,
55 His companies unletter'd, rude, and shallow,
His hours fill'd up with riots, banquets, sports,
And never noted in him any study,
Any retirement, any sequestration
From open haunts and popularity.
      Ely
60 The strawberry grows underneath the nettle,
And wholesome berries thrive and ripen best
Neighbour'd by fruit of baser quality.
And so the prince obscur'd his contemplation
Under the veil of wildness, which, no doubt,
65 Grew like the summer grass fastest by night,
Unseen, yet crescive in his faculty.
      Canterbury
It must be so, for miracles are ceas'd,
And therefore we must needs admit the means
How things are perfected.
      Ely
                              But my good lord,
70 How now for mitigation of this bill
Urg'd by the Commons? Doth his majesty
Incline to it or no?
      Canterbury
                        He seems indifferent,
Or rather swaying more upon our part
Than cherishing th'exhibiters against us,
75 For I have made an offer to his majesty
Upon our spiritual convocation
And in regard of causes now in hand
Which I have open'd to his grace at large,
As touching France, to give a greater sum
80 Than ever at one time the clergy yet
Did to his predecessors part withal.

74 *exhibiters*: sponsors, those who are presenting the bill.
76 *Upon*: on behalf of.
   spiritual convocation: assembly of the higher clergy.
77 *causes*: legal matters.
78 *open'd*: explained.
79 *touching*: concerning.
81 *withal*: with.
83 *of*: by.
85 *fain*: like to.
86 *severals*: separate details.
   unhidden passages: clear and undisputed lines of descent.
88 *seat*: throne.
89 *Deriv'd*: descended from; see 'Family Tree', p. x.

Ely
How did this offer seem receiv'd, my lord?
Canterbury
With good acceptance of his majesty,
Save that there was not time enough to hear,
85 As I perceiv'd his grace would fain have done,
The severals and unhidden passages
Of his true titles to some certain dukedoms,
And generally to the crown and seat of France
Deriv'd from Edward, his great-grandfather.
   Ely
90 What was th'impediment that broke this off?
   Canterbury
The French ambassador upon that instant
Crav'd audience, and the hour I think is come
To give him hearing. Is it four o'clock?
   Ely
It is.
   Canterbury

95 *embassy*: ambassador's message.

95 Then go we in, to know his embassy,
Which I could with a ready guess declare
Before the Frenchman speak a word of it.
   Ely
I'll wait upon you, and I long to hear it.   [*Exeunt*

Act 1 Scene 2
King Henry asks the archbishop if it is right that England should declare war on France. Henry knows that many lives will be lost in the fighting, and he wants to make sure that his cause is just. The archbishop explains, at great length, why Henry can lay claim to the throne of France, and he urges the king to fight for his right. King Henry is convinced, but he is reluctant to leave England in case the Scots attack the country whilst the best of its armed forces are abroad. The archbishop sets the king's mind at rest, and then delivers a short sermon on the proper ordering of a state. King Henry is determined to fight, and he calls in the ambassadors from the French court, who deliver a very insulting message from the Dauphin. The king declares war.

SCENE 2

London: Westminster. Enter the King, Gloucester, Bedford, Clarence, Westmorland, *and* Exeter *and* Attendants

King
Where is my gracious lord of Canterbury?
   Exeter
Not here in presence.
   King
                          Send for him, good uncle.
   Westmorland
Shall we call in th'ambassador, my liege?

0s.d. *Clarence*: the Duke of Clarence has no speaking part in this scene, and he does not appear anywhere else in the play. But his entrance is marked in both Q and F texts. See 'Source, Date, and Text', p. xxxix.

2 *presence*: the royal presence.

3 *liege*: royal lord.

4 *cousin*: Westmorland was related to Henry by marriage.
   we: King Henry speaks in 'the royal plural'.
   resolv'd: satisfied.

5 *of . . . weight*: about matters of importance.

6 *task*: burden.

8 *become*: grace it with your presence.

10 *justly . . . unfold*: honestly and in all good faith explain.

11 *the law Salic*: The Archbishop of Canterbury expounds the Salic law in lines 37–95.

12 *Or . . . or*: either . . . or.

13 *faithful*: of good Christian faith.

14 *fashion*: give a false shape to.
   bow: distort.

15 *nicely charge*: lay a burden on [your soul] with subtle arguments.
   understanding: comprehending, learned; and obedient to, standing under, God.

16 *opening*: raising the question of.
   titles miscreate: illegitimate claims.

17 *Suits . . . colours*: does not match up.

19 *approbation*: support.

20 *your reverence*: This is an appropriate form of address for the Archbishop of Canterbury—but it could be spoken with some sarcasm.

21 *impawn*: risk, hazard.

26 *sore*: serious.

27 *wrongs*: wrong-doings.
   gives edge: sharpens; singular verbs might be used with plural nouns.

29 *Under this conjuration*: in response to this solemn invocation.

32 *sin*: the 'original sin' of which—according to the Catholic Church—every human being is guilty: all share Adam's sin (see *1, 1, 29* note) until this is cleansed by Christian baptism.

King
Not yet, my cousin. We would be resolv'd,
5 Before we hear him, of some things of weight
That task our thoughts, concerning us and France.

Enter Canterbury *and* Ely

Canterbury
God and his angels guard your sacred throne,
And make you long become it.
    King
                    Sure, we thank you.
My learned lord, we pray you to proceed,
10 And justly and religiously unfold
Why the law Salic that they have in France
Or should or should not bar us in our claim.
And God forbid, my dear and faithful lord,
That you should fashion, wrest, or bow your reading,
15 Or nicely charge your understanding soul
With opening titles miscreate, whose right
Suits not in native colours with the truth.
For God doth know how many now in health
Shall drop their blood in approbation
20 Of what your reverence shall incite us to.
Therefore take heed how you impawn our person,
How you awake our sleeping sword of war.
We charge you in the name of God take heed,
For never two such kingdoms did contend
25 Without much fall of blood, whose guiltless drops
Are every one a woe, a sore complaint
'Gainst him whose wrongs gives edge unto the swords
That makes such waste in brief mortality.
Under this conjuration speak, my lord,
30 For we will hear, note, and believe in heart
That what you speak is in your conscience wash'd
As pure as sin with baptism.

Canterbury

Then hear me, gracious sovereign, and you peers
That owe your selves, your lives and services
35 To this imperial throne. There is no bar
To make against your highness' claim to France
But this which they produce from Pharamond:
In terram Salicam mulieres ne succedant,
—No woman shall succeed in Salic land—
40 Which Salic land the French unjustly glose
To be the realm of France, and Pharamond
The founder of this law and female bar.
Yet their own authors faithfully affirm
That the land Salic is in Germany,
45 Between the floods of Sala and of Elbe,
Where Charles the Great, having subdu'd the Saxons,
There left behind and settled certain French,
Who, holding in disdain the German women
For some dishonest manners of their life,
50 Establish'd then this law: to wit, no female
Should be inheritrix in Salic land,
Which Salic (as I said) 'twixt Elbe and Sala
Is at this day in Germany called Meissen.
Then doth it well appear the Salic law
55 Was not devised for the realm of France.
Nor did the French possess the Salic land
Until four hundred one-and-twenty years

35 *imperial*: having absolute sovereignty.
   bar: objection. The archbishop could
   have explained that Henry's claim to
   the French throne was through his
   descent from Queen Isabella, the
   mother of Edward III and daughter of
   Philip IV of France (see 'Family Tree',
   p. x).
37 *Pharamond*: legendary king of the
   Salian Franks.
39 *succeed*: inherit the throne.
40 *glose*: gloss, interpret.
42 *female bar*: prohibition against
   women; the law was in fact devised by
   the French nobles who had elected
   Philip of Valois to the throne of
   France.
43 *authors*: scholars.
45 *floods*: rivers.
46 *Charles the Great*: Charlemagne,
   AD 742–814.
47 Charlemagne colonized the 'Salic
   land' with Frenchmen.
49 *dishonest manners*: unchastity.

55 *devised*: devisèd.
57 *four hundred one-and-twenty*: In
   actual fact, it was 379 years later—
   four hundred less one-and-twenty; the
   arithmetical error came from
   Holinshed.

58 *defunction*: decease.

59 *Idly*: falsely.

60 *the year of our redemption*: anno
Domini, the year of the Lord—Jesus
Christ, whose birth and death
redeemed mankind from all their sins.

62 *seat*: settle.

64 *Besides*: in addition.
writers: scholars.

65 *deposed*: deposèd.

66 *heir general*: one who inherits
regardless of whether the descent is
through the male or female line.

72 *fine*: refine, complete.
shows: appearance.

73 *naught*: rubbish.

74 *Convey'd*: dishonestly presented.

75 *Charlemagne*: This was really Charles
the Bald; Shakespeare follows
Holinshed's slip.

76 *Louis*: The name was pronounced as
'Lewis' by the Elizabethans.

82 *lineal of*: descended in a straight line
from.

88 *Louis his satisfaction*: Louis's
satisfaction.

89 *title*: entitlement.

91 *Howbeit*: notwithstanding.

93 *hide them in a net*: take refuge in a
tangle of obvious contradictions.

94 *amply*: honestly and openly.
embar their crooked titles: prevent
discovery of the weakness of their own
titles (which are not in a direct line of
descent).

After defunction of King Pharamond,
Idly suppos'd the founder of this law,
60 Who died within the year of our redemption,
Four hundred twenty-six, and Charles the Great
Subdu'd the Saxons and did seat the French
Beyond the River Sala in the year
Eight hundred five. Besides, their writers say
65 King Pepin, which deposed Childeric,
Did as heir general, being descended
Of Blithild, which was daughter to King Clothair,
Make claim and title to the crown of France.
Hugh Capet also, who usurp'd the crown
70 Of Charles the Duke of Lorraine, sole heir male
Of the true line and stock of Charles the Great,
To fine his title with some shows of truth,
Though in pure truth it was corrupt and naught,
Convey'd himself as th'heir to the Lady Lingard,
75 Daughter to Charlemagne, who was the son
To Louis the emperor, and Louis the son
Of Charles the Great. Also King Louis the Ninth,
Who was sole heir to the usurper Capet,
Could not keep quiet in his conscience,
80 Wearing the crown of France, till satisfied
That fair Queen Isabel, his grandmother,
Was lineal of the Lady Ermengard,
Daughter to Charles the foresaid Duke of Lorraine;
By the which marriage the line of Charles the Great
85 Was reunited to the crown of France.
So that, as clear as is the summer's sun,
King Pepin's title, and Hugh Capet's claim,
King Louis his satisfaction, all appear
To hold in right and title of the female.
90 So do the kings of France unto this day.
Howbeit, they would hold up this Salic law
To bar your highness claiming from the female,
And rather choose to hide them in a net
Than amply to embar their crooked titles
95 Usurp'd from you and your progenitors.
      King
May I with right and conscience make this claim?

Canterbury
The sin upon my head, dread sovereign,
For in the Book of Numbers is it writ
'When the man dies, let the inheritance
100 Descend unto the daughter.' Gracious lord,
Stand for your own, unwind your bloody flag,
Look back into your mighty ancestors.
Go, my dread lord, to your great-grandsire's tomb,
From whom you claim. Invoke his warlike spirit,
105 And your great-uncle's, Edward the Black Prince,
Who on the French ground play'd a tragedy,
Making defeat on the full power of France,
Whiles his most mighty father on a hill
Stood smiling to behold his lion's whelp
110 Forage in blood of French nobility.
O noble English, that could entertain
With half their forces the full pride of France,
And let another half stand laughing by,
All out of work and cold for action.

98 *Book of Numbers*: In the Old Testament the Book of Numbers (27:8) rules that 'If a man die, and hath no son, then ye shall cause his inheritance to pass unto his daughter'. *writ*: written.
101 *unwind*: unfurl.
   bloody: bloodstained.
103 *great-grandsire*: Edward III.

106–10 The Black Prince defeated the French at the Battle of Crécy in 1346.

108 *Whiles*: whilst.
   on a hill: According to Holinshed, the king 'stood aloft on a windmill hill' for the entire duration of the battle.
109 *lion's whelp*: lion cub; see note to line 124.
110 *Forage in*: gorge himself with.
111 *entertain*: cope with.
112 *half*: The English army was arranged in three divisions, one of which remained with the king as a reserve force.
114 *for action*: i.e. for lack of action.

116 *puissant*: powerful.
118 *renowned them*: renownèd; made them famous.
119 *thrice-puissant*: triply powerful— (1) as heir to the throne; (2) as occupant of the throne; and (3) for his personal prowess. The bishop reckons up the points he made in lines 117–18.

Ely
115 Awake remembrance of these valiant dead,
And with your puissant arm renew their feats.
You are their heir, you sit upon their throne.
The blood and courage that renowned them
Runs in your veins, and my thrice-puissant liege

120 *the very May-morn*: right at the springtime; Henry was in fact 27 years old.

123 *rouse yourself*: come out of your lair.

124 *lions*: The lion, being king among beasts, was emblematic of the king among men; and heraldic lions characterize the royal coat-of-arms.

125 *They*: i.e. the French; the stress is on the first word of the line.
   cause: legal justification.

126 *So hath your highness*: and indeed you do.

129 *pavilion'd*: encamped; '*pavilions*' were tents used by the knights in jousting tournaments.

120 Is in the very May-morn of his youth,
Ripe for exploits and mighty enterprises.

   Exeter

Your brother kings and monarchs of the earth
Do all expect that you should rouse yourself,
As did the former lions of your blood.

   Westmorland

125 They know your grace hath cause, and means, and
      might;
So hath your highness. Never king of England
Had nobles richer and more loyal subjects,
Whose hearts have left their bodies here in England
And lie pavilion'd in the fields of France.

132 *spirituality*: clergy.
136–9 In Holinshed it is Westmorland, not the king, who raises this issue.
137 *lay down*: estimate.
proportions: number of troops required.
138 *make road*: attack.
140 *marches*: the border territories; the Lords of the Marches, bordering Scotland and Wales, maintained a military presence until the early seventeenth century.
143 *coursing snatchers*: snatch and grab raiders (who are like greyhounds hunting hares).
144 *main intendment*: general hostile purpose.
145 *still*: always.
giddy: unstable.
146 *read*: i.e. in history books; the king has learned his lessons—see *1, 1, 41–2*.
148 *unfurnish'd*: unprotected.
149 *breach*: break in the sea-wall.
151 *Galling*: wounding.
gleaned: gleanèd; stripped bare of all resources.
assays: expeditions, sorties.
152 *Girding*: surrounding.
154 *th'ill neighbourhood*: having such bad neighbours.
155 *fear'd*: frightened.
156 *hear . . . her self*: just consider the precedents in England's past.
157 *chivalry*: knights, men-at-arms.
158 *of*: for.
160 *take . . . stray*: captured and imprisoned like a stray beast which is put in the parish pound (= cattle-pen).
161 King David II, who was captured in 1346 during Edward III's absence in France. A play, *Edward III* (c. 1596), shows him being taken to Calais—but this has no basis in fact.
162 *fill*: enlarge.
163 *their chronicle*: the history of England and of Edward III.
rich with praise: full of praiseworthy deeds.
164 *ooze and bottom*: oozy bottom.
165 *wreck*: wreckage.
sumless treasuries: inestimable riches.

Canterbury

130 Oh, let their bodies follow, my dear liege,
With blood and sword and fire, to win your right.
In aid whereof we of the spirituality
Will raise your highness such a mighty sum
As never did the clergy at one time
135 Bring in to any of your ancestors.

    King

We must not only arm t'invade the French
But lay down our proportions to defend
Against the Scot, who will make road upon us
With all advantages.

    Canterbury

140 They of those marches, gracious sovereign,
Shall be a wall sufficient to defend
Our England from the pilfering borderers.

    King

We do not mean the coursing snatchers only,
But fear the main intendment of the Scot,
145 Who hath been still a giddy neighbour to us.
For you shall read that my great-grandfather
Never went with his forces into France
But that the Scot on his unfurnish'd kingdom
Came pouring like the tide into a breach
150 With ample and brim fullness of his force,
Galling the gleaned land with hot assays,
Girding with grievous siege castles and towns,
That England, being empty of defence,
Hath shook and trembled at th'ill neighbourhood.

    Canterbury

155 She hath been then more fear'd than harm'd, my liege.
For hear her but exampled by her self:
When all her chivalry hath been in France
And she a mourning widow of her nobles,
She hath herself not only well defended
160 But taken and impounded as a stray
The king of Scots, whom she did send to France
To fill King Edward's fame with prisoner kings,
And make their chronicle as rich with praise
As is the ooze and bottom of the sea
165 With sunken wreck and sumless treasuries.

166–73 It seems reasonable to give this speech to Westmorland, who was Warden of northern Marches (see line 140 note). In Q it is given to 'A Lord', whereas F attributes it to 'Ely'. But it is unlikely that the Bishop of Ely would dare dissent in this way to his archbishop's proposals.

169 *in prey*: in pursuit of her prey.

172 Compare, 'While the cat's away, the mice will play'.

173 *'tame*: attame, break in.
havoc: destroy.

175 *crush'd*: distorted.

177 *pretty*: ingenious.

178 *armed*: armèd.

179 *advised*: advisèd; prudent.

180–3 Exeter pursues a musical image throughout these lines.

180 *high and low and lower*: i.e. the verse notes.

181 *parts*: the separate lines for different voices or instruments.
one consent: a single harmony.

182 *Congreeing*: agreeing together, co-operating.
close: the cadence at the end of a musical phrase.

184 *state*: estate, body politic.
man: humankind.
divers: different.

185 *endeavour*: human effort.

186 *fixed*: fixèd.
butt: target.

187 *Obedience*: i.e. to the will of God.

187–204 The use of the bee-hive as an analogy for the well-governed state was very popular in Elizabethan political theory. The best-known classical source is Book IV of Virgil's *Georgics*, lines 152ff.

188 *rule in nature*: instinctive government.

189 *act of order*: orderly action.
peopled: human.

Westmorland
But there's a saying, very old and true,
'If that you will France win,
Then with Scotland first begin.'
For once the eagle England being in prey,
170 To her unguarded nest the weasel Scot
Comes sneaking, and so sucks her princely eggs,
Playing the mouse in absence of the cat
To 'tame and havoc more than she can eat.

Exeter
It follows, then, the cat must stay at home.
175 Yet that is but a crush'd necessity,
Since we have locks to safeguard necessaries
And pretty traps to catch the petty thieves.
While that the armed hand doth fight abroad
Th'advised head defends itself at home.
180 For government, though high and low and lower,
Put into parts, doth keep in one consent,
Congreeing in a full and natural close
Like music.
        Canterbury
            Therefore doth heaven divide
The state of man in diverse functions,
185 Setting endeavour in continual motion,
To which is fixed as an aim or butt
Obedience. For so work the honey bees,
Creatures that by a rule in nature teach
The act of order to a peopled kingdom.
190 They have a king, and officers of sorts,
Where some like magistrates correct at home,
Others like merchants venture trade abroad,
Others like soldiers, armed in their stings,
Make boot upon the summer's velvet buds,
195 Which pillage they with merry march bring home

190 *a king*: the queen bee; Aristotle had taught that the head of the hive was male, and it was not until the seventeenth century that English scientists recognized his error.
of sorts: of different ranks.
191 *correct*: administer justice.
193 *armed in their stings*: armèd; whose weapons are their stings.
194 *Make boot*: plunder.
197 *his majesties*: his royal duties; *and* his royal splendour.
199 *civil*: orderly, dutiful.
kneading: moulding.
200 *mechanic*: artisan, labouring.
202 *sad-ey'd justice*: serious-minded magistrate.
hum: the sound of the bee; *and* the expression, 'hmm', of the human magistrate.
203 *executors pale*: threatening executioners.
205–6 *having . . . consent*: being all related to a single common aim.
206 *contrariously*: in opposite ways.
207 *As*: just as.
loosed several ways: loosèd; shot from different angles.
210 *close*: converge.
dial: sundial.

211 *afoot*: set on foot, started off.
212 *borne*: sustained.
216 *withal*: with it.
Gallia: the Latin name for Gaul, the ancient France.
218 *the dog*: the dog of war.
219 *worried*: torn to pieces by the dog; *and* anxious.
220 *name*: reputation.
policy: statesmanship.
222 *well resolv'd*: freed from all doubts; *and* determined on action.
224 *France being ours*: since France belongs to the English throne (by right of inheritance).
bend it to our awe: make France recognize the authority of England.

To the tent royal of their emperor,
Who, busied in his majesties, surveys
The singing masons building roofs of gold,
The civil citizens kneading up the honey,
200 The poor mechanic porters crowding in
Their heavy burdens at his narrow gate,
The sad-ey'd justice with his surly hum
Delivering o'er to executors pale
The lazy yawning drone. I this infer,
205 That many things, having full reference
To one consent, may work contrariously.
As many arrows loosed several ways
Come to one mark; as many ways meet in one town
As many fresh streams meet in one salt sea,
210 As many lines close in the dial's centre,
So may a thousand actions, once afoot
End in one purpose, and be all well borne
Without defeat. Therefore to France, my liege.
Divide your happy England into four,
215 Whereof take you one quarter into France,
And you withal shall make all Gallia shake.
If we with thrice such powers left at home
Cannot defend our own doors from the dog
Let us be worried, and our nation lose
220 The name of hardiness and policy.
    King
Call in the messengers sent from the Dauphin.
                                    [*Exit* Attendant
Now are we well resolv'd, and by God's help
And yours, the noble sinews of our power,
France being ours, we'll bend it to our awe,
225 Or break it all to pieces. Or there we'll sit,
Ruling in large and ample empery
O'er France and all her almost kingly dukedoms,
Or lay these bones in an unworthy urn
Tombless, with no remembrance over them.
230 Either our history shall with full mouth
Speak freely of our acts, or else our grave
Like Turkish mute shall have a tongueless mouth,
Not worshipp'd with a waxen epitaph.

225–8 *Or . . . Or*: either . . . or.
225 *we'll sit*: i.e. on the throne.
226 *large and ample empery*: complete sovereignty.
227 *almost kingly dukedoms*: At the beginning of *Act 3* the Chorus refers to the French offer of 'some petty and unprofitable dukedoms' (line 31).
228 *unworthy urn*: dishonourable grave.
229 *Tombless*: without a monument.
230 *with full mouth*: loudly, with mouth widely stretched.
232 *mute*: dumb slave; some Turkish slaves had their tongues cut out, to make sure they kept the secrets of the royal household.
233 *worshipp'd*: venerated.
    waxen: carved in wax, perishable.
234–5 *know . . . Dauphin*: learn what the Dauphin has to say.
235 *fair*: honourable; the adjective may be applied politely or with sarcasm—as in the modern House of Commons.
    cousin: kinsman.
238 *Freely*: directly, in a straightforward manner.
    render: deliver.
    what we have in charge: the message we have been told to bring.
239 *sparingly . . . far off*: discreetly indicate in fairly general terms.
240 'What the Dauphin means and the reason for our presence.'
242 *grace*: Christian virtue.
    as subject: as much a subject.
    is: A singular verb with a plural subject is not uncommon in Elizabethan usage.
244 *uncurbed*: uncurbèd.
245 *mind*: intention.
    in few: briefly, in a few words.
246 *lately*: recently.
    sending: sending ambassadors.
250–97 Shakespeare here follows Hall's account of events, and not that of Holinshed.
250 *savour . . . youth*: seem too much like the lad you used to be.
251 *be advis'd*: be warned, take care.
252 *galliard*: a lively dance.
253 *revel*: frolic.
254 *meeter*: more appropriate.
255 *tun*: large treasure chest or casket.
    lieu of: return for.
258 *Tennis balls*: These were made of leather and stuffed with horsehair. The game of 'royal tennis', from which

Enter Ambassador of France *with* Attendants

Now are we well prepar'd to know the pleasure
235 Of our fair cousin Dauphin; for we hear
Your greeting is from him, not from the king.
    Ambassador
May't please your majesty to give us leave
Freely to render what we have in charge,
Or shall we sparingly show you far off
240 The Dauphin's meaning, and our embassy?
    King
We are no tyrant, but a Christian king,
Unto whose grace our passion is as subject
As are our wretches fetter'd in our prisons.
Therefore with frank and with uncurbed plainness
245 Tell us the Dauphin's mind.
    Ambassador
                    Thus then in few:
Your highness lately, sending into France,
Did claim some certain dukedoms, in the right
Of your great predecessor, King Edward the Third.
In answer of which claim the prince our master
250 Says that you savour too much of your youth,
And bids you be advis'd: there's naught in France
That can be with a nimble galliard won;
You cannot revel into dukedoms there.
He therefore sends you, meeter for your spirit,
255 This tun of treasure, and in lieu of this
Desires you let the dukedoms that you claim
Hear no more of you. This the Dauphin speaks.
    King
What treasure, uncle?
    Exeter
                [*Opens tun*] Tennis balls, my liege.
    King
We are glad the Dauphin is so pleasant with us.
260 His present and your pains we thank you for.
When we have match'd our rackets to these balls
We will in France, by God's grace, play a set
Shall strike his father's crown into the hazard.
Tell him he hath made a match with such a wrangler

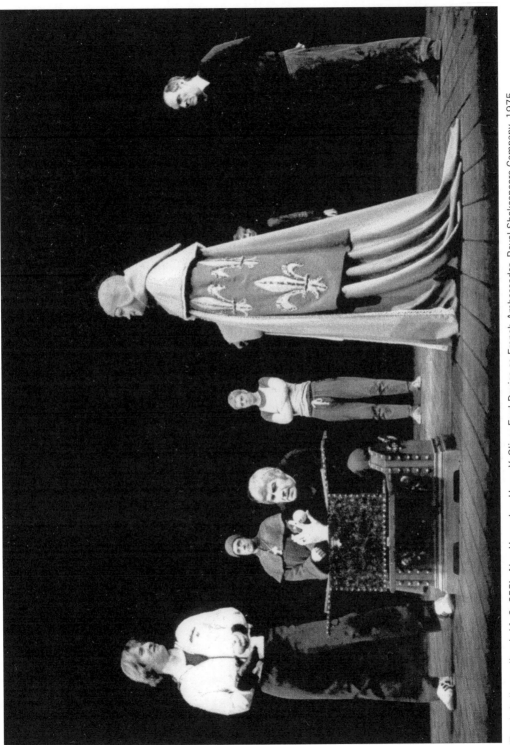

'Tennis balls, my liege', (1, 2, 258). Alan Howard as Henry V, Oliver Ford-Davies as French Ambassador, Royal Shakespeare Company, 1975.

modern lawn tennis is derived, was
very popular with the Elizabethan
nobility. It was played on an oblong
court, which was paved and enclosed
by walls. A rope or low net was
stretched between the two longer
walls, and the players used rackets,
netted with string, to drive their balls
from side to side. The two shorter
walls were pierced with holes called
'hazards', and points were scored by
driving a ball into one of these, or by
causing it to bounce twice before it
was struck by the opposing player
(making a 'chase').

259 *so pleasant with us*: can make such
     jokes at my expense.
260 *pains*: trouble (in bringing the
     message).
262 *set*: i.e. of tennis games.
263 *Shall*: that shall.
     into the hazard: See line 258 note.
264 *wrangler*: opponent—especially one
     who disputes in academic exercises.
265 *courts*: (a) royal; (b) tennis; (c) law.
266 *chases*: See line 258 note.
267 *comes o'er us*: throws in our face.
269 *seat*: estate, throne.
270 *hence*: away from it.
271 *barbarous licence*: uncivilized
     freedom.
     common: common practice, common
     knowledge.
272 *from*: away from.
273 *keep my state*: maintain my royal
     position.
274 *sail of greatness*: swelling powers of
     majesty (the image is from the full
     sails of a galleon).
275 *rouse me*: come out of my lair (see
     line 123); *and* raise myself up.
     my: King Henry re-asserts his claim.
276 *For that*: because.
     laid by: set aside.
277 *a man for working days*: a common
     man on working days.
281 *pleasant*: jesting.
282 *gun-stones*: cannon balls.
283 *sore charged*: chargèd; heavily
     burdened with guilt.
     wasteful: destructive.
     vengeance: revenge for the insult.
285 *mock out of*: cheat, deprive of.
287 *ungotten*: not yet begotten.
289 *lies all within*: all depends on.

265 That all the courts of France will be disturb'd
    With chases. And we understand him well,
    How he comes o'er us with our wilder days,
    Not measuring what use we made of them.
    We never valu'd this poor seat of England,
270 And therefore, living hence, did give ourself
    To barbarous licence, as 'tis ever common
    That men are merriest when they are from home.
    But tell the Dauphin I will keep my state,
    Be like a king, and show my sail of greatness
275 When I do rouse me in my throne of France.
    For that I have laid by my majesty
    And plodded like a man for working days.
    But I will rise there with so full a glory
    That I will dazzle all the eyes of France,
280 Yea, strike the Dauphin blind to look on us.
    And tell the pleasant prince this mock of his
    Hath turn'd his balls to gun-stones, and his soul
    Shall stand sore charged for the wasteful vengeance
    That shall fly with them; for many a thousand widows
285 Shall this his mock mock out of their dear husbands,
    Mock mothers from their sons, mock castles down,
    And some are yet ungotten and unborn
    That shall have cause to curse the Dauphin's scorn.
    But this lies all within the will of God,
290 To whom I do appeal, and in whose name

292 *venge*: avenge.
    as I may: as best I can.
293 *rightful hand*: King Henry constantly
    emphasizes the righteousness of his
    cause and the sacredness of his
    mission.
    well-hallow'd: most holy.
297 *Convey*: escort.

300 *omit no happy hour*: don't lose any
    convenient occasion.
301 *give furtherance*: advance.

303 'Except for our thoughts about God
    which must go before everything we
    do.'
304 *proportions*: forces.

307 *God before*: with God to guide us.
308 *chide*: reprove.
    at his father's door: on his home
    ground.
309 *task his thought*: give his mind to the
    job.
310 *on foot*: in motion.

Tell you the Dauphin I am coming on
To venge me as I may, and to put forth
My rightful hand in a well-hallow'd cause.
So get you hence in peace. And tell the Dauphin
295 His jest will savour but of shallow wit
When thousands weep more than did laugh at it.
[*To* Attendants] Convey them with safe conduct. Fare
    you well.
                    [*Exeunt* Ambassador *and* Attendants

Exeter
This was a merry message.
    King
We hope to make the sender blush at it.
300 Therefore, my lords, omit no happy hour
That may give furtherance to our expedition,
For we have now no thought in us but France,
Save those to God that run before our business.
Therefore let our proportions for these wars
305 Be soon collected, and all things thought upon
That may with reasonable swiftness add
More feathers to our wings. For, God before,
We'll chide this Dauphin at his father's door.
Therefore let every man now task his thought
310 That this fair action may on foot be brought.
                    [*Flourish. Exeunt*

ACT 2

London: the Globe. Enter Chorus

Chorus

Now all the youth of England are on fire
And silken dalliance in the wardrobe lies.
Now thrive the armourers, and honour's thought
Reigns solely in the breast of every man.
5   They sell the pasture now to buy the horse,
Following the mirror of all Christian kings
With winged heels, as English Mercuries.
For now sits expectation in the air,
And hides a sword from hilts unto the point
10   With crowns imperial, crowns and coronets
Promis'd to Harry and his followers.
The French, advis'd by good intelligence
Of this most dreadful preparation,
Shake in their fear, and with pale policy
15   Seek to divert the English purposes.
O England: model to thy inward greatness,
Like little body with a mighty heart,
What mightst thou do, that honour would thee do,
Were all thy children kind and natural?
20   But see, thy fault France hath in thee found out,
A nest of hollow bosoms, which he fills
With treacherous crowns, and three corrupted men—
One, Richard, Earl of Cambridge, and the second
Henry, Lord Scroop of Masham, and the third

Chorus

The Chorus tells how the English are preparing to invade France, and how three English lords have been bribed by the French king to betray and murder King Henry. The audience learns that the action of the play will now move from London to Southampton, and from there to France.

2   *silken dalliance . . . lies*: all frivolous behaviour has been set aside like the fine clothes of the courtiers which are left in the dressing-room ('wardrobe').
3   *honour's thought*: the thought of honour.
6   *mirror*: pattern of perfection.
7   *winged*: wingèd; Mercury was the messenger and herald of the classical gods; he is usually depicted with wings either on his heels or on his helmet.
8   *sits . . . air*: the air is full of expectation.
9   *a sword . . . point*: The heraldic device of Edward III was a sword ringed by crowns; Shakespeare could have seen a picture of this in his copy of Holinshed's Chronicles.
    hilts: the arms of the cross-piece.

10   *crowns imperial, crowns and coronets*: the king's crowns, gold coins (see line 22), and ducal coronets.
12   *advis'd*: warned.
      intelligence: secret reports, espionage.
14   *pale policy*: cowardly intrigue.
15   *divert*: change the course of.

16 *model*: miniature replica.
18 *that . . . do*: that would bring honour to you.
19 *kind and natural*: properly filial and obedient to the law of nature.
20 *fault*: weakness.
France: the king of France.
21 *hollow*: empty (of proper feelings), false.
bosoms: hearts; *and also* the clothes worn over the heart, in which money could be hidden.
22 *crowns*: gold coins—the French *écu*.
26 *gilt*: i.e. the crowns.
27 *fearful*: frightened.
28 *grace of kings*: model of kingship.
29 *hold*: keep.
30 *Ere*: before.
31 *Linger . . . on*: be patient.
31–2 *digest . . . distance*: set in order— help you to cope with—the problem of distance.
32 *force perforce*: cram, stuff by force feeding.
34 *is set*: has departed.
35 *gentles*: ladies and gentlemen.
38 *bring you back*: This is usually spoken as a joke.
charming: i.e. like a magician.
the narrow seas: the English Channel.
39 *gentle pass*: a good crossing.
if we may: if we can help it.
40 *offend one stomach*: displease anyone, cause anyone to be seasick.
41 *when the king come*: when the king comes.
41–2 These lines seem to contradict lines 35–6. Here we are told that the action will be set in Southampton only when the king appears: the scene that now follows is still set in London.

25 Sir Thomas Gray, knight of Northumberland—
Have for the gilt of France (oh, guilt indeed)
Confirm'd conspiracy with fearful France,
And by their hands this grace of kings must die,
If hell and treason hold their promises,
30 Ere he take ship for France, and in Southampton.
Linger your patience on, and we'll digest
Th'abuse of distance, force perforce a play.
The sum is paid, the traitors are agreed,
The king is set from London, and the scene
35 Is now transported, gentles, to Southampton.
There is the playhouse now, there must you sit,
And thence to France shall we convey you safe
And bring you back, charming the narrow seas
To give you gentle pass, for if we may
40 We'll not offend one stomach with our play.
But when the king come forth, and not till then,
Unto Southampton do we shift our scene   [*Exit*

Act 2 Scene 1
In a London street Bardolph encounters his mate, Nym, who is depressed because he has quarrelled with Pistol, another old crony. When Pistol comes on to the scene with his newly-married wife, Mistress Quickly, there is a violent slanging match, conducted in a mock-heroic style. Bardolph succeeds in averting bloodshed, and friendship is restored between the two antagonists when they are all called to the sickbed of Sir John Falstaff, the fat old knight who was once the close friend of Prince Hal, now King Henry V.

1 *Well met*: A common Elizabethan greeting—'Good to see you'.
  Corporal: the officer in charge of one quarter of a military company; Nym's is the lowest of the three rankings.
2 *morrow*: morning.
3 *Ancient*: a corruption of ensign (= standard bearer); the rank is mid-way between lieutenant and corporal.
4–5 *when time shall serve*: when the time is right.
5 *shall be smiles*: I shall be friendly enough.
6 *wink*: close my eyes.
  iron: sword.
7 *simple*: cheap.
  what though: so what; Nym's speech is usually sprinkled with such meaningless expressions.
7–8 *toast . . . cold*: be useful both as a toasting-fork and as a weapon.
8 *as*: as well as.
  another: any other.
9 *there's an end*: that's all there is to it.
10 *bestow a breakfast*: invite you to breakfast.
11 *sworn brothers*: joined in a brotherhood (usually said of chivalrous knights—or thieves).
13 *Faith*: in faith, indeed.
  the certain: for sure.
14–15 *when . . . may*: a proverbial expression: 'He that cannot do as he would [wants to] must do as he may'.
15 *That is my rest*: that is my final bid—an expression borrowed from the game of primero.
  rendezvous: last resort.
16 *Nell Quickly*: In *Henry IV Part 2* she was the hostess of the Boar's Head tavern in Eastcheap.

Scene 1

London: a street. Enter Corporal Nym *and* Lieutenant Bardolph

Bardolph
Well met, Corporal Nym.
  Nym
Good morrow, Lieutenant Bardolph.
  Bardolph
What, are Ancient Pistol and you friends yet?
  Nym
For my part, I care not. I say little, but when time shall
5 serve there shall be smiles, but that shall be as it may. I dare not fight, but I will wink and hold out mine iron. It is a simple one, but what though? It will toast cheese, and it will endure cold as another man's sword will, and there's an end.

Bardolph
10 I will bestow a breakfast to make you friends, and we'll be all three sworn brothers to France. Let's be so, good Corporal Nym.
  Nym
Faith, I will live so long as I may, that's the certain of it, and when I cannot live any longer I will do as I
15 may. That is my rest, that is the rendezvous of it.
  Bardolph
It is certain, corporal, that he is married to Nell Quickly, and certainly she did you wrong, for you were troth-plight to her.
  Nym
I cannot tell. Things must be as they may. Men may
20 sleep, and they may have their throats about them at that time, and some say knives have edges. It must be as

'if he be not hewn now, we shall see wilful adultery and murder committed.' (2, 1, 33–4) Patricia Routledge as Mistress Quickly and Bernard Horsfall as Pistol, Royal Shakespeare Company, 1984.

17–18 *troth-plight*: betrothed; the contract was more binding than the modern engagement.

22–3 *Though . . . plod*: although it may be tedious, patience will get there (i.e. succeed) in the end.

23 *conclusions*: some way of sorting things out.

26 *host*: Nym's form of address is insulting to his superior officer. Pistol became the host (= innkeeper) of the tavern through his marriage to Mistress Quickly, the hostess (= landlady).

27 *tyke*: mongrel, cur.

29 *my troth*: my word.
not long: Perhaps the lodgers will not stay long because the inn has a reputation for being a brothel—or perhaps it is a brothel.

31 *honestly*: respectably.
by the prick of their needles: as seamstresses—but the phrase is capable of bawdy innuendo.

32 *bawdy house*: brothel.
straight: at once.

33 *welladay*: oh dear me.
Lady: by Our Lady (the Virgin Mary)—a mild oath.
be not hewn: is not cut down.

34 *wilful adultery*: A characteristic of the Hostess's speech is her mistaking of words; here, perhaps, she means 'rape'—unwilling adultery.

35 *lieutenant*: Shakespeare seems to have forgotten that it is Bardolph who is the lieutenant—although at 3, 7,11–12 Pistol is addressed as 'ancient lieutenant' (= sub-lieutenant).
offer nothing: don't start a fight.

37 *Iceland dog*: These were small, hairy lap-dogs with pointed ('prick') ears, with a reputation for snappish bad-temper.

39 *show thy valour*: This is usually an exhortation to fight.
put up: put away, sheath.

41 *shog off*: go away, clear off.

42 *solus*: alone; the Latin word is often used in stage directions.

42–47 Pistol's speech is really an expansion of the phrase 'make him eat his words'. He visualizes throwing Nym's word back in his face, crushing it against his teeth, and thrusting it down his throat, into his lungs and stomach ('maw'), so that it even comes out by way of his bowels.

it may. Though patience be a tired mare, yet she will plod. There must be conclusions. Well, I cannot tell.

Enter Pistol *and* Hostess

Bardolph
Here comes Ancient Pistol and his wife. Good corporal,
25 be patient here.
Nym
How now, mine host Pistol?
Pistol
Base tyke, call'st thou me host? Now by this hand I swear I scorn the term, nor shall my Nell keep lodgers.
Hostess
No, by my troth, not long, for we cannot lodge and
30 board a dozen or fourteen gentlewomen that live honestly by the prick of their needles but it will be thought we keep a bawdy house straight. [Nym *draws his sword*] Oh, welladay, Lady, if he be not hewn now, we shall see wilful adultery and murder committed.

Pistol *draws his sword*

Bardolph
35 Good lieutenant, good corporal, offer nothing here.
Nym
Pish.
Pistol
Pish for thee, Iceland dog, thou prick-eared cur of Iceland.
Hostess
Good Corporal Nym, show thy valour, and put up your
40 sword.

They sheathe their swords

Nym
Will you shog off? [*To* Pistol] I would have you *solus*.
Pistol
Solus, egregious dog? O viper vile! The *solus* in thy most mervailous face, the *solus* in thy teeth, and in thy throat, and in thy hateful lungs, yea, in thy maw, perdy, and,

43 *mervailous*: marvellous; the accent is on the second syllable.

44 *perdy*: by God (French *par dieu*).

45 *nasty*: foul (the word had greater force in Shakespeare's time).

46 *take*: blast, curse.

46–7 *cock is up*: A gun is ready for firing when it is cocked up; here the sexual innuendo is obvious.

48 *Barbason*: The name is that of a French knight who fought Henry V at the siege of Melun; Nym probably refers to Barbas, a fiend who appeared in the likeness of a raging lion.
conjure: exorcise: Pistol's grandiose speech reminds Nym of the style of a magician.

49 *humour*: urge, whim.
knock: beat.
indifferently well: thoroughly.

49–50 *grow foul*: discharge your filth.

50 *scour*: cleanse.
rapier: a thin sword; Nym offers to run this through Pistol's body as a rod is drawn through a gun—or blocked-up pipe—for cleaning purposes.

50–1 *as I may, in fair terms*: to put it as decently as I can.

51 *walk off*: i.e. come to a more secluded area, away from a main street.

52–3 *that's the humour of it*: that's how it is.

54 *braggart*: boaster.
wight: person; the word was obsolescent at Shakespeare's time, but it suits Pistol's mock-heroic style.

55 *gape*: open wide.
doting death is near: death is eager to receive you very soon.
exhale: draw forth [your sword].

57 *hilts*: arms protecting the handle of the sword.

59 *mickle*: great.

60 *forefoot*: front paw.
tall: valiant.

63 *Couple a gorge*: Pistol intends the French *coupez la gorge* (= cut his throat).

64 *hound of Crete*: Only one reference (in Golding's translation of Ovid's *Metamorphoses*) describes Cretan hounds as being hairy.

65 *Spital*: hospital, especially for the treatment of venereal diseases.
powdering tub: heated tub generally used for salting beef but here

45 which is worse, within thy nasty mouth! I do retort the *solus* in thy bowels, for I can take, and Pistol's cock is up, and flashing fire will follow!

Nym

I am not Barbason, you cannot conjure me. I have an humour to knock you indifferently well. If you grow
50 foul with me, Pistol, I will scour you with my rapier, as I may, in fair terms. If you would walk off I would prick your guts a little in good terms, as I may, and that's the humour of it.

Pistol

O braggart vile, and damned furious wight, the grave
55 doth gape and doting death is near. Therefore exhale!

They draw their swords

Bardolph

Hear me, hear me what I say. [*Draws his sword*] He that strikes the first stroke, I'll run him up to the hilts, as I am a soldier.

Pistol

An oath of mickle might, and fury shall abate. Give me
60 thy fist, thy forefoot to me give. Thy spirits are most tall.

Nym

I will cut thy throat one time or other in fair terms, that is the humour of it.

Pistol

Couple a gorge, that is the word. I defy thee again! O hound of Crete, thinkst thou my spouse to get? No, to
65 the Spital go, and from the powdering tub of infamy fetch forth the lazar kite of Cressid's kind, Doll Tearsheet, she by name, and her espouse. I have, and I will hold the quondam Quickly for the only she, and *pauca*, there's enough. Go to.

specifically thought of as a treatment for venereal disease.

66 *the . . . kind*: that diseased carrion bird of Cressida's family. Medieval stories tell how Cressida was false to her lover Troilus and, as punishment, was afflicted with leprosy (sometimes, by the Elizabethans, equated with syphilis).

66–7 *Doll Tearsheet*: A prostitute in *Henry IV Part 2*; at the end of that play she was taken away to prison.

67 *espouse*: marry.

67–8 *I have . . . she*: Pistol, newly married, remembers the promise he has just made in the marriage service, 'to have, and to hold [his wife] . . . forsaking all other'.

68 *quondam*: former (Latin).
   the only she: the only woman in the world.

69 *pauca*: few words (Latin).
   Go to: get on with it, get away with you.

70 *my master*: i.e. Sir John Falstaff; the Boy is the page given to Falstaff by Prince Hal in *Henry IV Part 2*.

71 *would to bed*: wants to go to bed.

72 *thy face*: Bardolph's face was red and full of spots or boils; it was the subject of many good-humoured jokes in *Henry IV Part 1*.

73 *warming pan*: long-handled covered pan filled with hot coals used (like the modern hot-water bottle) to warm the sheets.

75 *yield . . . pudding*: become food for birds; the expression was often used to predict death by hanging—perhaps the Hostess refers to the Boy, although her next words speak of Falstaff.

76 *The king . . . heart*: In *Henry IV Part 2* the king, immediately after his coronation, rejected his former way of life and, in particular, his friend Sir John Falstaff. The rejection completely broke Falstaff's heart, so that he lost all pleasure in living; see p. xxxiii.

77 *presently*: at once.

78 *must*: must go.

81 Pistol's declaration of friendship (which will last until the rivers overflow their banks, and the devils cry out for lack of damned souls to

Enter the Boy

Boy
70 Mine host Pistol, you must come to my master, and your hostess. He is very sick, and would to bed. Good Bardolph, put thy face between his sheets and do the office of a warming pan. Faith, he's very ill.

Bardolph
Away, you rogue.

Hostess
75 By my troth, he'll yield the crow a pudding one of these days. The king has killed his heart. Good husband, come home presently.

[*Exeunt* Hostess *and* Boy

Bardolph
Come, shall I make you two friends? We must to France together. Why the devil should we keep knives to cut
80 one another's throats?

Pistol
Let floods o'erswell, and fiends for food howl on!

Nym
You'll pay me the eight shillings I won of you at betting?

Pistol
Base is the slave that pays.

Nym
85 That now I will have. That's the humour of it.

Pistol
As manhood shall compound. Push home.

They draw their swords

Bardolph
[*Draws his sword*] By this sword, he that makes the first thrust, I'll kill him, by this sword I will.

Pistol
Sword is an oath, and oaths must have their course.

Sheathes his sword

feed on) is as extreme as his
professions of enmity had been.

82 *eight shillings*: a considerable sum of
money in Elizabethan currency.
of: from.

84 This seems to be Pistol's version of
the saying, 'The poor man always
pays'.

86 *manhood*: courage.
compound: decide.
Push home: fight for it.

89 *Sword*: i.e. by God's word.
have their course: be fulfilled.

90 *an*: if.

91 *Prithee*: I pray you.

92 *put up*: sheath your sword.

93 *A noble*: a coin worth six shillings and
eight pence; Pistol wants discount for
cash.
present pay: ready money.

95–6 *I'll live . . . by me*: I'll live by the
help of a thief, and the thief shall live
by my help; Pistol puns on the
meaning ('nim' = to steal) of Nym's
name.

96 *sutler*: store-keeper, one who sells
provisions to the army.

97 *profits will accrue*: i.e. Pistol will
make some money for himself.

Bardolph

90 Corporal Nym, an thou wilt be friends, be friends. An thou wilt not, why then be enemies with me too. Prithee put up.

Nym sheathes his sword

Pistol

A noble shalt thou have, and present pay, and liquor likewise will I give to thee, and friendship shall
95 combine, and brotherhood. I'll live by Nym and Nym shall live by me; is not this just? For I shall sutler be unto the camp, and profits will accrue. Give me thy hand.

Nym

I shall have my noble?

Pistol

In cash, most justly paid.

Nym

100 Well, then that's the humour of it.

101 *come of*: are born of—i.e. have human
feelings.

103 *quotidian tertian*: The symptoms of
the *quotidian fever* occurred daily,
while those of the *tertian* appeared on
alternate days; the fevers may be
combined in Falstaff's sickness—or
perhaps the Hostess is confused.

Enter Hostess *and* Boy

Hostess

As ever you come of women, come in quickly to Sir John. Ah, poor heart, he is so shaked of a burning quotidian tertian that it is most lamentable to behold. Sweet men, come to him.

105 *run bad humours*: vented his bad
    mood on Falstaff; or caused Falstaff's
    melancholy.
106 *even*: plain truth.
107 *fracted*: broken.
108 *corroborate*: re-hardened; Pistol's
    Latinate vocabulary has led him into
    some confusion.
110 *passes . . . careers*: indulges some
    strange moods and wild actions; in
    terms of horsemanship, a 'career' is a
    short gallop during which the horse
    changes direction several times.
111 *condole*: sympathize with.
    lambkins: my little ones.
    we will live: i.e. they themselves will
    go on living even though Falstaff is
    dying.

Act 2 Scene 2
Three counsellors talk about some traitors
whom the king apparently trusts. They are
confident, however, that the treachery will
soon be revealed and that King Henry is
fully in control of the situation. The king
enters, along with three noblemen who
speak in praise of Henry's virtues and of
their own loyalty to him. When asked for
their opinions about a man who has abused
the monarch, they all recommend severe
punishment for him. King Henry confronts
them with evidence of their own conspiracy
against him—especially reproaching them,
especially Lord Scroop—for their betrayal of his love
and trust. He pronounces sentence of death
upon them all, and then turns his attention
to the war with France.

 1 *'Fore*: before, in the name of.
   bold: rash.
 2 *apprehended*: arrested.
 3 *smooth and even*: confidently.
 4 *bosoms*: hearts.
 5 *Crowned*: crownèd.
   constant: firm.
 7 *By interception*: i.e. their schemes
   have been intercepted and the king
   has been informed.
   dream not of: The conspiracy was
   revealed to the king by the Earl of
   March, the very man who would have
   gained most from its success; see
   line 153 note.

Nym
105 The king hath run bad humours on the knight; that's
the even of it.
    Pistol
Nym, thou hast spoke the right, his heart is fracted and
corroborate.
    Nym
The king is a good king, but it must be as it may. He
110 passes some humours and careers.
    Pistol
Let us condole the knight, for, lambkins, we will live.
                                                  [*Exeunt*

SCENE 2

Southampton: enter Exeter, Bedford, *and*
Westmorland

Bedford
'Fore God, his grace is bold to trust these traitors.
    Exeter
They shall be apprehended by and by.
    Westmorland
How smooth and even they do bear themselves,
As if allegiance in their bosoms sat,
5 Crowned with faith and constant loyalty.
    Bedford
The king hath note of all that they intend
By interception which they dream not of.
    Exeter
Nay, but the man that was his bedfellow,
Whom he hath dull'd and cloy'd with gracious favours;
10 That he should for a foreign purse so sell
His sovereign's life to death and treachery!

Sound trumpets. Enter the King, Scroop, Cambridge,
Gray, *and* Officers

8 *bedfellow*: closest friend—i.e. Lord Scroop; see lines 91–139. It was very common for friends to share a bed in the sixteenth and seventeenth centuries.
9 *dull'd and cloy'd*: more than satisfied, even surfeited, his appetite.
10 *foreign purse*: bribes from a foreign country.
15 *powers*: forces, army.
17 *the execution and the act*: performing the deed.
18 *in head*: as an army.

20 *well persuaded*: fully believe.

22 *grows . . . consent*: is not in full agreement.

25 *fear'd and lov'd*: In a well-known book *The Prince*, the sixteenth-century statesman Niccolo Machiavelli discussed the question of whether a ruler should be feared more than loved.
27 *heart-grief*: melancholy.
28 *sweet shade*: gentle protection.
30 *steep'd their galls*: drowned their bitterness.

32 *cause of*: reason for.
33 *forget . . . hand*: forget how to use my hand. The king's words seem to echo those of Psalm 137: 'If I forget thee, O Jerusalem, let my right hand forget her cunning'.
34 *quittance*: repayment.
   desert: worth.
35 *weight*: value.
36 *service*: each man's service.
   steeled: steelèd; toughened.
37 *labour*: every man's work.
38 *incessant*: unceasing.
40 *Enlarge*: set free.
41 *rail'd against*: offered verbal abuse to.
42 *set him on*: excited him.
43 *his more advice*: when he has thought more about it.

King
Now sits the wind fair, and we will aboard.
My lord of Cambridge and my kind lord Masham,
And you my gentle knight, give me your thoughts.
15 Think you not that the powers we bear with us
Will cut their passage through the force of France,
Doing the execution and the act
For which we have in head assembled them?
Scroop
No doubt, my liege, if each man do his best.
King
20 I doubt not that, since we are well persuaded
We carry not a heart with us from hence
That grows not in a fair consent with ours,
Nor leave not one behind that doth not wish
Success and conquest to attend on us.
Cambridge
25 Never was monarch better fear'd and lov'd
Than is your majesty. There's not I think a subject
That sits in heart-grief and uneasiness
Under the sweet shade of your government.
Gray
True. Those that were your father's enemies
30 Have steep'd their galls in honey, and do serve you
With hearts create of duty and of zeal.
King
We therefore have great cause of thankfulness,
And shall forget the office of our hand
Sooner than quittance of desert and merit,
35 According to the weight and worthiness.
Scroop
So service shall with steeled sinews toil
And labour shall refresh itself with hope,
To do your grace incessant services.
King
We judge no less. Uncle of Exeter,
40 Enlarge the man committed yesterday
That rail'd against our person. We consider
It was excess of wine that set him on,
And on his more advice we pardon him.

44 *security*: over-confidence.

46 *by his sufferance*: by allowing him to go unpunished.

49 *give him life*: allow him to live.
50 *the taste of much correction*: suffering severe punishment.

51 *too much*: very great.

52 *heavy orisons*: pleas that weigh heavily.
53–6 *If . . . us*: if we cannot close our eyes ('wink') to such little faults, how wide must we open ('stretch') them when we see major crimes.
53 *proceeding on distemper*: caused by a disordered state of mind.
55 *capital crimes*: crimes punishable by death.
   chew'd, swallow'd, and digested: i.e. very well planned.
58 *preservation*: protection.

60 *late*: recently appointed.
   commissioners: regents who will govern the kingdom in the king's absence.
61 *it*: the written commission; from this remark, it becomes evident to the nobles—and to the audience—that Henry has stage-managed this entire business.

Scroop
That's mercy, but too much security.
45 Let him be punish'd, sovereign, lest example
Breed by his sufferance more of such a kind.
   King
Oh, let us yet be merciful.
   Cambridge
So may your highness, and yet punish too.
   Gray
Sir, you show great mercy if you give him life
50 After the taste of much correction.
   King
Alas, your too much love and care of me
Are heavy orisons 'gainst this poor wretch.
If little faults, proceeding on distemper,
Shall not be wink'd at, how shall we stretch our eye
55 When capital crimes, chew'd, swallow'd, and digested,
Appear before us? We'll yet enlarge that man,
Though Cambridge, Scroop, and Gray, in their dear care
And tender preservation of our person
Would have him punish'd. And now to our French causes.
60 Who are the late commissioners?
   Cambridge
                                    I one, my lord.
Your highness bade me ask for it today.
   Scroop
So did you me, my liege.
   Gray
                              And I, my royal sovereign.
   King
Then Richard, Earl of Cambridge, there is yours.
There yours, Lord Scroop of Masham, and sir knight,
65 Gray of Northumberland, this same is yours.

   Gives them papers

Read them and know I know your worthiness.
My lord of Westmorland and uncle Exeter,
We will aboard tonight. Why, how now, gentlemen?

70 *complexion*: colour from your cheeks.
71 *paper*: the colour—white—of paper.
72 *cowarded*: turned into a coward.
73 *appearance*: sight.

What see you in those papers, that you lose
70 So much complexion? Look ye how they change.
Their cheeks are paper. Why, what read you there,
That have so cowarded and chas'd your blood
Out of appearance?
    Cambridge
                I do confess my fault,
And do submit me to your highness' mercy.

Kneels

Gray and **Scroop**
75 To which we all appeal.

They kneel

King
The mercy that was quick in us but late
By your own counsel is suppress'd and kill'd.
You must not dare for shame to talk of mercy,
For your own reasons turn into your bosoms,
80 As dogs upon their masters, worrying you.
See you, my princes and my noble peers,
These English monsters. My lord of Cambridge here,
You know how apt our love was to accord,
To furnish him with all appurtenants
85 Belonging to his honour, and this man
Hath for a few light crowns lightly conspir'd
And sworn unto the practices of France
To kill us here in Hampton. To the which
This knight, no less for bounty bound to us
90 Than Cambridge is, hath likewise sworn. But oh,
What shall I say to thee, Lord Scroop, thou cruel,
Ingrateful, savage, and inhuman creature?
Thou that didst bear the key of all my counsels,
That knew'st the very bottom of my soul,
95 That almost mightst have coin'd me into gold,
Wouldst thou have practis'd on me for thy use?
May it be possible that foreign hire
Could out of thee extract one spark of evil
That might annoy my finger? 'Tis so strange

76 *quick*: alive.
   but late: just now.
80 *worrying you*: tearing you to pieces.
82 *English monsters*: Unnatural or
   deformed creatures, usually said to be
   of foreign origin, were often on
   exhibition in Elizabethan fairs.
83 *apt*: ready.
   accord: consent, agree.
84 *appurtenants*: things appropriate.
86 *light crowns*: treacherous money.
   lightly conspir'd: readily plotted.
87 *practices*: schemes.
88 *Hampton*: Southampton.
89 *This knight*: i.e. Lord Gray.
   no less . . . us: was equally obliged to
   my generosity.
92 *Ingrateful*: ungrateful; the Elizabethan
   form of the word seems more forceful
   than the modern one.
93 *bear . . . counsels*: had access to all
   my secrets.
94 *bottom*: deepest part.
95 *coin'd me into gold*: used me as the
   mint; Scroop was Lord Treasurer until
   1411.
96 *Wouldst . . . use*: if you had wanted to
   use your schemes against me for your
   own purposes.
97 *May*: can.
   hire: bribery.

99 *might annoy*: could hurt.

100–1 *stands off . . . white*: stands out as plainly as if it were written in black and white.
101 *my eye . . . it*: i.e. I can hardly believe it.
102 *kept*: lived, worked.
103 *yoke-devils*: devils harnessed—yoked—together like oxen.
either's: each other's.
104 *grossly*: obviously.
natural: i.e. for devils.
105 *That . . . them*: that they raised no outcry of amazement.
106 *proportion*: natural order.
109 *preposterously*: unnaturally.
110 *got the voice*: won the vote.
111 *suggest*: tempt.
112–14 *Do . . . piety*: The damnation is less perfectly achieved by the other devils because the traitor is deceived into thinking that he has some virtuous reason for what he is doing.
112 *botch*: patch, cobble.
113 *patches*: pretences.
colours: false pretexts.
forms: devices.
fetch'd: derived.
114 *glistering*: falsely glittering, flashy.
semblances: appearances.
piety: loyalty.
115 *he that temper'd thee*: the devil that moulded you to fit his cause.
bade thee stand up: ordered you to rebel.
116 *instance*: reason.
117 *dub*: confer a knighthood (so that Scroop would have been 'Sir Traitor').
118 *gull'd*: deceived.
119 *lion gait*: moving like a lion; the king's words echo those of the Bible; 'your adversary the devil, as a roaring lion, walketh about, seeking whom he may devour' (1 Peter, 5:8).
120 *vasty Tartar*: the vast depths of Tartarus; in classical mythology this was the equivalent of hell.
121 *legions*: a Roman legion was composed of more than 6,000 soldiers; in the Bible the unclean spirit said he was called Legion, 'for we are many' (Mark, 5:9).
123 *jealousy*: suspicion.
124 *affiance*: trust.
Show men: do men seem.
128 *spare in diet*: moderate in what they eat.

100 That though the truth of it stands off as gross
     As black on white my eye will scarcely see it.
     Treason and murder ever kept together,
     As two yoke-devils sworn to either's purpose,
     Working so grossly in a natural cause
105 That admiration did not whoop at them.
     But thou 'gainst all proportion didst bring in
     Wonder to wait on treason and on murder,
     And whatsoever cunning fiend it was
     That wrought upon thee so preposterously
110 Hath got the voice in hell for excellence.
     All other devils that suggest by treasons
     Do botch and bungle up damnation
     With patches, colours, and with forms being fetch'd
     From glistering semblances of piety;
115 But he that temper'd thee bade thee stand up,
     Gave thee no instance why thou shouldst do treason,
     Unless to dub thee with the name of traitor.
     If that same demon that hath gull'd thee thus
     Should with his lion gait walk the whole world
120 He might return to vasty Tartar back
     And tell the legions 'I can never win
     A soul so easy as that Englishman's.'
     Oh, how hast thou with jealousy infected
     The sweetness of affiance? Show men dutiful?
125 Why, so didst thou. Seem they grave and learned?
     Why, so didst thou. Come they of noble family?
     Why, so didst thou. Seem they religious?
     Why, so didst thou. Or are they spare in diet,
     Free from gross passion, or of mirth or anger,
130 Constant in spirit, not swerving with the blood,
     Garnish'd and deck'd in modest complement,
     Not working with the eye without the ear,
     And but in purged judgement trusting neither?
     Such and so finely bolted didst thou seem.
135 And thus thy fall hath left a kind of blot
     To mark the full fraught man, and best endow'd
     With some suspicion. I will weep for thee,
     For this revolt of thine, methinks, is like
     Another fall of man. Their faults are open.
140 Arrest them to the answer of the law,
     And God acquit them of their practices.

129 *or . . . or*: either . . . or.

130 *swerving with the blood*: carried away by passion.

131 *Garnish'd*: adorned.
complement: outward appearance; *or* personal qualities.

132 *Not . . . ear*: not trusting the evidence of either eye or ear alone.

133 *but*: except.
purged: purgèd; purified.

134 *bolted*: sifted (like flour).

136 *full fraught*: fully laden (i.e. with rich experience and wisdom); the words usually describe merchant ships.
best endow'd: endowed with the best qualities.

139 *fall of man*: The first fall of man was brought about when Satan tempted Adam and Eve (Genesis chs. 2–3).
open: manifest.

140 *answer of the law*: answer charges brought by the law.

141 *practices*: scheming.

147 *purposes*: schemes.

151 *For me*: as far as I am concerned.

152 *admit*: accept.

153 *effect*: accomplish.
what I intended: Cambridge was part of a conspiracy to put Edmund Mortimer, the Earl of March, on the English throne (see 'Family Tree', p. x).

154 *thanked*: thankèd.

155 *in sufferance*: in enduring the penalty.

159 *joy o'er myself*: rejoice over the discovery of my own treachery.

160 *damned*: damnèd.

162 *quit*: forgive.

165 *earnest*: part-payment in advance.

170 *Touching*: as regards.

171 *tender*: cherish.

175 *taste*: suffering.

177 *dear*: costing dearly.

Exeter
I arrest thee of high treason, by the name of Richard
Earl of Cambridge. I arrest thee of high treason, by the
name of Henry, Lord Scroop of Masham. I arrest thee of
145 high treason, by the name of Thomas Gray, knight of
Northumberland.
Scroop
Our purposes God justly hath discover'd,
And I repent my fault more than my death,
Which I beseech your highness to forgive,
150 Although my body pay the price of it.
Cambridge
For me, the gold of France did not seduce
Although I did admit it as a motive
The sooner to effect what I intended.
But God be thanked for prevention,
155 Which I in sufferance heartily will rejoice,
Beseeching God and you to pardon me.
Gray
Never did faithful subject more rejoice
At the discovery of most dangerous treason
Than I do at this hour joy o'er myself,
160 Prevented from a damned enterprise.
My fault, but not my body, pardon, sovereign.
King
God quit you in His mercy. Hear your sentence.
You have conspir'd against our royal person,
Join'd with an enemy proclaim'd, and from his coffers
165 Receiv'd the golden earnest of our death;
Wherein you would have sold your king to slaughter,
His princes and his peers to servitude,
His subjects to oppression and contempt,
And his whole kingdom into desolation.
170 Touching our person seek we no revenge,
But we our kingdom's safety must so tender,
Whose ruin you have sought, that to her laws
We do deliver you. Get you therefore hence,
Poor miserable wretches, to your death,
175 The taste whereof God of His mercy give
You patience to endure, and true repentance
Of all your dear offences. Bear them hence.
[*Exeunt* Cambridge, Scroop, Gray, *and* Officers

179 *like*: equally.

184 *rub*: obstacle.
    smoothed: smoothèd.
186 *puissance*: power, forces.
187 *straight*: immediately.
    in expedition: in motion.
188 *Cheerly*: cheerfully.
    signs: ensigns, standards.
    advance: raise.
189s.d. *Flourish*: trumpet call.

Act 2 Scene 3
Sir John Falstaff is dead. His friends grieve,
telling how he died, and remembering
details of his life. At last the men set off to
go to France with the king's army, leaving
the Hostess behind to look after things at
home.

2 *Staines*: a town about twenty miles
    from London on the road to
    Southampton.
3 *yearn*: grieve, mourn.
4 *vaunting veins*: swaggering spirits.
    bristle: rouse.
5 *we . . . therefore*: consequently we
    shall have to provide for ourselves;
    Falstaff was also a source of cash for
    his followers.
6 *Would*: I wish.
    wheresome're: wheresoever.
8 *Arthur's bosom*: The Hostess confuses
    King Arthur, the legendary ruler of the
    Knights of the Round Table and the
    model of English chivalry, with the
    Biblical patriarch, Abraham. The
    parable of Dives and Lazarus (Luke
    16:19–31) tells how Dives, the rich
    man, died and went to hell, whereas
    the beggar Lazarus was carried away
    to heaven—'Abraham's bosom'.
9 *A*: he.
10 *went away*: died.
    an: as if.

Now lords, for France, the enterprise whereof
Shall be to you as us, like glorious.
180 We doubt not of a fair and lucky war,
Since God so graciously hath brought to light
This dangerous treason lurking in our way
To hinder our beginnings. We doubt not now
But every rub is smoothed on our way.
185 Then forth, dear countrymen. Let us deliver
Our puissance into the hand of God,
Putting it straight in expedition.
Cheerly to sea, the signs of war advance.
No king of England if not king of France!

[*Flourish. Exeunt*

Scene 3

London: a tavern. Enter Pistol, Nym, Bardolph, Boy,
and Hostess

Hostess
Prithee, honey-sweet husband, let me bring thee to
Staines.
    Pistol
No, for my manly heart doth yearn. Bardolph, be blithe.
Nym, rouse thy vaunting veins. Boy, bristle thy courage
5 up, for Falstaff he is dead, and we must earn therefore.
    Bardolph
Would I were with him, wheresome're he is, either in
heaven or in hell.
    Hostess
Nay, sure, he's not in hell. He's in Arthur's bosom if ever
man went to Arthur's bosom. A made a finer
10 end, and went away an it had been any christom child.
A parted e'en just between twelve and one, e'en at the
turning o'the tide, for after I saw him fumble with the
sheets, and play with flowers, and smile upon his
finger's end, I knew there was but one way. For his nose
15 was as sharp as a pen, and a babbled of green fields.
'How now, Sir John,' quoth I, 'what man, be o' good
cheer!' So a cried out 'God, God, God' three or four

10 *christom child*: newly christened baby. For the first month after baptism the infant was dressed in a white robe called a 'chrism-cloth' ('chrism' = the oil then used for anointing at baptism).

11–12 *A parted . . . tide*: he died between midnight and one o'clock, just as the tide was turning. It was a very old superstition that the life of a dying man ebbed away with the ebbing of the tide.

12–15 *fumble . . . pen*: These were said to be classical signs of impending death.

15 *a pen*: a sharpened goose quill.
a babbled: This is one of the most famous of textual problems; F reads 'a Table', but an eighteenth-century editor, Lewis Theobald, emended to the present reading.
green fields: Falstaff may have been remembering the 'green pastures' of Psalm 23.

20 *bade*: told (the past tense of 'bid').

23 *up-peered*: upward; this may be an attempt to indicate the Hostess's dialectal pronunciation.

25 *of sack*: against drinking sack; this Spanish wine was Falstaff's favourite drink in *Henry IV Part 1*.

27 *of women*: against women.

29 *incarnate*: made flesh; but the Hostess misunderstands.

30 *carnation*: Sixteenth-century carnations were pink—an appropriate colour for devils.

33 *handle*: talk about.

34 *rheumatic*: The Hostess would stress the first syllable; she probably means 'lunatic' (= confused, deranged).
Whore of Babylon: the 'scarlet woman' of the Book of Revelation (17:4–5); the term was often applied by English Protestants to the pope and hence to the Roman Catholic Church. The Hostess's speech moves by association from 'incarnate' and 'carnation' and perhaps from 'rheumatic' to 'Rome' (which was then pronounced 'Room').

37 *fuel*: i.e. the drink paid for by Falstaff.

39 *shog*: get on our way.

times. Now I, to comfort him, bid him a should not think of God; I hoped there was no need to trouble
20 himself with any such thoughts yet. So a bade me lay more clothes on his feet. I put my hand into the bed, and felt them, and they were as cold as any stone. Then I felt to his knees, and so up-peered and upward, and all was as cold as any stone.

Nym

25 They say he cried out of sack.

Hostess

Ay, that a did.

Bardolph

And of women.

Hostess

Nay, that a did not.

Boy

Yes, that a did, and said they were devils incarnate.

Hostess

30 A could never abide carnation, 'twas a colour he never liked.

Boy

A said once, the Devil would have him about women.

Hostess

A did in some sort, indeed, handle women. But then he was rheumatic, and talked of the Whore of Babylon.

Boy

35 Do you not remember a saw a flea stick upon Bardolph's nose, and a said it was a black soul burning in hell?

Bardolph

Well, the fuel is gone that maintained that fire. That's all the riches I got in his service.

Nym

Shall we shog? The king will be gone from
40 Southampton.

'A made a finer end, and went away an it had been any christom child.' (*2*, 3, 9–10) Joanna McCallum as Mistress Quickly, Royal Shakespeare Company, 1994.

Pistol

Come, let's away. My love, give me thy lips. Look to my
chattels and my moveables. Let senses rule: the word is,
pitch and pay. Trust none, for oaths are straws, men's
faiths are wafer cakes, and Hold-fast is the only dog, my
45 duck. Therefore *caveto* be thy counsellor. Go, clear thy
crystals. Yoke-fellows in arms, let us to France, like
horseleeches, my boys, to suck, to suck, the very blood
to suck!

Boy

And that's but unwholesome food, they say.

Pistol

50 Touch her soft mouth, and march.

Bardolph

Farewell, hostess.

Kisses her

Nym

I cannot kiss, that is the humour of it, but adieu.

Pistol

Let housewifery appear. Keep close, I thee command.

Hostess

Farewell, adieu.   [*Exeunt*

Scene 4

France: the French king's palace. Flourish. Enter the
French King, *the* Dauphin, *the* Dukes of Berri *and*
Bourbon, *the* Constable, *and other* Lords

French King

Thus comes the English with full power upon us,
And more than carefully it us concerns
To answer royally in our defences.
Therefore the Dukes of Berri and of Bourbon,
5 Of Brabant and of Orléans, shall make forth,
And you, Prince Dauphin, with all swift despatch
To line and new repair our towns of war
With men of courage and with means defendant,

Notes (left column):

41–2 *Look to . . . moveables*: look after
    everything I have (which could be
    stolen).
42 *Let senses rule*: keep on the alert.
43 *pitch and pay*: cash down, no credit.
    straws: no stronger than straws.
44 *wafer cakes*: promises are like thin
    cakes (compare the proverb 'Promises
    and pie-crusts are made to be
    broken').
    Hold-fast . . . dog: There was a
    proverbial saying, 'Brag is a good dog,
    but Holdfast is a better'; both 'brag'
    and 'dog' were names for nails, and a
    'holdfast' was a clamp.
45 *caveto*: beware.
45–6 *clear thy crystals*: wipe your eyes.
46 *Yoke-fellows in arms*: fellow-soldiers.
49 *unwholesome food*: Culinary writers
    advised that the blood of beasts and
    fowl was indigestible.

58 *let housewifery appear*: show yourself
    to be a careful housewife.
    Keep close: keep yourself occupied in
    the house.

Act 2 Scene 4
The King of France recognizes the need to
defend his country against the English
invasion. The Dauphin speaks scathingly of
King Henry, but the Constable, who has
been impressed by the Ambassador's report
of his reception at the English court,
reproves the Dauphin. The embassy from
England arrives, led by the Duke of Exeter
who delivers King Henry's challenge. The
French king is warned that there will be war
if he does not surrender his crown.

0s.d. *Constable*: The Lord Constable
    was head of the royal household, and
    commander of the army.
2 *more than . . . concerns*: we must be
    more than usually concerned.
3 *To . . . defences*: to defend ourselves
    with all our royal power.
5 *make forth*: set out.

6 *swift despatch*: with all haste.
7 *line*: reinforce.
8 *means defendant*: defensive equipment.
9 *England*: the King of England.
10 *gulf*: whirlpool.
11 *fits*: befits, is necessary.
12 *late examples*: recent example—i.e. the Battles of Crécy (1346) and Poitiers (1356).
13 *fatal and neglected*: fatally underrated.
14 *fields*: battlefields.
   redoubted: respected.
15 *meet*: proper.
16 *dull*: make lazy.
17 *Though*: even though.
   known: particular, declared.
18 *musters*: armies.
19 *maintain'd . . . collected*: The verbs correspond in order to the nouns of line 18.
25 *Whitsun morris dance*: The traditional morris dance, often performed at Whitsuntide, sometimes featured a comic king and queen who were attended by the dancers with bells and wooden swords; the Dauphin compares England to the morris queen, with King Henry as her comic king.
26 *idly king'd*: foolishly ruled.
27 *sceptre . . . borne*: her royal power so absurdly exercised.
28 *giddy*: unstable.
   humorous: whimsical.
29 *attends*: accompanies.

For England his approaches makes as fierce
10 As waters to the sucking of a gulf.
It fits us then to be as provident
As fear may teach us, out of late examples
Left by the fatal and neglected English
Upon our fields.
    Dauphin
                    My most redoubted father,
15 It is most meet we arm us 'gainst the foe,
For peace itself should not so dull a kingdom,
Though war nor no known quarrel were in question,
But that defences, musters, preparations
Should be maintain'd, assembled, and collected
20 As were a war in expectation.
Therefore I say 'tis meet we all go forth
To view the sick and feeble parts of France.
And let us do it with no show of fear,
No, with no more than if we heard that England
25 Were busied with a Whitsun morris dance.
For, my good liege, she is so idly king'd,
Her sceptre so fantastically borne,
By a vain, giddy, shallow, humorous youth,
That fear attends her not.

Constable

Oh peace, Prince Dauphin,

30 You are too much mistaken in this king.
Question, your grace, the late ambassadors,
With what great state he heard their embassy,
How well supplied with noble counsellors,
How modest in exception, and withal

35 How terrible in constant resolution,
And you shall find his vanities, forespent,
Were but the outside of the Roman Brutus,
Covering discretion with a coat of folly,
As gardeners do with ordure hide those roots

40 That shall first spring and be most delicate.

Dauphin

Well, 'tis not so, my Lord High Constable.
But though we think it so, it is no matter.
In cases of defence, 'tis best to weigh
The enemy more mighty than he seems,

45 So the proportions of defence are fill'd,
Which of a weak and niggardly projection
Doth like a miser spoil his coat, with scanting
A little cloth.

French King

Think we King Harry strong,
And, princes, look you strongly arm to meet him.

50 The kindred of him hath been flesh'd upon us,
And he is bred out of that bloody strain
That haunted us in our familiar paths.
Witness our too-much memorable shame
When Crécy battle fatally was struck,

55 And all our princes captiv'd, by the hand
Of that black name, Edward, black Prince of Wales,
Whilst that his mountant sire, on mountain standing,
Up in the air, crown'd with the golden sun,
Saw his heroical seed, and smil'd to see him

60 Mangle the work of nature and deface
The patterns that by God and by French fathers
Had twenty years been made. This is a stem
Of that victorious stock, and let us fear
The native mightiness and fate of him.

---

31 *the late ambassadors*: i.e. those who have just returned from England.
32 *great state*: dignity.
   embassy: ambassadorial message.
34 *in exception*: in raising objections.
   withal: altogether.
35 *in constant resolution*: in his firm determination.
36 *vanities, forespent*: former frivolousness, now exhausted.
37 *outside . . . Brutus*: Lucius Junius Brutus (not the Brutus who murdered Julius Caesar) gave the appearance of stupidity in order to preserve his life from the Roman tyrant Tarquin—whom he later helped to expel from Rome.
38 *coat of folly*: the fool's costume, worn at the morris dance.
39 *ordure*: mulch, compost.
42 *though*: even if.
43 *weigh*: esteem.
45 *So . . . fill'd*: in this way all possible means of defence will be provided.
46 *projection*: estimated scale.
47 *scanting*: begrudging, trying to economize on.
48 *Think we*: let us think.
50 *The kindred of him*: his ancestors.
   flesh'd: trained in warfare (the image is from the training of hawks and hounds, which are fed with the flesh of the quarries they must hunt).
51 *bloody strain*: bloodthirsty breed.
52 *haunted . . . paths*: pursued us on our home ground.
54 *When Crécy . . . struck*: when the Battle of Crécy was fought and we were defeated.
55 *captiv'd*: taken captive.
56 *black*: evil (from the French point of view); the French king speaks as though the Prince of Wales had been a devil.
57 *mountant*: in the ascendant, climbing up to the peak of success; early texts have 'mountain'.
   on mountain standing: See *1, 2, 108* note.
59 *seed*: offspring.
61 *patterns*: models.
62 *stem*: offshoot.
63 *stock*: root.
64 *The native . . . him*: the great destiny to which he was born.

Enter a Messenger

Messenger
65 Ambassadors from Harry, king of England,
Do crave admittance to your majesty.
        French King
We'll give them present audience.
Go, and bring them.   [*Exit* Messenger
You see this chase is hotly follow'd, friends.
        Dauphin
70 Turn head and stop pursuit, for coward dogs
Most spend their mouths when what they seem to
        threaten
Runs far before them. Good my sovereign,
Take up the English short, and let them know
Of what a monarchy you are the head.
75 Self love, my liege, is not so vile a sin
As self neglecting.

        Enter Exeter

French King
                    From our brother of England?
        Exeter
From him, and thus he greets your majesty:
He wills you in the name of God almighty
That you divest yourself, and lay apart
80 The borrow'd glories that by gift of heaven,
By law of nature and of nations, 'longs
To him and to his heirs, namely, the crown,
And all wide-stretched honours that pertain
By custom and the ordinance of times
85 Unto the crown of France. That you may know
'Tis no sinister nor no awkward claim
Pick'd from the wormholes of long vanish'd days,
Nor from the dust of old oblivion rak'd,
He sends you this most memorable line

67 *give . . . audience*: hear them immediately.

69 *this chase*: The king picks up the hunting imagery from line 50.

70 *Turn head*: turn to face them (like a stag at bay; 'head' = antlers).
71 *spend their mouths*: give tongue, bark loudly.

73 *short*: abruptly.
76 *brother*: brother king.
78 *wills*: desires.
79 *divest*: strip off.
80–1 *by gift . . . of nations*: by all laws—divine, natural, and human. Divine law (which could only be learned through revelation) controlled all things; working within this was the law of nature (whose scientific truths were discoverable by human reasoning powers); and subordinate to these were the laws of nations (which were often decided by custom).
81 *'longs*: belongs.
83 *all . . . pertain*: every title that derives, no matter how remotely, from this. *wide-stretched*: stretchèd.
84 *ordinance of times*: established practice, tradition.
85 *That*: in order that.
86 *sinister*: irregular; in heraldry, the 'bend sinister' on a shield indicated the bearer's illegitimacy of birth. *awkward*: oblique, illegitimate.
87 *Pick'd . . . worm-holes*: found with much research into worm-eaten manuscripts.
88 *from . . . rak'd*: from raking amongst the dust of things that have been forgotten for years.
89 *line*: i.e. of the family tree (see p. x).

Delivers scroll

90 In every branch truly demonstrative,
Willing you overlook this pedigree,
And when you find him evenly deriv'd
From his most fam'd of famous ancestors,
Edward the Third, he bids you then resign
95 Your crown and kingdom, indirectly held
From him, the native and true challenger.
    French King
Or else what follows?
    Exeter
Bloody constraint, for if you hide the crown
Even in your hearts, there will he rake for it.
100 Therefore in fierce tempest is he coming,
In thunder and in earthquake, like a Jove,
That if requiring fail, he will compel,
And bids you, in the bowels of the Lord,
Deliver up the crown, and to take mercy
105 On the poor souls for whom this hungry war
Opens his vasty jaws, and on your head
Turning the widow's tears, the orphan's cries,
The dead men's blood, the prived maiden's groans,
For husbands, fathers, and betrothed lovers
110 That shall be swallow'd in this controversy.
This is his claim, his threatening, and my message—
Unless the Dauphin be in presence here,
To whom expressly I bring greeting to.

91 *Willing you overlook*: desiring you to read through.
92 *evenly deriv'd*: directly descended.

95 *indirectly*: wrongfully, illegitimately.
96 *native*: natural by right of birth.
  challenger: claimant.
98 *constraint*: compulsion, force.
99 *rake*: search for.
100–1 *coming . . . in earthquake*: In the Bible (Isaiah 29:6) it is prophesied that Jehovah, the Lord of Hosts, will come to earth in this manner.
101 *Jove*: Jupiter, king of the Roman gods; he is often depicted with a thunderbolt.
102 *requiring*: requesting.
103 *in the bowels of the Lord*: in all compassion; the phrase was biblical (see Philippians 1:8, 'in the bowels of Jesus Christ').
106 *vasty*: immense.
106–7 *on your head Turning*: taking the guilt on yourself.
108 *prived*: privèd; deprived.
109 *betrothed*: betrothèd.
110 *swallow'd*: i.e. by the 'vasty jaws of war'.

112 *in presence*: in the presence chamber.
113 *expressly*: particularly.

115 *full intent*: considered reply.

117 *stand here*: represent.

118 *slight regard*: disdain.
119 *misbecome*: be inappropriate.
120 *prize*: reckon, rate.
121 *and if*: An intensive form of 'if'.
122 *in grant . . . at large*: satisfying all my demands in full.

125 *womby vaultages*: hollow caverns.

127 *second accent*: echo.
ordinance: artillery.

128 *fair return*: polite response.

130 *odds*: quarrel.
131 *matching to*: appropriate for, *and* making a match with.
vanity: shallowness.
132 *Paris balls*: tennis balls; the French ones were particularly lightweight.
133 *Louvre*: the Royal Court of France; the word was pronounced 'Lover'—which leads to word-play in the next line.
134 *mistress-court*: chief court.

137 *greener*: more immature.
138 *masters*: possesses.
139 *utmost grain*: last grain of sand in the hour-glass.
read: recognize; perhaps there is also a pun with 'rede' (= regret).
141 *at full*: completely.
Flourish: The trumpets sound as the king rises and prepares to depart; but Exeter boldly interrupts. The trumpeters might renew or repeat their 'flourish' when the king leaves the stage after line 147.

French King
For us, we will consider of this further.
115 Tomorrow shall you bear our full intent
Back to our brother of England.
    Dauphin
                        For the Dauphin,
I stand here for him. What to him from England?
    Exeter
Scorn and defiance, slight regard, contempt,
And anything that may not misbecome
120 The mighty sender, doth he prize you at.
Thus says my king, and if your father's highness
Do not, in grant of all demands at large,
Sweeten the bitter mock you sent his majesty,
He'll call you to so hot an answer of it
125 That caves and womby vaultages of France
Shall chide your trespass and return your mock
In second accent of his ordinance.
    Dauphin
Say, if my father render fair return
It is against my will, for I desire
130 Nothing but odds with England. To that end,
As matching to his youth and vanity,
I did present him with the Paris balls.
    Exeter
He'll make your Paris Louvre shake for it,
Were it the mistress-court of mighty Europe.
135 And be assur'd, you'll find a difference,
As we his subjects have in wonder found,
Between the promise of his greener days
And these he masters now. Now he weighs time
Even to the utmost grain. That you shall read
140 In your own losses, if he stay in France.
    French King
Tomorrow shall you know our mind at full.

    Flourish

142 *Dispatch us*: send us away.
  our king: the king of England. Exeter's pronoun emphasizes that the King of France is subject to King Henry just as much as he himself.
144 *footed . . . already*: In historical fact, Exeter's embassy was in February 1415, and the king did not land in France until August of that year.
146 *small breath*: little breathing-space.

Exeter
Dispatch us with all speed, lest that our king
Come here himself to question our delay,
For he is footed in this land already.
    French King
145 You shall be soon dispatch'd, with fair conditions.
A night is but small breath and little pause
To answer matters of this consequence.
                       [*Flourish. Exeunt*

ACT 3

Act 3 Chorus
The Chorus continues to exhort the audience that they must make full use of their imaginations. They must visualize the scene at Southampton as the king embarks his troops, and then conjure up for themselves the sight of all the ships crossing the English Channel. And then they must picture the scene when the army is besieging Harfleur. The French king's attempt at appeasement has been rejected, and the fighting is about to start.

1 *imagin'd wing*: wing of imagination.
  scene: setting, locality.
2–3 *In . . . thought*: as quick as thought.
4 *well-appointed*: well-equipped.
  Hampton: Southampton.
5 *royalty*: majesty—himself and his entourage.
  brave: spectacular.
6 *streamers*: banners.
  young Phoebus feigning: looking like the rising sun (Phoebus Apollo was the classical god of the sun).
7 *Play with your fancies*: exercise your imaginations.
8 *hempen tackle*: rigging, the ship's ropes.
9 *whistle*: i.e. the one blown by the master-mariner to communicate with the ship-boys.
10 *threaden*: stitched with strengthening cords, or, strung on the 'hempen tackle'.
12 *bottoms*: vessels.

London: the Globe. Enter Chorus

Chorus
Thus with imagin'd wing our swift scene flies
In motion of no less celerity
Than that of thought. Suppose that you have seen
The well-appointed king at Hampton Pier
5 Embark his royalty, and his brave fleet
With silken streamers the young Phoebus feigning.
Play with your fancies, and in them behold
Upon the hempen tackle ship-boys climbing.
Hear the shrill whistle, which doth order give
10 To sounds confus'd. Behold the threaden sails,
Borne with the invisible and creeping wind,
Draw the huge bottoms through the furrow'd sea,
Breasting the lofty surge. O do but think

14 *rivage*: shore.
15 *inconstant*: unsteady, heaving.
17 *holding due course to Harfleur*: headed directly for Harfleur (see map, p. 60).
18 *Grapple*: hook on, fasten with grappling irons.
   sternage: the rear ends.
19 *as . . . still*: as silent as midnight.
20 *grandsires*: grandfathers.
21 *to pith and puissance*: at strength and full power.
22 *but*: only.
24 *cull'd and choice-drawn cavaliers*: hand-picked and specially selected knights.
26 *ordnance on their carriages*: guns mounted on their carriages.
27 *fatal mouths*: deadly muzzles.
   girded: fortified.
28 *Suppose*: imagine.
30 *to dowry*: for a dowry.
31 *petty and unprofitable dukedoms*: The Chorus now scorns what were once called 'almost kingly dukedoms'. (*1, 2, 227*). In historical fact, these offers were made about two months before Henry landed in France.
32 *likes not*: does not please.
   nimble: adroit, agile.
33 *linstock*: stick holding the gunner's match.
   devilish: fireworks were usually associated with devils (especially on the Elizabethan stage).
33s.d. *Alarm*: trumpet signal ordering battle to commence.
   chambers: small cannons; in the theatre these would be positioned above the stage.
35 *eke*: fill, complete.
   mind: invention.

You stand upon the rivage, and behold
15 A city on th'inconstant billows dancing,
   For so appears this fleet majestical,
   Holding due course to Harfleur. Follow, follow!
   Grapple your minds to sternage of this navy,
   And leave your England as dead midnight, still,
20 Guarded with grandsires, babies, and old women,
   Either past or not arriv'd to pith and puissance.
   For who is he whose chin is but enrich'd
   With one appearing hair that will not follow
   These cull'd and choice-drawn cavaliers to France?
25 Work, work your thoughts, and therein see a siege.
   Behold the ordnance on their carriages
   With fatal mouths gaping on girded Harfleur.
   Suppose th'ambassador from the French comes back,
   Tells Harry that the king doth offer him
30 Katherine his daughter, and with her to dowry
   Some petty and unprofitable dukedoms.
   The offer likes not, and the nimble gunner
   With linstock now the devilish cannon touches

   Alarm, and chambers go off

   And down goes all before them. Still be kind,
35 And eke out our performance with your mind.   [*Exit*

Act 3 Scene 1

A single speech from King Henry. The English army has burst open part of the city wall surrounding Harfleur, but the soldiers are now in retreat. The king urges his troops to make just one more assault. He calls upon their loyalty, patriotism, and their sense of honour; and at last he sounds the battle-cry.

0s.d. *scaling ladders*: apparently the cannon shots have destroyed part of the parapets, thus enabling the soldiers to climb over ('scale') the city wall.

1 *breach*: break in the wall made by the cannon.

2 *the wall*: i.e. the 'breach'.

4 *stillness*: quietness.

7 *conjure up the blood*: call up your vital spirits; the Elizabethans believed that these resided in the blood, and gave rise to all manly actions.

8 *fair nature*: naturally attractive appearance.
hard-favour'd: grim-featured.

9 *aspect*: expression; the word is stressed on the second syllable.

10 *pry*: peer.
portage: portholes.

11 *o'erwhelm it*: over-hang the threatening glare of the eyes, frown.

12 *galled rock*: gallèd; cliff which is being washed away.

13 *jutty*: jut out over.
confounded: eroded.

14 *Swill'd*: violently washed.

16–17 *bend up . . . full height*: The image is of a bow, bent until the bowstring is taut.

17 *his*: its.

18 *fet*: fetched, inherited.
war-proof: tested and experienced in war.

SCENE 1

France: before Harfleur. Enter the King, Exeter, Bedford, *and* Gloucester

Alarm. Enter soldiers *with scaling ladders at Harfleur*

King
Once more unto the breach, dear friends, once more,
Or close the wall up with our English dead!
In peace there's nothing so becomes a man
As modest stillness and humility.
5 But when the blast of war blows in our ears,
Then imitate the action of the tiger:
Stiffen the sinews, conjure up the blood,
Disguise fair nature with hard-favour'd rage.
Then lend the eye a terrible aspect,
10 Let it pry through the portage of the head,
Like the brass cannon. Let the brow o'erwhelm it
As fearfully as doth a galled rock
O'erhang and jutty his confounded base,
Swill'd with the wild and wasteful ocean.
15 Now set the teeth and stretch the nostril wide,
Hold hard the breath, and bend up every spirit
To his full height. On, on, you noble English,
Whose blood is fet from fathers of war-proof,

'Cry "God for Harry, England, and Saint George!"' (*3*,1, 34) Iain Glen as Henry V, Royal Shakespeare Company, 1994.

19 *Alexander*: Alexander the Great, who is said to have lamented that there were no more worlds for him to conquer.

20 *from morn till even*: from morning to night; King Henry's language becomes momentarily romantic and 'poetic'.

21 *argument*: opposition.

22 *Dishonour not your mothers*: i.e. by casting doubt on your paternity.
attest: bear witness, prove.

24 *copy*: example.
grosser: thicker, less refined.

25 *war*: fight.
yeomen: countrymen who fought as foot-soldiers, particularly archers; their service was especially distinguished at Crécy, Poitiers, and Agincourt.

27 *mettle of your pasture*: quality of the land which bred you.

28 *worth your breeding*: deserve all that it has cost to bring you up.

29 *mean and base*: however humble and lowly by birth.

31 *slips*: leashes.

32 *Straining upon the start*: eager to get started.
The game's afoot: the quarry—the hare that greyhounds would chase—has set off.

33 *upon this charge*: as you charge.

34 *Saint George*: the patron saint of England, to whom Henry was especially devoted. The name was pronounced to rhyme with 'charge'.

34s.d. *Alarm . . . off*: The trumpet signals the fresh assault, and the cannons are fired again.

Fathers that like so many Alexanders
20 Have in these parts from morn till even fought,
And sheath'd their swords for lack of argument.
Dishonour not your mothers. Now attest
That those whom you call'd fathers did beget you.
Be copy now to men of grosser blood,
25 And teach them how to war. And you, good yeomen,
Whose limbs were made in England, show us here
The mettle of your pasture. Let us swear
That you are worth your breeding, which I doubt not,
For there is none of you so mean and base
30 That hath not noble lustre in your eyes.
I see you stand like greyhounds in the slips,
Straining upon the start. The game's afoot.
Follow your spirit, and upon this charge
Cry 'God for Harry, England, and Saint George!'
[*Alarm, and chambers go off. Exeunt*

Act 3 Scene 2
Four characters whom we last saw in the London tavern re-appear on the battlefields of France. They sing to keep up their spirits before the soldiers return to the fight, leaving the Boy alone on the stage to speak confidentially to the audience.

2 *corporal*: Bardolph seems to have been demoted from his rank (*2, 1, 2*) of lieutenant.
   knocks: fighting.
3 *I . . . lives*: I've only got one life; a 'case' is a set of two pistols.
   humour: temper; the word has many different senses, allowing for easy word-play—as in line 5.
4 *the very plain-song*: the simple truth; in music, plain-song is the air without variations.
5 *most just*: right word (French *mot juste*).
   humours: bad airs, mists; there would even be smoke in the playhouse—as on the battlefield—caused by the cannon.
6 *vassals*: servants.
7–18 Pistol and the Boy sing fragments of old songs.
9 *Doth*: Shakespeare often mixes singular and plural verbs and nouns.
10 *Would*: I wish.
13 *prevail with*: succeed.
15 *hie*: go quickly.
16 *duly*: accurately.
17 *truly*: honourably.

19 *preach*: breach (= break in the wall); the p/b substitution is one of Shakespeare's indications of the character's Welsh accent.
   Avaunt: get away.
   cullions: rascals.
20 *duke*: leader (from the Latin *dux*).
   men of mould: men of earth, mere mortals.
22 *bawcock*: fine fellow.
   bate: abate.
   use lenity: be lenient.
   chuck: good lad.
23 *These . . . humours*: this is a fine change of mood.
   wins: conquers.

Scene 2

France: the battlefield. Enter Nym, Bardolph, Pistol, *and* Boy

Bardolph
On, on, on, on, on, to the breach, to the breach!
   Nym
Pray thee, corporal, stay. The knocks are too hot, and for mine own part I have not a case of lives. The humour of it is too hot, that is the very plain-song of it.
   Pistol
5 'The plain-song' is most just, for humours do abound.
Knocks go and come, God's vassals drop and die,
      [*Sings*] And sword and shield,
      In bloody field,
      Doth win immortal fame.
   Boy
10 Would I were in an ale-house in London. I would give all my fame for a pot of ale, and safety.
   Pistol
And I.
      [*Sings*] If wishes would prevail with me,
      My purpose should not fail with me,
15   But thither would I hie.
   Boy
      [*Sings*] As duly
      But not as truly
      As bird doth sing on bough.

Enter Llewellyn

Llewellyn
Up to the preach, you dogs! Avaunt, you cullions!
   Pistol
20 Be merciful, great duke, to men of mould! Abate thy rage, abate thy manly rage! Abate thy rage, great duke! Good bawcock, bate thy rage. Use lenity, sweet chuck.
   Nym
These be good humours! Your honour wins bad humours!
      [*Exeunt* Pistol, Bardolph, *and* Nym, *pursued by* Llewellyn

25 *swashers*: swaggerers.
26 *boy to*: (a) servant to; (b) younger than.
27 *man to me*: (a) my manservant; (b) more manly than I am.
28 *antics*: clowns.
29 *white-livered*: bloodless, cowardly (the liver was thought to be the seat of courage).
    red-faced: courageous in appearance—but Bardolph's face was covered in spots and boils (see *2, 1, 72* note).
30 *a*: he.
31 *killing tongue*: foul mouth.
32 *breaks words*: fights verbal battles, *and* does not keep his promises.
33–4 *men . . . best men*: Nym must have heard the proverbial saying: *vir sapit qui pauca loquitur*—it's a wise man who doesn't talk much.
39 *purchase*: fair exchange.
40 *league*: a French mile (equivalent to three English miles).
41 *filching*: pilfering.
    Calais: At this time Calais was an English property.
42 *piece of service*: little job.
43 *carry coals*: do any degrading work, *and*, be damned in hell.
43–4 *as familiar*: as often on the inside.
45–6 *makes much . . . manhood*: greatly offends my self-respect.
47 *pocketing up of wrongs*: (a) putting up with insults; *and* (b) receiving stolen goods.
49 *goes against*: upsets.
50 *cast it up*: throw—or vomit—it back again, give up this employment.

Act 3 Scene 3
Three army officers—a Scotsman, a Welshman, and an Irishman—engage in cautious nationalistic sparring. The English captain stands neutral.

1 *presently*: immediately.
2 *mines*: tunnels dug underneath fortifications for the purpose of laying explosives.
4 *look you*: An emphatic phrase which, like the p/b confusion (*3, 2, 19*), indicates Llewellyn's Welsh accent.
5 *disciplines of war*: conventions of warfare.

Boy
25 As young as I am, I have observed these three swashers.
I am boy to them all three, but all they three, though they would serve me, could not be man to me, for indeed three such antics do not amount to a man. For Bardolph, he is white-livered and red-faced, by the
30 means whereof a faces it out but fights not. For Pistol, he hath a killing tongue and a quiet sword, by the means whereof a breaks words and keeps whole weapons. For Nym, he hath heard that men of few words are the best men, and therefore he scorns to say his prayers lest a
35 should be thought a coward, but his few bad words are matched with as few good deeds, for a never broke any man's head but his own, and that was against a post when he was drunk. They will steal anything and call it purchase. Bardolph stole a lute-case, bore it twelve
40 leagues and sold it for three halfpence. Nym and Bardolph are sworn brothers in filching, and in Calais they stole a fire-shovel. I knew by that piece of service the men would carry coals. They would have me as familiar with men's pockets as their gloves or their
45 handkerchiefs, which makes much against my manhood if I should take from another's pocket to put into mine, for it is plain pocketing up of wrongs. I must leave them and seek some better service. Their villainy goes against my weak stomach, and therefore I must
50 cast it up.   [*Exit*

SCENE 3

France: the battlefield. Enter Gower *and* Llewellyn

Gower
Captain Llewellyn, you must come presently to the mines. The Duke of Gloucester would speak with you.
Llewellyn
To the mines? Tell you the duke it is not so good to come to the mines, for, look you, the mines is not according to
5 the disciplines of the war, the concavities of it is not sufficient. For, look you, th'athversary, you may discuss

5–6 *the . . . sufficient*: Llewellyn means that there is not enough space in the tunnels for the explosives to be effective.

6 *athversary*: the enemy.

6–7 *discuss unto*: inform.

7–8 *is . . . countermines*: has dug countermines for himself four yards underneath our mines.

8 *Cheshu*: Jesus.
plow: blow.

9 *directions*: instructions.

10 *order*: management.

12 *gentleman*: The captains in the play are all referred to as 'gentlemen', a social rank between the nobles and the yeomen.

16 *verify . . . beard*: prove it to his face.

18 *Roman disciplines*: These were thought to be superior to any modern theories of warfare; Llewellyn clearly thinks that the Irishman will be ignorant of such refinements.
is: has.

21 *falorous*: valorous.

22 *expedition*: quick-thinking.

23 *anchient*: ancient.

26 *pristine*: faultless, perfectly conducted.

27 *guidday*: good day—Shakespeare now attempts to suggest a Scottish accent.

28 *Goodden*: God give you good day.

30 *pioneers*: sappers.

31 *law*: This is an intensifier for the oath, not quite 'lord'.
'tish: 'tis; Shakespeare tries to suggest Irish speech.

32 *retreat*: order to retreat.

---

unto the duke, look you, is digged himself, four yard under, the countermines! By Cheshu, I think a will plow up all, if there is not better directions.

Gower

10 The Duke of Gloucester, to whom the order of the siege is given, is altogether directed by an Irishman, a very valiant gentleman, i'faith.

Llewellyn

It is Captain Macmorris, is it not?

Gower

I think it be.

Llewellyn

15 By Cheshu, he is an ass, as in the world. I will verify as much in his beard. He has no more directions in the true disciplines of the wars, look you, of the Roman disciplines, than is a puppy dog.

Enter Macmorris *and* Captain Jamy

Gower

Here a comes, and the Scots captain, Captain Jamy,
20 with him.

Llewellyn

Captain Jamy is a marvellous falorous gentleman, that is certain, and of great expedition and knowledge in th'anchient wars, upon my particular knowledge of his directions. By Cheshu, he will maintain his argument as
25 well as any military man in the world, in the disciplines of the pristine wars of the Romans.

Jamy

I say guidday, Captain Llewellyn.

Llewellyn

Goodden to your worship, good Captain James.

Gower

How now, Captain Macmorris, have you quit the mines?
30 Have the pioneers given o'er?

Macmorris

By Chrish law, 'tish ill done. The work ish give over, the trumpet sound the retreat. By my hand I swear, and my father's soul, the work ish ill done. It ish give over. I

34 *law*: Macmorris intensifies his oath.

39 *touching*: regarding.

46 *'quite*: requite, answer.

51 *besieched*: besieged.
52 *be*: by.

55 *sa'*: save.

56 *By the mess*: The Protestant
Elizabethans would find it acceptable
for Jamy, being a Roman Catholic
Scot, to swear by the mass.
57 *lig*: lie.
grund: ground.
59 *the breff*: short (brief).
60 *wad full fain*: would very much like to.
some question: discussion, argument.
twae: two.

63 *Of my nation*: Macmorris is sensitive
about his nationality. The
Elizabethans had special martial rules
to prevent this kind of quarrelling in
camps.

67 *peradventure*: it may be.

would have blowed up the town, so Chrish save me law,
35 in an hour. O, 'tish ill done, 'tish ill done. By my hand,
'tish ill done.
   Llewellyn
Captain Macmorris, I beseech you now, will you
vouchsafe me, look you, a few disputations with you, as
partly touching or concerning the disciplines of the war,
40 the Roman wars, in the way of argument, look you, and
friendly communication? Partly to satisfy my opinion,
and partly for the satisfaction, look you, of my mind, as
touching the direction of the military discipline, that is
the point.
   Jamy
45 It sall be vary guid, guid faith, guid captains baith, and I
sall 'quite you with guid leave, as I may pick occasion,
that sall I, marry.
   Macmorris
It is no time to discourse, so Chrish save me. The day is
hot, and the weather, and the wars, and the king, and
50 the dukes. It is no time to discourse, the town is
besieched! An the trumpet call us to the breach, and we
talk and be Chrish do nothing, 'tis shame for us all! So
God sa' me, 'tis shame to stand still, it is shame, by my
hand. And there is throats to be cut, and works to be
55 done, and there ish nothing done, so Christ sa' me law.
   Jamy
By the mess, ere these eyes of mine take themselves to
slumber I'll dee guid service, or I'll lig i'the grund for it.
I owe Got a death, and I'll pay't as valorously as I may,
that sal I surely do, that is the breff and the long. Marry,
60 I wad full fain hear some question 'tween you twae.
   Llewellyn
Captain Macmorris, I think, look you, under your
correction, there is not many of your nation—
   Macmorris
Of my nation? What ish my nation? Ish a villain, and a
bastard, and a knave, and a rascal. What ish my nation?
65 Who talks of my nation?
   Llewellyn
Look you, if you take the matter otherwise than is
meant, Captain Macmorris, peradventure I shall think

68 *use*: treat.

you do not use me with that affability as in discretion
you ought to use me, look you, being as good a man as
70 yourself, both in the disciplines of war, and in the
derivation of my birth, and in other particularities.
    Macmorris
I do not know you so good a man as myself. So Chrish
save me, I will cut off your head!
    Gower
Gentlemen both, you will mistake each other.
    Jamy
75 Ah, that's a foul fault.

74 *you will mistake*: you persist in
misunderstanding.

    A parley

75s.d. *parley*: trumpet-call signalling a
cease-fire for the two sides to begin
negotiations.

    Gower
The town sounds a parley.
    Llewellyn
Captain Macmorris, when there is more better
opportunity to be required, look you, I will be so bold
as to tell you I know the disciplines of war, and there is
80 an end.   [*Exeunt*

78 *to be required*: presents itself.

Act 3 Scene 4
Outside Harfleur, King Henry addresses the
enemy soldiers who are drawn up on the
city walls. He demands the surrender of the
city, painting a graphic picture of the
sufferings that must be endured by its
citizens if they refuse to submit. The
Governor acknowledges the superiority of
the English power, and yields up Harfleur.

SCENE 4

France: outside Harfleur. Enter the King, Exeter, *and
all his train before the gates*

    King
How yet resolves the governor of the town?
This is the latest parle we will admit,
Therefore to our best mercy give yourselves,
Or like to men proud of destruction
5 Defy us to our worst. For as I am a soldier,
A name that in my thoughts becomes me best,
If I begin the battery once again
I will not leave the half-achiev'd Harfleur
Till in her ashes she lie buried.
10 The gates of mercy shall be all shut up
And the flesh'd soldier, rough and hard of heart,
In liberty of bloody hand shall range

1 *resolves*: decides.
2 *latest parle*: final attempt at
negotiation.
4 *proud of*: excited by, glorying in.
5 *to our worst*: to do our worst.
6 *in my thoughts*: in my opinion.
becomes: suits.
7 *battery*: assaults.
8 *half-achiev'd*: already half-conquered.
9 *buried*: buri̇èd.
10 'We shall show no compassion.'
11 *flesh'd*: trained in slaughter (see
2, 4, 50).
12 *In liberty*: given complete freedom.
range: go anywhere.

13 *With . . . hell*: with a conscience that will accommodate all hellish deeds.

15 *impious war*: civil war (Latin *bellum impium*). It could be so described because Harfleur was supposed to be English, and the Governor was withholding the city from its rightful ruler.

16 *prince of fiends*: Lucifer, the leading devil in hell; he was also the bringer of light (and fire).

17 *smirch'd*: blackened (with gunpowder).
fell feats: cruel deeds.

18 *Enlink'd*: connected with, linked together (as by a chain); a 'link' was also a flaming torch used to light travellers in dark streets.

19 *you yourselves*: i.e. because (from King Henry's point of view) they are fighting against their lawful sovereign.

23 *career*: headlong gallop.

24 *bootless*: unrewarding.
vain: futile.

25 *enraged*: enragèd.
spoil: looting.

26 *precepts*: written summons; the word is stressed on the second syllable.
the Leviathan: the whale; its massive strength was described for the Elizabethans in the Book of Job chap. 41.

30 *grace*: human kindness.

31 *filthy . . . clouds*: i.e. the storm and smoke of battle.

32 *heady*: intoxicating.

33 *look*: expect.

34 *blind*: reckless.
bloody: bloodthirsty.

35 *Defile the locks*: tear the hair, *and also* ravish the chastity.

38 *spitted*: pierced on spits (like roasting pigs).

40–1 *wives . . . slaughtermen*: Jewish mothers were wild with grief when Herod (the King of Israel—'Jewry'), hearing of the birth of Jesus Christ, commanded the slaughter of all male babies (see Matthew 2: 16–18).

With conscience wide as hell, mowing like grass
Your fresh fair virgins and your flowering infants.
15 What is it then to me if impious war,
Array'd in flames like to the prince of fiends,
Do with his smirch'd complexion all fell feats
Enlink'd to waste and desolation?
What is't to me, when you yourselves are cause,
20 If your pure maidens fall into the hand
Of hot and forcing violation?
What rein can hold licentious wickedness
When down the hill he holds his fierce career?
We may as bootless spend our vain command
25 Upon th'enragèd soldiers in their spoil
As send precepts to the Leviathan
To come ashore. Therefore, you men of Harfleur,
Take pity of your town and of your people
Whiles yet my soldiers are in my command,
30 Whiles yet the cool and temperate wind of grace
O'erblows the filthy and contagious clouds
Of heady murder, spoil, and villainy.
If not, why, in a moment look to see
The blind and bloody soldier with foul hand
35 Defile the locks of your shrill-shrieking daughters,
Your fathers taken by the silver beards,
And their most reverend heads dash'd to the walls,
Your naked infants spitted upon pikes
Whiles the mad mothers with their howls confus'd
40 Do break the clouds, as did the wives of Jewry
At Herod's bloody-hunting slaughtermen.

43 *in defence*: because you are defending the city from its rightful king.

What say you? Will you yield, and this avoid?
Or guilty in defence be thus destroy'd?

43s.d. *above*: i.e. on the stage balcony, representing the city walls.

Enter Governor *above*

Governor
Our expectation hath this day an end.

45 *of succours*: for aid.

45 The Dauphin, whom of succours we entreated,

46 *Returns us*: sends back the reply. *yet not*: still not.

Returns us that his powers are yet not ready
To raise so great a siege. Therefore, great king,
We yield our town and lives to thy soft mercy.
Enter our gates, dispose of us and ours,

50 *defensible*: capable of being defended.

50 For we no longer are defensible.
   King
Open your gates. Come, uncle Exeter,
                    [*Exit* Governor *above*
Go you and enter Harfleur. There remain
And fortify it strongly 'gainst the French.

54 *Use mercy*: show mercy; according to Holinshed, the town was cruelly sacked.
55 *sickness*: The English army was suffering badly from dysentery.
58 *address'd*: prepared.
58s.d. *Flourish*: The trumpets herald the king's entry into Harfleur.

Use mercy to them all. For us, dear uncle,

55 The winter coming on, and sickness growing
Upon our soldiers, we will retire to Calais.
Tonight in Harfleur we will be your guest,
Tomorrow for the march we are address'd.
                    [*Flourish, and enter the town*

Act 3 Scene 5
A scene of quiet comedy follows the bloody violence threatened outside Harfleur as Princess Katherine takes her first lesson in English.

1 *tu . . . langage*: you have been in England and you speak the language well.

2 *Un peu*: a little.

3–4 *Je te . . . anglais*: I beg you, teach me; I've got to learn to speak it. How do you say 'hand' in English?

5 *Elle est appelée de hand*: It is called *de hand*.

6 *Et les doigts*: And the 'fingers'?

7–9 *Les . . . fingres*: The 'fingers'? Oh my word, I forgot 'fingers', but I'll remember, the 'fingers'. I think they are called *de fingres*. Yes, *de fingres*.

10–12 *Je . . . ongles*: I think I'm a good pupil. I have learned two words of English very quickly. What do you call the 'nails'?

13 *nous . . . nails*: we call them '*de nails*'.

14 *Ecoutez . . . bien*: Listen! Tell me if I speak correctly.

16 *C'est . . . anglais*: That's well spoken, madam. It is very good English.

17 *Dites . . . bras*: Tell me the English for the 'arm'.

21–2 *Je m'en fais . . . présent*: I'm going to repeat all the words that you have taught me so far.

Scene 5

France: Rouen. Enter Katherine *and* Alice, *an old gentlewoman*

Katherine
Alice, tu as été en Angleterre, et tu bien parles le langage.
    Alice
Un peu, madame.
    Katherine
Je te prie, m'enseignez. Il faut que j'apprenne à parler. Comment appelez-vous la main en anglais?
    Alice
5 La main. Elle est appelée *de hand*.
    Katherine
De hand. Et les doigts?
    Alice
Les doigts, ma foi, j'ai oublié les doigts, mais je me souviendrai les doigts. Je pense qu'ils sont appelés *de fingres*. Oui, *de fingres*.
    Katherine
10 La main, *de hand*. Les doigts, les *fingres*. Je pense que je suis le bon écolier. J'ai gagné deux mots d'anglais vitement. Comment appelez-vous les ongles?
    Alice
Les ongles, nous les appelons *de nails*.
    Katherine
De nails. Écoutez! Dites-moi si je parle bien: *de hand, de*
15 *fingres*, et *de nails*.
    Alice
C'est bien dit, madame. Il est fort bon anglais.
    Katherine
Dites-moi l'anglais pour le bras.
    Alice
De arm, madame.
    Katherine
Et le coude.
    Alice
20 *D'elbow*.
    Katherine
D'elbow. Je m'en fais la répétition de tous les mots que vous m'avez appris dès à présent.

'Écoutez, *d'hand, de fingres, de nails, d'arma, de bilbow.*' (*3*, 5, 24–5) Ludmilla Mikael as Princess Katherine, Yvonne Coulette as Alice, Royal Shakespeare Company, 1975.

Alice

Il est trop difficile, madame, comme je pense.

Katherine

Excusez-moi, Alice. Écoutez, *d'hand, de fingres, de*
25 *nails, d'arma, de bilbow.*

Alice

D'elbow, madame.

Katherine

O Seigneur Dieu, je m'en oublié *d'elbow*! Comment
appelez-vous le col?

Alice

De nick, madame.

Katherine

30 *De nick.* Et le menton?

Alice

De chin.

Katherine

De sin. Le col, *de nick.* Le menton, *de sin.*

Alice

Oui. Sauf votre honneur, en vérité vous prononcez les
mots aussi droit que les natifs d'Angleterre.

Katherine

35 Je ne doute point d'apprendre, par la grâce de Dieu, et
en peu de temps.

Alice

N'avez-vous pas déjà oublié ce que je vous ai enseigné?

Katherine

Non, et je réciterai à vous promptement: *d'hand, de
fingre, de mailés—*

Alice

40 *De nails,* madame.

Katherine

De nails, de arma, de ilbow—

Alice

Sauf votre honneur, *de elbow.*

Katherine

Ainsi dis-je. *D'elbow, de nick,* et *de sin.* Comment
appelez-vous les pieds et la robe?

Alice

45 *De foot,* madame, et *de count.*

---

23 *Il est . . . pense*: It's too difficult, madam, I think.

24 *Excusez-moi*: not at all. *Écoutez*: listen.
25 *bilbow*: The bilbow was a short sword, or a bar shackling the legs of prisoners.

27 *O Seigneur Dieu*: oh good heavens. *je m'en oublié*: I have forgotten.
27–8 *Comment . . . le col*: What do you call the 'neck'. Both *nick* and *cul* were slang names for the vulva.

33–4 *Sauf . . . d'Angleterre*: If it please your honour, you really do pronounce the words just as well as the natives of England.
35–6 *Je . . . temps*: I've no doubt I shall be able to learn it with God's help, and very quickly.

37 *N'avez . . . enseigné*: Haven't you already forgotten what I have taught you?
38 *Non . . . promptement*: No, I'll recite it to you straightaway.

42 *Sauf votre honneur*: If it please your honour.

43 *Ainsi dis-je*: That's what I said.

46 Katherine hears Alice's words as the French *foutre* (= to fuck) and *con* (= cunt).

46–51 *ils sont . . . ensemble*: these words sound wicked, corrupting, obscene, and rude, and not to be spoken by ladies of honour. I would not like to utter these words in front of French gentlemen for all the world. Ugh! the 'foot' and the 'count'! All the same, I will recite my lesson once more, altogether.

55 *C'est . . . dîner*: That's enough for one time. Let's go in to dinner.

Katherine
De foot et *de count*? O Seigneur Dieu, ils sont les mots de son mauvais, corruptible, gros, et impudique, et non pour les dames d'honneur d'user! Je ne voudrais prononcer ces mots devant les seigneurs de France pour
50 tout le monde! Foh! *De foot* et *de count*! Néanmoins, je réciterai une autre fois ma leçon ensemble: *de hand, de fingre, de nails, d'arma, d'elbow, de nick, de sin, de foot,* le *count.*

Alice
Excellent, madame!

Katherine
55 C'est assez pour une fois. Allons-nous à dîner.

[*Exeunt*

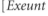

Act 3 Scene 6
The French king, dismayed by the English success at Harfleur, urges his nobles to make greater efforts to expel King Henry from their country.

SCENE 6

France: Rouen. Enter the King of France, *the* Dauphin, *the* Constable of France, *the* Duke of Bourbon, *and others*

1 *pass'd the River Somme*: i.e. on the retreat to Calais (see *3, 4, 56*); the river is halfway between Calais and Harfleur—see map above.

2 *And if*: An intensive form of 'if'. *withal*: with.

3 *quit*: to give up.

French King
'Tis certain he hath pass'd the River Somme.
    Constable
And if he be not fought withal, my lord,
Let us not live in France. Let us quit all
And give our vineyards to a barbarous people.

Dauphin

5 *O Dieu vivant!* Shall a few sprays of us,
The emptying of our fathers' luxury,
Our scions, put in wild and savage stock,
Spurt up so suddenly into the clouds
And overlook their grafters?

Bourbon

10 Normans, but bastard Normans, Norman bastards!
Mort de ma vie, if they march along
Unfought withal, but I will sell my dukedom
To buy a slobbery and a dirty farm
In that nook-shotten isle of Albion.

Constable

15 *Dieu de batailles*, where have they this mettle?
Is not their climate foggy, raw, and dull,
On whom, as in despite, the sun looks pale,
Killing their fruit with frowns? Can sodden water,
A drench for sur-rein'd jades, their barley-broth,
20 Decoct their cold blood to such valiant heat?
And shall our quick blood, spirited with wine,
Seem frosty? Oh, for honour of our land
Let us not hang like roping icicles
Upon our houses' thatch whiles a more frosty people
25 Sweat drops of gallant youth in our rich fields!
'Poor' may we call them, in their native lords!

Dauphin

By faith and honour,
Our madams mock at us and plainly say
Our mettle is bred out, and they will give
30 Their bodies to the lust of English youth
To new-store France with bastard warriors.

---

5 *O Dieu vivant*: Oh living God.
sprays of us: of our bastards; the English are descendants—'offshoots'—of the Normans who invaded England in 1066.

6 *The emptying*: that which was emptied out.
luxury: lust.

7 *scions*: sprigs for grafting.
stock: the parent plants on to which the shoots are grafted.

8 *Spurt*: sprout.

9 *overlook*: grow bigger than, dominate.
grafters: plants from which the grafts were originally taken.

11 *Mort de ma vie*: death of my life.

13 *slobbery*: wet and slimy.

14 *nook-shotten*: full of corners—the reference is to England's jagged coastline.
Albion: an old name (deriving from the white—Latin *alba*—cliffs) for the kingdoms of England, Scotland, and Wales.

15 *Dieu de batailles*: God of battles.
have . . . mettle: do they get this spirit.

17 *as in despite*: as though in scorn.

18–19 *sodden . . . broth*: The Constable scorns the English beer as being no stronger than boiled water, suitable only as a medicine for over-ridden horses.

20 *Decoct*: infuse, warm up.

21 *quick*: lively.

23 *roping*: hanging down.

25 *drops of gallant youth*: i.e. the blood shed in fighting.

26 *'Poor' . . . lords*: we should call our land poor, not rich, because its nobles are so feeble.

28 *madams*: fashionable ladies.

29 *bred out*: exhausted.

31 *new-store*: restock.

32 *bid us . . . dancing-schools*: tell us to become dancing-teachers to the English.
33 *lavoltas*: dances with jumping and leaping steps.
   corantos: dances with swift running steps.
34 *grace*: elegant movement, skill.
   heels: dancing, *and* running away.
35 *lofty runaways*: high born (*or* accomplished, high leaping) deserters.

39 *hie*: go quickly.
40–5 These names, all except Berri and Charolais, are from Holinshed's list of those slain at Agincourt.
47 *For*: for the sake of.
   seats: positions, family-seats.
   quit you of: clear yourselves of.
48 *Bar*: block the path of.
   Harry England: Henry king of England.
49 *pennons*: streamers carried on cavalry lances.

50 *host*: army.
51 *vassal*: servile.
52 *The Alps . . . rheum*: The king describes an avalanche of white snow from the Alps (spoken of as a single mountain).
   void: empty.
   rheum: phlegm.
54 *captive chariot*: i.e. a triumphal chariot designed to show off the captive.

Bourbon

They bid us to the English dancing-schools,
And teach lavoltas high and swift corantos,
Saying our grace is only in our heels,
35   And that we are most lofty runaways.

French King

Where is Montjoy the herald? Speed him hence,
Let him greet England with our sharp defiance.
Up, princes, and with spirit of honour edg'd
More sharper than your swords hie to the field.
40   Charles Delabret, High Constable of France,
You Dukes of Orléans, Bourbon, and of Berri,
Alençon, Brabant, Bar, and Burgundy,
Jacques Châtillon, Rambures, Vaudemont,
Beaumont, Grandpré, Roussi, and Fauconbridge,
45   Foix, Lestrelles, Boucicault, and Charolais,
High dukes, great princes, barons, lords, and knights,
For your great seats, now quit you of great shames.
Bar Harry England that sweeps through our land
With pennons painted in the blood of Harfleur.
50   Rush on his host as doth the melted snow
Upon the valleys, whose low vassal seat
The Alps doth spit and void his rheum upon.
Go down upon him. You have power enough,
And in a captive chariot into Rouen

55 Bring him our prisoner.
    Constable
                    This becomes the great.
Sorry am I his numbers are so few,
His soldiers sick, and famish'd in their march,
For I am sure when he shall see our army
He'll drop his heart into the sink of fear
60 And for achievement offer us his ransom.
    French King
Therefore, Lord Constable, haste on Montjoy,
And let him say to England that we send
To know what willing ransom he will give.
Prince Dauphin, you shall stay with us in Rouen.
    Dauphin
65 Not so, I do beseech your majesty.
    French King
Be patient, for you shall remain with us.
Now forth, Lord Constable and princes all,
And quickly bring us word of England's fall.

                                        [Exeunt

SCENE 7

France: the English camp. Enter Captains, *English and Welsh,* [Gower *and* Llewellyn]

Gower
How now, Captain Llewellyn, come you from the bridge?
    Llewellyn
I assure you there is very excellent services committed at the bridge.
    Gower
5 Is the Duke of Exeter safe?
    Llewellyn
The Duke of Exeter is as magnanimous as Agamemnon, and a man that I love and honour with my soul, and my heart, and my duty, and my life, and my living, and my uttermost power. He is not, God be praised and blessed,

---

Glossary (left column):

55 *becomes*: is appropriate for.

59 *sink*: pit.
60 *for achievement*: to settle the business (rather than engage in honourable encounter).
61 *haste on*: hasten, tell him to hurry.

63 *know*: learn.
   willing . . . give: he is willing to give.

66 *shall*: must.

Act 3 Scene 7
Llewellyn has been at the battle-front and can report the successful capture of a strategic bridge. But Bardolph has got himself into serious trouble, and Pistol pleads for his life. Llewellyn is unmoved: the disciplines of war must be maintained. King Henry supports Llewellyn. Montjoy brings a message from the French king which is both boastful and threatening. Henry hears with patience, and returns a courteous but defiant answer.

2 *the bridge*: A detachment of English soldiers was sent ahead to capture the bridge over the Ternoise at Blangy; the main army crossed over on 24 October, the night before the battle of Agincourt.
3 *services*: exploits.
5 *Exeter*: According to the historians, he was not at the bridge—but Shakespeare has work for him in this scene!
6 *magnanimous*: great in heart.
   Agamemnon: the leader of the Greek expedition in the Trojan war.

10 *woreld*: world—an attempt to indicate
Welsh pronunciation.
keeps: is in control of.
11–12 *ancient lieutenant*: ensign (=
first, or sub-) lieutenant.
13 *Mark Antony*: The Roman hero, friend
of Julius Caesar; Llewellyn seems to
have forgotten his earlier encounter
with Pistol (*Act 3*, Scene 2).
14 *estimation*: reputation.

10 any hurt in the woreld, but keeps the pridge most
valiantly with excellent discipline. There is an ancient
lieutenant there at the pridge. I think in my very
conscience he is as valiant a man as Mark Antony, and
he is a man of no estimation in the world, but I did see
15 him do as gallant service.

Gower

What do you call him?

Llewellyn

He is called Ancient Pistol.

Gower

I know him not.

Enter Pistol

Llewellyn

Here is the man.

Pistol

20 Captain, I thee beseech to do me favours. The Duke
of Exeter doth love thee well.

Llewellyn

Ay, I praise God, and I have merited some love at his
hands.

Pistol

Bardolph, a soldier firm and sound of heart, and of
25 buxom valour, hath by cruel fate and giddy Fortune's
furious fickle wheel, that goddess blind that stands
upon the rolling restless stone—

Llewellyn

By your patience, Ancient Pistol, Fortune is painted
plind, with a muffler afore her eyes to signify to you that
30 Fortune is plind. And she is painted also with a wheel to
signify to you, which is the moral of it, that she is
turning and inconstant and mutability and variation.
And her foot, look you, is fixed upon a spherical stone,
which rolls and rolls and rolls. In good truth, the poet
35 makes a most excellent description of it. Fortune is an
excellent moral.

Pistol

Fortune is Bardolph's foe, and frowns on him. For he
hath stolen a pax, and hanged must a be. A damned

25 *buxom*: sturdy.
25–6 *Fortune's . . . wheel*: Pistol
confuses two icons of the blind
goddess: in one she holds a wheel,
and in the other she balances
precariously on a rolling stone.
Llewellyn expounds the iconography in
lines 28–34.
26 *furious*: cruel.

36 *moral*: message, emblem.
37 *Fortune . . . him*: Pistol paraphrases a
popular song, 'Fortune my foe, why
dost thou frown on me?'.
38 *pax*: a small metal plate with a
crucifix impressed on it, which was
kissed by the communicants at mass.
a: he.

39 *dog*: Dogs and cats were regularly hanged for misdemeanours.
40 *hemp*: the hangman's rope.
40–1 *given . . . death*: The king had decreed that any man caught stealing from a church should be hanged immediately.
43 *vital thread*: thread of life which (in classical mythology) was cut by one of the three Fates.
44 *vile reproach*: reproach of being despicable.
45 *requite*: repay.

death! Let gallows gape for dog, let man go free, and let
40 not hemp his windpipe suffocate! But Exeter hath given
the doom of death, for pax of little price. Therefore go
speak. The duke will hear thy voice, and let not
Bardolph's vital thread be cut with edge of penny cord
and vile reproach! Speak, captain, for his life, and I will
45 thee requite.

Llewellyn
Ancient Pistol, I do partly understand your meaning.
        Pistol
Why then, rejoice therefore.
        Llewellyn

46 *partly understand*: Llewellyn understands that he is being offered a bribe.

Certainly, ancient, it is not a thing to rejoice at. For if, look you, he were my brother I would desire the duke
50 to use his good pleasure and put him to execution. For discipline ought to be used.
        Pistol

51 *used*: maintained.
52 *fico*: a term of contemptuous dismissal, usually accompanied by an obscene gesture in which the thumb was thrust between two fingers, or into the mouth.
54 *fig of Spain*: a more emphatic insult.

Die and be damned, and *fico* for thy friendship!
        Llewellyn
It is well.
        Pistol
The fig of Spain!   [*Exit*
        Llewellyn
55 Very good.
        Gower

56 *arrant*: utter.
        counterfeit: cheating.
57 *bawd*: brothel-keeper.
        cutpurse: petty thief, pickpocket.
58 *prave words*: Llewellyn has been deceived by the bombast of Pistol's language.
60–1 *when time is serve*: Llewellyn will be revenged at some opportune moment.

Why, this is an arrant counterfeit rascal. I remember him now: a bawd, a cutpurse.
        Llewellyn
I'll assure you, a uttered as prave words at the pridge as you shall see in a summer's day. But it is very well. What
60 he has spoke to me, that is well, I warrant you, when time is serve.

62 *gull*: stupid oaf.

63 *grace*: dignify.

64–5 *perfect . . . names*: know the names of all senior officers.

65–6 *learn you by rote*: learn by heart from themselves; the 'you' is merely intensive.

66 *services were done*: there was action.

67 *sconce*: fortification.
convoy: military escort.

67–8 *came off bravely*: acquitted himself well.

68 *terms*: conditions for surrender.

69 *stood on*: accepted.
con: study.

70 *the phrase of war*: military language.
trick up: dress up, embellish.
new-tuned: freshly-coined.

71 *of the general's cut*: trimmed in the same fashion of the general's beard.

72 *horrid suit of the camp*: fearsome battle-dress.

74 *slanders of the age*: those who bring disgrace on their times.

77 *make show*: pretend.

78 *find . . . coat*: A proverbial expression meaning 'find a weak spot', 'take him at a disadvantage'.

78s.d. *within*: off-stage.

80 *from*: about.

80s.d. *colours*: banners, heading the royal procession.

85 *passages*: i.e. of arms, fighting.

86 *was have*: did have.

Gower
Why, 'tis a gull, a fool, a rogue, that now and then goes to the wars, to grace himself at his return into London under the form of a soldier. And such fellows are perfect
65 in the great commanders' names, and they will learn you by rote where services were done—at such and such a sconce, at such a breach, at such a convoy; who came off bravely, who was shot, who disgraced, what terms the enemy stood on. And this they con perfectly in the
70 phrase of war, which they trick up with new-tuned oaths. And what a beard of the general's cut and a horrid suit of the camp will do among foaming bottles and ale-washed wits is wonderful to be thought on. But
75 you must learn to know such slanders of the age, or else you may be marvellously mistook.

Llewellyn
I tell you what, Captain Gower: I do perceive he is not the man that he would gladly make show to the woreld he is. If I find a hole in his coat I will tell him my mind.

A drum within

Hark you, the king is coming, and I must speak with
80 him from the pridge.

Drum and colours. Enter the King, Gloucester, *and his poor soldiers*

Llewellyn
God pless your majesty.
King
How now, Llewellyn? Camest thou from the bridge?
Llewellyn
Ay, so please your majesty. The Duke of Exeter has very gallantly maintained the pridge. The French is gone off,
85 look you, and there is gallant and most prave passages. Marry, th'athversary was have possession of the pridge, but he is enforced to retire, and the Duke of Exeter is master of the pridge. I can tell your majesty, the duke is a prave man.

91 *perdition*: losses.
93 *never a man*: not a single man.
   like: likely.
95 *bubuckles*: Llewellyn conflates 'bubo'
   (= abscess) and 'carbukles'
   (= carbuncles).
   whelks: pimples.
96 *lips . . . nose*: i.e. his lips protruded
   under his nose.
98 *nose is executed*: A thief's nose was
   slit before he was executed.
   his: its.
100–4 *give . . . language*: The sentence is
   repeated exactly from Holinshed and
   Hall.
101 *express charge*: specific orders.
102 *compelled*: extorted.
103 *upbraided*: reviled.
105 *play*: i.e. with dice.
   gamester: gambler.
106s.d. *Tucket*: trumpet-call.
   Montjoy: the name given to the chief
   herald of France.

107 *habit*: uniform: the herald wore a
   tabard emblazoned with the arms of
   the authority he represented.
   Montjoy's address is curt—almost
   insolent—and King Henry replies in
   the same manner.
108 *know of*: learn from.
112 *Advantage*: seizing the right
   opportunity.
115 *bruise an injury*: squeeze an abscess.
115–16 *speak upon our cue*: i.e. like an
   actor.
116 *England*: the king of England.
117–18 *admire our sufferance*: wonder at
   our patience.
118 *consider of*: think about.
119 *proportion*: balance.

King

90 What men have you lost, Llewellyn?

Llewellyn

The perdition of th'athversary hath been very great,
reasonable great. Marry, for my part I think the duke
hath lost never a man, but one that is like to be executed
for robbing a church, one Bardolph, if your majesty

95 know the man. His face is all bubuckles and whelks, and
knobs, and flames o'fire, and his lips blows at his nose,
and it is like a coal of fire, sometimes plue and
sometimes red. But his nose is executed and his fire's
out.

King

100 We would have all such offenders so cut off, and we give
express charge that in our marches through the country
there be nothing compelled from the villages, nothing
taken but paid for, none of the French upbraided or
abused in disdainful language. For when lenity and

105 cruelty play for a kingdom, the gentler gamester is the
soonest winner.

Tucket. Enter Montjoy

Montjoy

You know me by my habit.

King

Well then, I know thee. What shall I know of thee?

Montjoy

My master's mind.

King

110 Unfold it.

Montjoy

Thus says my king: 'Say thou to Harry of England,
though we seemed dead, we did but sleep. Advantage is
a better soldier than rashness. Tell him, we could have
rebuked him at Harfleur, but that we thought not good

115 to bruise an injury till it were full ripe. Now we speak
upon our cue, and our voice is imperial. England shall
repent his folly, see his weakness and admire our
sufferance. Bid him therefore consider of his ransom,
which must proportion the losses we have borne, the

120 *digested*: endured.
121 *in weight . . . re-answer*: to make complete compensation.
    pettiness: meagre strength.
122 *exchequer*: entire wealth.
123 *effusion*: pouring out.
    muster: whole roll-call of soldiers.

127 *betrayed*: The subject of a king's responsibility for his soldiers is debated in *Act 4, Scene 1*.
128 *condemnation*: who are condemned to death.
129 *office*: duty as herald.
130 *quality*: professional ability.

134 *could be willing*: would like to.
135 *impeachment*: hindrance.
    say the sooth: tell you the truth.
137 *of craft and vantage*: who is cunning and who has superior strength.

142–3 *upon . . . Frenchmen*: i.e. one Englishman was equal to three Frenchmen.
144 *brag*: boast.
    air: weather; the French were conventionally regarded as braggarts (and cowards). There is also a pun on '*heir*' (to the throne)—i.e. the Dauphin.
147 *this . . . trunk*: his body (and not a trunk full of treasure).
150 *France himself*: the king of France.
151 *There's for thy labour*: Both Holinshed and Hall report that Henry gave the herald a generous reward.
152–5 Holinshed used the same words: 'yet I wish not any of you so unadvised as to be the occasion that I dye your tawny ground with your red blood'.
152 *well advise himself*: take good warning.
157 *would not*: do not want to.

120 subjects we have lost, the disgrace we have digested,
which in weight to re-answer, his pettiness would bow
under. For our losses, his exchequer is too poor. For
th'effusion of our blood, the muster of his kingdom too
faint a number. And for our disgrace, his own person
125 kneeling at our feet but a weak and worthless
satisfaction. To this add defiance, and tell him for
conclusion, he hath betrayed his followers, whose
condemnation is pronounced.' So far my king and
master, so much my office.
      King
130 What is thy name? I know thy quality.
      Montjoy
Montjoy.
      King
Thou dost thy office fairly. Turn thee back
And tell thy king I do not seek him now,
But could be willing to march on to Calais
135 Without impeachment. For to say the sooth,
Though 'tis no wisdom to confess so much
Unto an enemy of craft and vantage,
My people are with sickness much enfeebled,
My numbers lessen'd, and those few I have
140 Almost no better than so many French,
Who when they were in health, I tell thee, herald,
I thought upon one pair of English legs
Did march three Frenchmen. Yet forgive me, God,
That I do brag thus. This your air of France
145 Hath blown that vice in me. I must repent.
Go therefore, tell thy master here I am.
My ransom is this frail and worthless trunk,
My army but a weak and sickly guard.
Yet, God before, tell him we will come on
150 Though France himself and such another neighbour
Stand in our way. There's for thy labour, Montjoy.
Go, bid thy master well advise himself.
If we may pass, we will. If we be hinder'd,
We shall your tawny ground with your red blood
155 Discolour. And so, Montjoy, fare you well.
The sum of all our answer is but this:
We would not seek a battle as we are,

Nor as we are we say we will not shun it.
So tell your master.
    Montjoy
160 I shall deliver so. Thanks to your highness.   [*Exit*
    Gloucester
I hope they will not come upon us now.
    King
We are in God's hand, brother, not in theirs.
March to the bridge. It now draws toward night.
Beyond the river we'll encamp ourselves,
165 And on tomorrow. Bid them march away.   [*Exeunt*

161 *come upon*: attack.

Act 3 Scene 8
The French lords are impatient as they wait for the dawn, when battle can commence. The Lord Bourbon has extravagant praise for his horse, and the other lords tease him about his rhapsodies. Bourbon departs to get his armour, leaving the other lords to joke idly until a messenger brings news of the English approach.

Os.d. *Bourbon*: In the Folio text it is the Dauphin who enters now and who speaks the lines here assigned to Bourbon, *but* in historical fact the Dauphin was not present at the battle of Agincourt, and in *Act 3*, Scene 5 of the play Shakespeare's character was expressly ordered to remain in Rouen.
1 *armour*: suit of armour.
3–4 *his due*: the credit he deserves (compare the saying, 'Give the devil his due').

SCENE 8

France: the French camp. Enter the Constable *of France, the* Lord Rambures, Orléans, Bourbon, *with others*

Constable
Tut, I have the best armour of the world! Would it were day.
    Orléans
You have an excellent armour, but let my horse have his due.
    Constable
5 It is the best horse of Europe.

9 *provided of*: equipped with.

11–38 Bourbon's speech is in the form of an exercise in rhetoric which takes a theme—here, 'my horse'—and develops it with variations (as in music) which include references, quotations, and illustrations. A comparable description of a warhorse is in the Bible, Job 39: 19–25.

12 *pasterns*: the part of a horse's leg between the fetlock and the hoof. *Ch'ha*: Bourbon imitates his horse's neigh; see Job 39:25, 'he saith among the trumpets, "Ha ha"'.

13 *as if . . . hairs*: as though he were stuffed with hair (like a tennis ball).

14 *Pegasus*: the flying horse ('*le cheval volant*') of Greek mythology. When Perseus cut off the head of the Gorgon Medusa, Pegasus rose up from the monster's blood. The horse's hoof, striking the earth, caused Hippocrene (the fountain of the Muses and source of all poetic inspiration) to spring up on Mount Helicon.
qui a les narines de feu: which has nostrils of fire: see Job 39:20, 'the glory of his nostrils is terrible'.

15 *trots the air*: trots on air.

16 *basest horn*: lowest part of *both* the hoof and the hunting-horn.

17 *Hermes*: the Greek god who invented the lyre and the reed pipe.

18 *nutmeg*: i.e. mid-brown. Orléans seems to offer a criticism of the horse, since it was commonly believed that colour was an indication of temperament—which was determined in every creature by the mixture of the four elements, earth, air, fire, and water.

23 *jades*: poor nags.
beasts: i.e. not worthy of the name of 'horse'.

24 *absolute*: perfect.

26 *palfreys*: A 'poetic' word for the horses ridden by heroic knights in chivalric romance.

29–30 *rising . . . lamb*: morning until night.

30 *vary*: speak variations on a theme (as he himself is now doing).

31 *fluent*: flowing, eloquent.

31–2 *Turn . . . tongues*: i.e. if there were as many orators as the sands of the sea.

Orléans

Will it never be morning?

Bourbon

My lord of Orléans, and my lord High Constable, you talk of horse and armour?

Orléans

You are as well provided of both as any prince in the world.

Bourbon

What a long night is this! I will not change my horse with any that treads but on four pasterns. Ch'ha! He bounds from the earth as if his entrails were hairs—*le cheval volant*, the Pegasus, *qui a les narines de feu*! When I bestride him I soar, I am a hawk! He trots the air. The earth sings when he touches it. The basest horn of his hoof is more musical than the pipe of Hermes.

Orléans

He's of the colour of the nutmeg.

Bourbon

And of the heat of the ginger. It is a beast for Perseus. He is pure air and fire, and the dull elements of earth and water never appear in him but only in patient stillness while his rider mounts him. He is indeed a horse, and all other jades you may call beasts.

Constable

Indeed, my lord, it is a most absolute and excellent horse.

Bourbon

It is the prince of palfreys. His neigh is like the bidding of a monarch, and his countenance enforces homage.

Orléans

No more, cousin.

Bourbon

Nay, the man hath no wit that cannot from the rising of the lark to the lodging of the lamb vary deserved praise on my palfrey. It is a theme as fluent as the sea. Turn the sands into eloquent tongues and my horse is argument for them all. 'Tis a subject for a sovereign to reason on, and for a sovereign's sovereign to ride on, and for the world, familiar to us and unknown, to lay apart their particular functions and wonder at him. I once writ a

32 *argument*: subject matter.
33 *subject*: theme, and subordinate.
   reason: discourse.
36 *particular*: individual.
   writ: wrote.

41 *courser*: horse ('poetic').

42 *bears well*: carries the rider *and* (of a
   female) breeds.

43 *prescript*: prescribed.

44 *particular*: belonging to one man only.

45 *shrewdly*: sharply, like a shrew (= a
   nagging woman; shrews could be
   punished with bridles to keep their
   mouths closed).

48 *bridled*: i.e. like a horse or shrew.

50 *kern of Ireland*: barefoot Irish peasant
   soldier.
   French hose: loose-fitting breeches.
51 *strait strossers*: tight trousers, leggings
   (but Bourbon probably means 'bare-
   legged').
52 *horsemanship*: The Constable puns on
   'whoresmanship'.
54 *foul bogs*: dirty places—in Ireland *and*
   with whores.

56 *as lief*: would rather.
   jade: female (or horse) of inferior
   quality.
57 *wears his own hair*: Bourbon implies
   that the Constable's mistress wears a
   wig, presumably because her own hair
   has been lost through venereal
   disease.

60–1 *Le chien . . . bourbier*: 'The dog is
   turned to his own vomit again, and the
   sow that was washed to her wallowing
   in the mire', 2 Peter 2:22.
62 *use*: i.e. sexually.
63 *kin*: related, relevant.

sonnet in his praise, and began thus: 'Wonder of
nature! . . . '
   Orléans
I have heard a sonnet begin so to one's mistress.
   Bourbon
40 Then did they imitate that which I composed to my
courser, for my horse is my mistress.
   Orléans
Your mistress bears well.
   Bourbon
Me well, which is the prescript praise and perfection of
a good and particular mistress.
   Constable
45 Nay, for methought yesterday your mistress shrewdly
shook your back.
   Bourbon
So perhaps did yours.
   Constable
Mine was not bridled.
   Bourbon
Oh, then belike she was old and gentle, and you rode
50 like a kern of Ireland, your French hose off, and in your
strait strossers.
   Constable
You have good judgement in horsemanship.
   Bourbon
Be warned by me, then. They that ride so and ride not
warily fall into foul bogs. I had rather have my horse to
55 my mistress.
   Constable
I had as lief have my mistress a jade.
   Bourbon
I tell thee, Constable, my mistress wears his own hair.
   Constable
I could make as true a boast as that, if I had a sow to my
mistress.
   Bourbon
60 'Le chien est retourné à son propre vomissement, et la
truie lavée au bourbier.' Thou makest use of anything.
   Constable
Yet do I not use my horse for my mistress, or any such
proverb so little kin to the purpose.

Rambures
My lord Constable, the armour that I saw in your tent
65 tonight, are those stars or suns upon it?
Constable
Stars, my lord.
Bourbon
Some of them will fall tomorrow, I hope.
Constable
And yet my sky shall not want.
Bourbon
That may be, for you bear a many superfluously, and
70 'twere more honour some were away.
Constable
Even as your horse bears your praises, who would trot
as well were some of your brags dismounted.
Bourbon
Would I were able to load him with his desert. Will it
never be day? I will trot tomorrow a mile, and my way
75 shall be paved with English faces.
Constable
I will not say so, for fear I should be faced out of my way.
But I would it were morning, for I would fain be about
the ears of the English.
Rambures
Who will go to hazard with me for twenty prisoners?
Constable
80 You must first go yourself to hazard, ere you have them.
Bourbon
'Tis midnight. I'll go arm myself.   [*Exit*
Orléans
The Duke of Bourbon longs for morning.
Rambures
He longs to eat the English.
Constable
I think he will eat all he kills.
Orléans
85 By the white hand of my lady, he's a gallant prince.
Constable
Swear by her foot, that she may tread out the oath.
Orléans
He is simply the most active gentleman of France.

65 *stars or suns*: i.e. as decoration; Rambures tries to change the subject.

68 *want*: be deficient.

69 *a many superfluously*: far many more than you need.
70 *away*: taken off.

72 *brags*: boasts.

73 *Would*: I wish.
desert: what he deserves.

76 *faced . . . way*: put to shame; *and* turned away.
77–8 *fain . . . English*: would like to get on with fighting the English.

79 *go to hazard*: make a bet.

80 *go . . . hazard*: put yourself in danger.

84 *eat all he kills*: i.e. none of them.

85 *prince*: nobleman.

86 *tread out*: stamp out.

87 *simply*: absolutely.

88 *Doing*: fornicating.
still: always.

99 *lackey*: stable-lad (the only one he
   dared to beat).
99–100 *hooded . . . bate*: The image is
   from falconry: hawks were blindfolded
   until the quarry was in sight, and then
   the hood was removed so that the
   trained bird would fly in pursuit. But
   an untrained bird would 'bate' (= flap
   its wings wildly and ineffectually).
101 *Ill . . . well*: The lords begin a game of
   swapping proverbs with each other.

105 *placed*: answered.
   stands . . . for: stands in the position
   of.
106 *have at the very eye*: let me aim right
   at the heart.
108 *bolt*: arrow.

109 *shot over*: missed the target.

110 *overshot*: mistaken, *and* drunk.

Constable
Doing is activity, and he will still be doing.
Orléans
He never did harm that I heard of.
Constable
90 Nor will do none tomorrow. He will keep that good
name still.
Orléans
I know him to be valiant.
Constable
I was told that, by one that knows him better than you.
Orléans
What's he?
Constable
95 Marry, he told me so himself, and he said he cared not
who knew it.
Orléans
He needs not, it is no hidden virtue in him.
Constable
By my faith, sir, but it is. Never anybody saw it but his
lackey. 'Tis a hooded valour, and when it appears it will
100 bate.
Orléans
Ill will never said well.
Constable
I will cap that proverb with 'There is flattery in
friendship'.
Orléans
And I will take up that with 'Give the devil his due'.
Constable
105 Well placed. There stands your friend for the devil. Have
at the very eye of that proverb with 'A pox of the devil'.
Orléans
You are the better at proverbs, by how much 'a fool's
bolt is soon shot'.
Constable
You have shot over.
Orléans
110 'Tis not the first time you were overshot.

Enter a Messenger

Messenger
My lord High Constable, the English lie within fifteen
hundred paces of your tents.
Constable
Who hath measured the ground?
Messenger
The lord Grandpré.
Constable
115 A valiant and most expert gentleman. Would it were
day! Alas, poor Harry of England! He longs not for the
dawning as we do.
Orléans
What a wretched and peevish fellow is this king of
England, to mope with his fat-brained followers so far
120 out of his knowledge.
Constable
If the English had any apprehension they would run
away.
Orléans
That they lack, for if their heads had any intellectual
armour they could never wear such heavy headpieces.
Rambures
125 That island of England breeds very valiant creatures.
Their mastiffs are of unmatchable courage.

Orléans
Foolish curs, that run winking into the mouth of a
Russian bear and have their heads crushed like rotten
apples. You may as well say that's a valiant flea that dare
130 eat his breakfast on the lip of a lion.

111–12 *fifteen hundred paces*: According to Holinshed, the armies were 250 paces apart (a 'pace' = 75cm or 30 inches).

113 *measured the ground*: estimated the distance.

118 *peevish*: tiresome.

119 *mope*: blunder aimlessly about.
fat-brained: brainless.

121 *apprehension*: understanding, appreciation of the situation.

124 *headpieces*: helmets; if the English had any sense, they would not be fighting at all.

126 *mastiffs*: huge fighting-dogs, comparable to the modern pit bull-terrier.

127 *winking*: with their eyes shut.

131 *sympathize with*: behave like.

132 *robustious*: wildly energetic.
coming on: attack.

Constable
Just, just. And the men do sympathize with the mastiffs
in robustious and rough coming on, leaving their wits
with their wives. And then, give them great meals of
beef and iron and steel, they will eat like wolves and
135 fight like devils.

Orléans
Ay, but these English are shrewdly out of beef.

136 *shrewdly*: cruelly.

Constable
Then shall we find tomorrow they have only stomachs
to eat and none to fight. Now is it time to arm. Come,
shall we about it?

137 *stomachs*: appetites.

139 *about it*: get on with it.

Orléans
140 It is now two o'clock. But let me see, by ten
We shall have each a hundred Englishmen!   [*Exeunt*

ACT 4

Act 4 Chorus
The Chorus now exhorts the audience to move, in imagination, from the tent of the French lords across to the English camp, where the knights are arming for the next day's battle. The common soldiers are waiting restlessly by their camp-fires, and the figure of the king can be discerned as he goes from one fire to another.

1 *entertain conjecture*: open your minds to the imagination.
2 *creeping . . . dark*: The soldiers are creeping and whispering, straining their eyes to see in the darkness.
3 *wide vessel*: hollow vault.
4 *foul womb*: Night is personified as a witch (line 21) who gives birth to foul things—both nightmares, and the next day's hideous battle.
5 *either army*: both the armies.
   stilly: quietly and constantly—*and also* in the still of the night.
6 *fix'd sentinels*: guards who do not leave the posts at which they have been positioned.
7 *each other's watch*: the other side's guard; the night is so silent (and the armies so close) that they can hear each other.
8 *answers*: reflects.
   paly: pale and flickering.
9 *battle*: army already drawn up to fight—i.e. in battle order.
   umber'd: orange-brown, fire-lit.
11 *dull*: unresponsive.
12 *accomplishing the knights*: fitting the knights into their armour.
14 *note*: sound, notice.
17 *secure in soul*: over-confident in their minds.
18 *over-lusty*: excessively merry.
19 *low-rated*: despised, under-estimated.
   play: gamble for.
20 *tardy-gaited*: slow-paced.
22 *condemned*: condemnèd.
23 *watchful fires*: watch-fires; it is the soldiers who are 'watchful'.
24 *inly*: inwardly.

London: the Globe. Enter Chorus

Chorus
Now entertain conjecture of a time
When creeping murmur and the poring dark
Fills the wide vessel of the universe.
From camp to camp, through the foul womb of night,
5 The hum of either army stilly sounds,
That the fix'd sentinels almost receive
The secret whispers of each other's watch.
Fire answers fire, and through their paly flames
Each battle sees the other's umber'd face.
10 Steed threatens steed, in high and boastful neighs,
Piercing the night's dull ear. And from the tents
The armourers accomplishing the knights
With busy hammers closing rivets up
Give dreadful note of preparation.
15 The country cocks do crow, the clocks do toll,
And the third hour of drowsy morning name.
Proud of their numbers and secure in soul
The confident and over-lusty French
Do the low-rated English play at dice,
20 And chide the cripple tardy-gaited night
Who like a foul and ugly witch doth limp
So tediously away. The poor condemned English,
Like sacrifices, by their watchful fires
Sit patiently and inly ruminate
25 The morning's danger; and their gesture sad,
Investing lank-lean cheeks and war-worn coats,
Presented them unto the gazing moon
So many horrid ghosts. O now, who will behold
The royal captain of this ruin'd band
30 Walking from watch to watch, from tent to tent?
Let him cry 'Praise and glory on his head!'
For forth he goes and visits all his host,
Bids them good morrow with a modest smile,

25 *gesture*: bearing, 'body-language'.
26 *Investing*: pervading.
   lank-lean: drawn and hollow.
28 *so many*: like so many.
   horrid: horrifying.
   who will behold: who wishes to imagine.
30 *watch*: watch-fire
32 *host*: army.
33 *good morrow*: good morning.
35 *note*: sign.
36 *enrounded*: surrounded.
37–8 *nor . . . night*: and he does not look at all pale for this tiring and sleepless night.
38 *all-watched*: watchèd.
39 *overbears attaint*: overcomes all physical and mental strain.
40 *semblance*: appearance.
   sweet majesty: gracious royal bearing.
43 *A largess . . . sun*: a bounty as generous as that of the sun.
45 *mean and gentle*: humble and noble by birth.
46 *as . . . define*: what I might humbly describe as.
47 *A . . . night*: some little feeling tonight of what our king is really like.
48 *our scene*: this stage production.
50 *vile and ragged foils*: crude and blunted swords.
51 *Right ill dispos'd*: most clumsily handled.
53 *Minding*: calling to mind, 'entertain[ing] conjecture'.
   mockeries: imitations.

And calls them brothers, friends, and countrymen.
35 Upon his royal face there is no note
How dread an army hath enrounded him,
Nor doth he dedicate one jot of colour
Unto the weary and all-watched night,
But freshly looks and overbears attaint
40 With cheerful semblance and sweet majesty,
That every wretch, pining and pale before,
Beholding him, plucks comfort from his looks.
A largess universal like the sun
His liberal eye doth give to everyone,
45 Thawing cold fear, that mean and gentle all
Behold, as may unworthiness define,
'A little touch of Harry in the night'.
And so our scene must to the battle fly,
Where (O for pity!) we shall much disgrace,
50 With four or five most vile and ragged foils
Right ill dispos'd in brawl ridiculous,
The name of Agincourt. Yet sit and see,
Minding true things by what their mockeries be.   [*Exit*

Act 4 Scene 1

As the Chorus promised, we now see King Henry doing the rounds of the English camp, and speaking (in disguise) to all the different ranks of soldiers. He hears their complaints, and he tries to answer their questions. Finally he remains alone on the stage, meditating on the moral responsibilities of a king.

0s.d. *another door*: i.e. from different sides of the stage.

5 *observingly*: by taking notice.
   distil it out: extract it.
6 *stirrers*: risers; the expression was proverbial.
7 *husbandry*: management, economy.

10 *dress . . . end*: get dressed properly for the work we have to do; *and also*, prepare ourselves spiritually to meet our deaths.
11 *gather . . . weed*: find some good in everything: a proverbial saying.
12 *make a moral of*: learn a lesson from.

15 *churlish*: rough, unfriendly.

16 *likes me*: suits me.
18–23 *'Tis . . . legerity*: Probably King Henry keeps these thoughts to himself, speaking them 'aside' to the play's audience.
19 *Upon example so*: with such an example [as Sir Thomas Erpingham].
20 *quicken'd*: stirred, brought to life.
21 *organs*: bodily functions, limbs.
   defunct: lifeless.
22 *Break . . . grave*: awaken from sleep (as though bursting out of a tomb).
23 *with casted slough*: having shaken off their despondency (like snakes shedding their old skins).
   legerity: quickness, nimbleness.
26 *do my good morrow*: say 'good morning' to them for me.
   anon: shortly.
27 *Desire . . . to*: ask them to come.
   pavilion: tent.

SCENE 1

France: the English camp. Enter the King *and* Gloucester *and* Bedford *by another door*

King
Gloucester, 'tis true that we are in great danger.
The greater therefore should our courage be.
Good morrow, brother Bedford. God almighty,
There is some soul of goodness in things evil
5 Would men observingly distil it out.
For our bad neighbour makes us early stirrers,
Which is both healthful and good husbandry.
Besides, they are our outward consciences
And preachers to us all, admonishing
10 That we should dress us fairly for our end.
Thus may we gather honey from the weed
And make a moral of the devil himself.

Enter Erpingham

Good morrow, old Sir Thomas Erpingham.
A good soft pillow for that good white head
15 Were better than a churlish turf of France.
Erpingham
Not so, my liege. This lodging likes me better
Since I may say 'now lie I like a king'.
    King
'Tis good for men to love their present pains.
Upon example so the spirit is eased,
20 And when the mind is quicken'd, out of doubt
The organs, though defunct and dead before,
Break up their drowsy grave and newly move
With casted slough and fresh legerity.
Lend me thy cloak, Sir Thomas. Brothers both,
25 Commend me to the princes in our camp.
Do my good morrow to them, and anon
Desire them all to my pavilion.
    Gloucester
We shall, my liege.

Erpingham
Shall I attend your grace?
   King
                  No, my good knight.
30 Go with my brothers to my lords of England.
I and my bosom must debate awhile,
And then I would no other company.
   Erpingham
The Lord in heaven bless thee, noble Harry.
               [*Exeunt all but* King

   King
God a mercy, old heart, thou speak'st cheerfully.

Enter Pistol

   Pistol
35 *Qui vous là?*
   King
A friend.
   Pistol
Discuss unto me, art thou officer, or art thou base, common, and popular?
   King
I am a gentleman of a company.
   Pistol
40 Trail'st thou the puissant pike?
   King
Even so. What are you?
   Pistol
As good a gentleman as the emperor.
   King
Then you are better than the king.
   Pistol
The king's a bawcock and a heart of gold, a lad of life, an
45 imp of fame, of parents good, of fist most valiant. I kiss his dirty shoe, and from heartstring I love the lovely bully. What is thy name?
   King
Harry *le roi.*
   Pistol
Leroy? A Cornish name. Art thou of Cornish crew?

31 *bosom*: heart.
32 *would*: want.
34 *a*: have.
35 *Qui vous là?*: Pistol's French is not very good: he wants to say '*Qui va là?*' (= who goes there?).
37 *Discuss*: explain.
37–8 *base, common, and popular*: of low degree, a common soldier, and an ordinary man.
39 *gentleman of a company*: non-commissioned officer.
40 *Trail'st . . . pike*: i.e. are you in the infantry. The pike ('puissant' = powerful) was a wooden staff, at least 12 feet (4 metres) long, with multi-bladed spearhead.
42 *As . . . emperor*: a proverbial comparison.
44 *bawcock*: good lad.
45 *imp of fame*: lucky young devil.
46 *heartstring*: bottom of my heart.
46–7 *lovely bully*: splendid chap.
48 *le roi*: the king.
49 *crew*: mob, crowd.

King

50 No, I am a Welshman.

Pistol

Knowest thou Llewellyn?

King

Yes.

Pistol

53 *leek*: the emblem of Wales, worn (and eaten) by all Welshmen on St David's Day, 1st March.
pate: head.

Tell him I'll knock his leek about his pate upon St Davy's day.

King

55 Do not you wear your dagger in your cap that day, lest he knock that about yours.

Pistol

Art thou his friend?

King

And his kinsman too.

Pistol

59 *The fico*: a term of contemptuous dismissal; see 3, 7, 52 note.

The *fico* for thee, then.

King

60 I thank you. God be with you.

Pistol

My name is Pistol called.   [*Exit*

King

62 *sorts*: fits.

It sorts well with your fierceness.

63s.d. *separate doors*: different sides of the stage.

Enter Llewellyn *and* Gower *by separate doors*

Gower

Captain Llewellyn!

Llewellyn

64 *speak fewer*: don't talk so loud.
65 *admiration*: amazing thing.
66 *ancient prerogatives*: traditional rights.

So! In the name of Jesu Christ, speak fewer. It is the 65 greatest admiration in the universal woreld when the true and ancient prerogatives and laws of the wars is not kept. If you would take the pains but to examine the wars of Pompey the Great you shall find, I warrant you, that there is no tiddle taddle nor pibble pabble in

68 *Pompey the Great*: A distinguished Roman general (d. 48 BC).
69 *tiddle taddle . . . pibble babble*: chattering and babbling.

70 Pompey's camp. I warrant you, you shall find the ceremonies of the wars, and the cares of it, and the forms of it, and the sobriety of it, and the modesty of it, to be otherwise.

72 *sobriety*: seriousness.
modesty: decency.

Gower
Why, the enemy is loud. You hear him all night.
Llewellyn

75–6 *prating coxcomb*: prattling idiot.
76 *meet*: right, suitable.

75 If the enemy is an ass and a fool and a prating
coxcomb, is it meet, think you, that we should also, look
you, be an ass and a fool and a prating coxcomb, in your
own conscience, now?
Gower
I will speak lower.
Llewellyn
80 I pray you, and beseech you, that you will.
[*Exeunt* Gower *and* Llewellyn
King
Though it appear a little out of fashion,
There is much care and valour in this Welshman.

81 *out of fashion*: old fashioned,
unconventional.

Enter three soldiers, John Bates, Alexander Court,
and Michael Williams

Court
Brother John Bates, is not that the morning which
breaks yonder?
Bates
85 I think it be. But we have no great cause to desire the
approach of day.
Williams
We see yonder the beginning of the day, but I think we
shall never see the end of it. Who goes there?
King
A friend.
Williams
90 Under what captain serve you?
King
Under Sir Thomas Erpingham.
Williams
A good old commander, and a most kind gentleman. I
pray you, what thinks he of our estate?
King
Even as men wrecked upon a sand, that look to be
95 washed off the next tide.

93 *estate*: situation, chances.

94 *wrecked upon a sand*: shipwrecked on
a sandbank.
look: expect.

Bates

He hath not told his thought to the king?

King

No. Nor it is not meet he should. For though I speak it to you, I think the king is but a man as I am. The violet smells to him as it doth to me. The element shows to
100 him as it doth to me. All his senses have but human conditions. His ceremonies laid by, in his nakedness he appears but a man; and though his affections are higher mounted than ours, yet when they stoop they stoop with the like wing. Therefore when he sees reason
105 of fears as we do, his fears, out of doubt, be of the same relish as ours are. Yet in reason no man should possess him with any appearance of fear, lest he by showing it should dishearten his army.

Bates

He may show what outward courage he will, but I
110 believe, as cold a night as 'tis, he could wish himself in Thames up to the neck. And so I would he were, and I by him, at all adventures, so we were quit here.

King

By my troth, I will speak my conscience of the king. I think he would not wish himself anywhere but where he
115 is.

Bates

Then I would he were here alone. So should he be sure to be ransomed and a-many poor men's lives saved.

King

I dare say you love him not so ill to wish him here alone, howsoever you speak this to feel other men's minds.
120 Methinks I could not die anywhere so contented as in the king's company, his cause being just and his quarrel honourable.

Williams

That's more than we know.

Bates

Ay, or more than we should seek after, for we know
125 enough if we know we are the king's subjects. If his cause be wrong our obedience to the king wipes the crime of it out of us.

97–8 *though . . . you*: I'll tell you in confidence.

99 *element shows*: sky appears.

101 *conditions*: qualities.
ceremonies: symbols of royalty.
laid by: set aside, apart.
102 *affections*: emotions.
102–3 *higher mounted*: set on higher things, soar higher (the metaphor is from hawking).
103 *stoop*: plunge down, drop (like a hawk).
104 *like*: same.
106 *relish*: taste, appreciation.
106–7 *possess him with*: put on himself.

111 *I would*: I wish.
112 *at all adventures*: at any price.
so . . . here: as long as we were out of this.
113 *By my troth*: by my word, in truth.
speak my conscience: say what I really believe to be true.

116 *So*: in that way.
117 *a-many*: a lot of.

119 *howsoever . . . minds*: whatever you may say in order to find out what others are thinking.
121 *his . . . just*: so long as his legal case is sound.

124 *seek after*: enquire into.

Williams

But if the cause be not good the king himself hath a
heavy reckoning to make, when all those legs and arms
130 and heads chopped off in a battle shall join together at
the latter day and cry all 'We died at such a place', some
swearing, some crying for a surgeon, some upon their
wives left poor behind them, some upon the debts they
owe, some upon their children rawly left. I am afeard
135 there are few die well that die in a battle, for how can
they charitably dispose of anything when blood is their
argument? Now if these men do not die well it will be a
black matter for the king that led them to it, who to
disobey were against all proportion of subjection.

King

140 So if a son that is by his father sent about merchandise
do sinfully miscarry upon the sea, the imputation of his
wickedness, by your rule, should be imposed upon his
father that sent him. Or if a servant, under his master's
command transporting a sum of money, be assailed by
145 robbers and die in many irreconciled iniquities, you
may call the business of the master the author of the
servant's damnation. But this is not so. The king is not
bound to answer the particular endings of his soldiers,
the father of his son, nor the master of his servant, for
150 they purpose not their death when they purpose their
services. Besides, there is no king, be his cause never so
spotless, if it come to the arbitrament of swords can try
it out with all unspotted soldiers. Some, peradventure,
have on them the guilt of premeditated and contrived
155 murder, some of beguiling virgins with the broken seals
of perjury, some, making the wars their bulwark, that
have before gored the gentle bosom of peace with
pillage and robbery. Now, if these men have defeated the
law and outrun native punishment, though they can
160 outstrip men they have no wings to fly from God. War is
His beadle, war is His vengeance, so that here men are
punished for before-breach of the king's laws in now the
king's quarrel. Where they feared the death they have
borne life away, and where they would be safe they
165 perish. Then, if they die unprovided, no more is the

129 *heavy . . . make*: a serious charge to
answer, a big account to settle.
129–31 *when . . . day*: It was believed that
on the Day of Judgement ('the latter
day') the dead would rise again, and
all lost limbs would be re-united with
their bodies.
134 *rawly left*: unprovided for.
afeard: afraid.
135 *die well*: i.e. spiritually prepared for
death.
136 *charitably dispose*: settle in a proper
Christian manner.
136–7 *blood is their argument*: killing is
their business.
139 *proportion of subjection*: rightful
duties of a subject.

141 *sinfully miscarry*: die in a state of sin.
imputation of: blame, responsibility,
for.
142 *by your rule*: according to your
interpretation.

145 *in . . . iniquities*: with many
unrepented sins.
146 *the author of*: the one responsible for.

148 *answer*: take responsibility for.
particular: individual.

150 *purpose*: intend.

152 *arbitrament of swords*: decision by
battle.
try: fight.
153 *unspotted*: sinless.
peradventure: perhaps.
154 *contrived*: plotted, intentional.
155 *beguiling*: cheating.
155–6 *seals of perjury*: promises of
marriage.
156 *bulwark*: defence.
157 *gored*: wounded.
158 *defeated*: cheated.
159 *outrun*: run away from.
native punishment: punishment at
home, in their native land.
161 *beadle*: policeman, agent of the law.
162 *before-breach*: a previous breach.
163–5 *Where . . . perish*: they ran for life
to escape punishment for their
crimes, but where they hoped to be
safe (i.e. in the army) they were killed.
165 *unprovided*: not spiritually prepared.

167 *visited*: punished.

168 *the king's*: to the king.

169 *his own*: i.e. his own responsibility.

170 *mote*: blemish, stain of sin.

171 *so*: in this way—i.e. purged of all sin.
death . . . advantage: For a Christian,
death is the beginning of eternal life:
see Philippians 1:21, 'For Christ is to
me life, and death is to me
advantage'.

172 *lost*: spent.

173–4 *it were not sin*: it would not be
sinful.

174 *free*: generous.

177 *dies ill*: in a state of sin.
the ill: the sin.

king guilty of their damnation than he was before guilty
of those impieties for the which they are now visited.
Every subject's duty is the king's, but every subject's soul
is his own. Therefore should every soldier in the wars do
170 as every sick man in his bed, wash every mote out of his
conscience. And dying so, death is to him advantage; or,
not dying, the time was blessedly lost wherein such
preparation was gained. And in him that escapes it were
not sin to think that, making God so free an offer, He let
175 him outlive that day to see His greatness, and to teach
others how they should prepare.

Williams
'Tis certain, every man that dies ill, the ill upon his own
head; the king is not to answer it.

Bates
I do not desire he should answer for me, and yet I
180 determine to fight lustily for him.

King
I myself heard the king say he would not be ransomed.

Williams
Ay, he said so to make us fight cheerfully, but when our
throats are cut he may be ransomed and we ne'er the
wiser.

King
185 If I live to see it, I will never trust his word after.

Williams
You pay him then! That's a perilous shot out of an elder
gun, that a poor and a private displeasure can do against
a monarch. You may as well go about to turn the sun to
ice with fanning in his face with a peacock's feather.
190 You'll never trust his word after! Come, 'tis a foolish
saying.

King
Your reproof is something too round. I should be angry
with you if the time were convenient.

Williams
Let it be a quarrel between us, if you live.

King
195 I embrace it.

Williams
How shall I know thee again?

186 *pay him*: make him pay, punish him.

186–7 *elder gun*: pop-gun, made from
hollowed-out stick of elder.

187 *a poor . . . displeasure*: the grievance
of a humble individual.

189 *his face*: i.e. the sun's face.

192 *round*: blunt.

194 *quarrel*: bone of contention.

197 *gage*: pledge, glove thrown down in
  challenge.

198 *bonnet*: cap.
199 *make it*: recognize it as.

204 *I will take*: I will give.

207 *I take thee*: I find you.

211 *reckon*: count.
212 *lay*: bet.
  crowns: heads; *and also* gold coins
  (*écus*).
215 *crowns*: heads *and* coins; it was a
  treasonable act to clip the edges of
  English coins (in order to steal the
  gold).
216 *clipper*: one of those clipping the
  French crowns.
218 *careful*: anxious, full of care.
220–72 The king muses on the difference
  between kings and their subjects. He
  apostrophizes the 'idol ceremony'
  (lines 228–239), then addresses
  himself (lines 239–45), and finally
  (lines 245–72) denounces
  'ceremony'.
221 *twin-born with*: born the twin of—i.e.
  an inevitable accompaniment.
222 *breath*: utterance, words.
  sense: understanding, awareness.
223 *his own wringing*: his own stomach-
  ache—i.e. only his own pains.

King
Give me any gage of thine and I will wear it in my
bonnet. Then, if ever thou darest acknowledge it, I will
make it my quarrel.
Williams
200 Here's my glove. Give me another of thine.
King
There.

They exchange gloves

Williams
This will I also wear in my cap. If ever thou come to me
and say, after tomorrow, 'This is my glove', by this hand
I will take thee a box on the ear.
King
205 If ever I live to see it, I will challenge it.
Williams
Thou darest as well be hanged.
King
Well, I will do it, though I take thee in the king's
company.
Williams
Keep thy word. Fare thee well.
Bates
210 Be friends, you English fools, be friends! We have
French quarrels enough if you could tell how to reckon.
King
Indeed, the French may lay twenty French crowns to
one they will beat us, for they bear them on their
shoulders. But it is no English treason to cut French
215 crowns, and tomorrow the king himself will be a
clipper.   [*Exeunt* Soldiers
Upon the king! 'Let us our lives, our souls, our debts,
our careful wives, our children and our sins, lay on the
king.'
220 We must bear all.
O hard condition, twin-born with greatness,
Subject to the breath of every fool, whose sense
No more can feel but his own wringing.

224 *neglect*: renounce, deprive themselves of.
225 *private*: ordinary.
231 *comings-in*: income, benefits.
232 *show me but*: just show me.
233 *Is . . . adoration*: are you nothing more than adoration.
234 *place*: public position.
    degree: social rank.
    form: ritual.
239 *great greatness*: King Henry is sarcastic as he speaks to himself.
242 *blown from adulation*: fanned (and flyblown, corrupted) by flattery.
243 *it*: i.e. the fever.
    give place: yield.
    flexure and low bending: kneeling and bowing (by flattering courtiers).
245 *proud dream*: The king addresses 'ceremony' again.
247 *find*: expose, judge.
248 *balm*: holy oil with which the king is annointed at his coronation.
    ball: orb.

250 *intertissued*: interwoven.
251 *farced title*: farcèd; pompous, long-winded titles with which the king is addressed.
252 *tide of pomp*: The king envisages grand ceremonial proceedings as a high tide whose waves swell up to the cliffs.
258 *distressful bread*: food he has laboured for.
259 *horrid*: full of horrors; see Chorus 4, line 4.
260 *lackey*: footman running beside a chariot.
261 *the eye of Phoebus*: under the gaze of Phoebus Apollo, the sun-god—i.e. in the heat of the sun.
262 *Elysium*: the 'heaven' of Greek mythology, and home of Phoebus the sun-god.
263 *Hyperion*: the oldest god of the sun: the peasant is up before sunrise to help the god harness his horses.

What infinite heart's ease must kings neglect
225 That private men enjoy?
    And what have kings that privates have not too,
    Save ceremony, save general ceremony?
    And what art thou, thou idol ceremony?
    What kind of god art thou, that suffer'st more
230 Of mortal griefs than do thy worshippers?
    What are thy rents? What are thy comings-in?
    O ceremony, show me but thy worth!
    What? Is thy soul of adoration?
    Art thou ought else but place, degree, and form,
235 Creating awe and fear in other men,
    Wherein thou art less happy being fear'd
    Than they in fearing?
    What drink'st thou oft, instead of homage sweet,
    But poison'd flattery? Oh, be sick, great greatness,
240 And bid thy ceremony give thee cure.
    Thinkst thou the fiery fever will go out
    With titles blown from adulation?
    Will it give place to flexure and low bending?
    Canst thou, when thou command'st the beggar's knee,
245 Command the health of it? No, thou proud dream,
    That playst so subtly with a king's repose.
    I am a king that find thee, and I know
    'Tis not the balm, the sceptre, and the ball,
    The sword, the mace, the crown imperial,
250 The intertissued robe of gold and pearl,
    The farced title running 'fore the king,
    The throne he sits on, nor the tide of pomp
    That beats upon the high shore of this world;
    No, not all these, thrice-gorgeous ceremony,
255 Not all these, laid in bed majestical,
    Can sleep so soundly as the wretched slave
    Who, with a body fill'd and vacant mind,
    Gets him to rest, cramm'd with distressful bread;
    Never sees horrid night, the child of hell,
260 But like a lackey from the rise to set
    Sweats in the eye of Phoebus, and all night
    Sleeps in Elysium; next day after dawn
    Doth rise and help Hyperion to his horse
    And follows so the ever-running year

267 *Winding up*: completely occupied with.
268 *forehand*: superior hold in wrestling. *vantage of*: advantage over.
269 *member . . . peace*: limb of the body politic, one who shares in the peace of the nation.
270 *gross*: dull, thick. *wots*: knows.
271 *watch*: wakefulness.
272 *best advantages*: gets most benefit from.

273 *jealous of*: worried about.

279 *steel*: harden, strengthen.
280 *possess . . . fear*: do not let them be afraid.
281 *reckoning*: counting, adding up. *opposed numbers*: opposèd; numbers of soldiers on the opposite side.
283 *fault*: sin.
284 *My father*: See 'About the Play' p. v. *compassing*: obtaining.
285 *interred new*: interrèd; At the beginning of his reign, Henry caused the body of Richard II to be brought to London and buried in Westminster Abbey.
287 *forced*: forcèd; i.e. in the act of murder.

265 With profitable labour to his grave.
And but for ceremony such a wretch,
Winding up days with toil and nights with sleep,
Had the forehand and vantage of a king.
The slave, a member of the country's peace,
270 Enjoys it, but in gross brain little wots
What watch the king keeps to maintain the peace,
Whose hours the peasant best advantages.

Enter Erpingham

Erpingham
My lord, your nobles, jealous of your absence,
Seek through your camp to find you.
King
275 Good old knight,
Collect them all together at my tent.
I'll be before thee.
Erpingham
I shall do't, my lord.   [*Exit*
King
O God of battles, steel my soldiers' hearts.
280 Possess them not with fear. Take from them now
The sense of reckoning ere th'opposed numbers
Pluck their hearts from them. Not today, O Lord,
Oh, not today, think not upon the fault
My father made in compassing the crown.
285 I Richard's body have interred new,
And on it have bestow'd more contrite tears
Than from it issued forced drops of blood.

289   *who . . . hold up*: i.e. in prayer.

290   *blood*: bloodshed.

291   *chantries*: chapels where requiem masses could be sung every day.
sad: grave.

292   *Sing*: i.e. sing requiem masses.
still: always.

293   *all . . . worth*: i.e. because not even good deeds are valuable (in the sight of God) without faith.

294   *after all*: Repentance should come before atonement.

296   *liege*: royal lord.

298   *stay*: wait for.

Five hundred poor I have in yearly pay
Who twice a day their wither'd hands hold up
290   Toward heaven to pardon blood. And I have built
Two chantries where the sad and solemn priests
Sing still for Richard's soul. More will I do,
Though all that I can do is nothing worth
Since that my penitence comes after all,
295   Imploring pardon.

Enter Gloucester

Gloucester
My liege.
    King
        My brother Gloucester's voice? Ay,
I know thy errand. I will go with thee.
The day, my friends, and all things stay for me.
[*Exeunt*

Act 4 Scene 2
The French lords, anticipating an easy victory, gloat over the miserable little English army.

2   *Montez à cheval*: to horse, mount up.
varlet lackey: you wretched groom.

4   *Via . . . terres*: go across water and land.

5   *Rien . . . feu*: not air and fire then (Orléans is sarcastic).

6   *Cieux*: heavens.

SCENE 2

France: the French camp. Enter Bourbon, Orléans,
Rambures, *and* Beaumont

Orléans
The sun doth gild our armour. Up, my lords!
    Bourbon
Montez à cheval! My horse, varlet lackey! Ha!
    Orléans
Oh, brave spirit!
    Bourbon
Via les eaux et terres!
    Orléans
5   *Rien puis l'air et feu?*
    Bourbon
Cieux, cousin Orléans!

Enter Constable

Now, my lord Constable?

8 *present service*: immediate action.

9 *make . . . hides*: spur them on.

10 *spin*: spray.

11 *dout*: douse, quench.

Constable
Hark how our steeds for present service neigh.
   Bourbon
Mount them, and make incision in their hides
10 That their hot blood may spin in English eyes
And dout them with superfluous courage! Ha!
   Rambures
What, will you have them weep our horses' blood?
How shall we then behold their natural tears?

Enter Messenger

   Messenger
The English are embattled, you French peers.
   Constable
15 To horse, you gallant princes, straight to horse!
Do but behold yon poor and starved band
And your fair show shall suck away their souls,
Leaving them but the shells and husks of men.
There is not work enough for all our hands,
20 Scarce blood enough in all their sickly veins
To give each naked curtal-axe a stain,
That our French gallants shall today draw out
And sheathe for lack of sport. Let us but blow on them,
The vapour of our valour will o'erturn them.
25 'Tis positive 'gainst all exceptions, lords,
That our superfluous lackeys and our peasants
Who in unnecessary action swarm
About our squares of battle were enough

14 *embattled*: drawn up in fighting line.

15 *straight*: at once.

16 *starved*: starvèd.

17 *your . . . souls*: the impressive appearance will take away their hearts.

21 *curtal-axe*: cutlass—a short, broad-bladed, sword (for chopping).

25 *'gainst all exceptions*: without any question.

28 *squares of battle*: military formations of soldiers.

29 *hilding*: contemptible.
30–1 *Though . . . speculation*: even though we ourselves stood by as mere spectators: the Constable refers to the French king's description of Edward III 'on mountain standing' at the battle of Crécy (*2, 4, 55–62*).

35 *The tucket sonance*: trumpet call for the infantry to march.
note to mount: order for the cavalry to mount their horses.
36 *dare*: terrify.
37 *couch*: lie.

39 *island*: i.e. from the British Isles.
carrions: corpses, food for carrion birds.
desperate of: careless about.
40 *Ill-favouredly become*: look unsightly.
41 *curtains*: i.e. military banners.
let loose: unfolded.
42 *passing*: exceedingly.
43 *Big Mars . . . host*: all the spirit of fighting seems to be exhausted in this worn-out army; *Mars* was the Roman god of war—to whom Henry was compared in the Prologue (line 6).
44 *faintly*: timidly.
beaver: visor, the face-piece of a helmet.
45 *fixed candlesticks*: fixèd; i.e. suits of armour placed (e.g. at the foot of a great staircase) to look like knights holding torches or candles.
46 *torch staves*: candle holders.
jades: nags.
47 *Lob*: droop down.
48 *down-roping*: hanging down.
49 *gemell'd*: jointed.
51 *executors*: those who dispose of what the dead leave behind them—in this case, the bodies.
54 *demonstrate*: depict.
the life of: to the life.
battle: army drawn up ready to fight.
56 *stay*: wait.
58 *provender*: hay, horse-food.
60 *guidon*: standard, pennant.
61 *trumpet*: trumpeter.
62 *for my haste*: so that I can get moving.
63 *outwear*: waste.

To purge this field of such a hilding foe,
30 Though we upon this mountain's basis by
Took stand for idle speculation,
But that our honours must not. What's to say?
A very little little let us do
And all is done. Then let the trumpets sound
35 The tucket sonance and the note to mount,
For our approach shall so much dare the field
That England shall couch down in fear, and yield.

Enter Grandpré

Grandpré
Why do you stay so long, my lords of France?
Yon island carrions, desperate of their bones,
40 Ill-favouredly become the morning field.
Their ragged curtains poorly are let loose
And our air shakes them passing scornfully.
Big Mars seems bankrupt in their beggar'd host,
And faintly through a rusty beaver peeps.
45 The horsemen sit like fixed candlesticks
With torch staves in their hand, and their poor jades
Lob down their heads, dropping the hides and hips,
The gum down-roping from their pale dead eyes,
And in their pale dull mouths the gemell'd bit
50 Lies foul with chew'd-grass, still and motionless.
And their executors the knavish crows
Fly o'er them all, impatient for their hour.
Description cannot suit itself in words
To demonstrate the life of such a battle,
55 In life so lifeless, as it shows itself.
    Constable
They have said their prayers, and they stay for death.
    Bourbon
Shall we go send them dinners and fresh suits
And give their fasting horses provender,
And after fight with them?
    Constable
60 I stay but for my guidon. To the field!
I will the banner from a trumpet take
And use it for my haste. Come, come, away!
The sun is high and we outwear the day.   [*Exeunt*

Act 4 Scene 3
The English lords are gloomy about their chances in the battle now imminent. King Henry invigorates them with a rousing speech, and seems undaunted even with the arrival of the French herald asking questions about ransom money.

2 *is rode*: has ridden.
   battle: formal battle-array.

3 *full*: at least; historians vary in their accounts of the actual number of troops involved in the fighting (Shakespeare gives Holinshed's estimate), but all agree that the English were desperately out-numbered.

6 *wi'*: with.
   charge: division.

10 *kind kinsman*: Westmorland's son was married to Salisbury's daughter.

13 *mind*: remind.
14 *fram'd*: composed.

16s.d. The king probably enters unobserved—perhaps still disguised in Erpingham's cloak.

17 *one ten thousand*: one in every ten thousand.

SCENE 3

France: the English camp. Enter Gloucester, Bedford, Exeter, Erpingham *with all his host,* Salisbury, *and* Westmorland

Gloucester
Where is the king?
Bedford
The king himself is rode to view their battle.
Westmorland
Of fighting men they have full threescore thousand.
Exeter
There's five to one. Besides, they all are fresh.
Salisbury
5 God's arm strike with us! 'Tis a fearful odds.
God be wi'you, princes all. I'll to my charge.
If we no more meet till we meet in heaven
Then joyfully, my noble lord of Bedford,
My dear lord Gloucester and my good lord Exeter,
10 And my kind kinsman, warriors all, adieu.
Bedford
Farewell, good Salisbury, and good luck go with thee.
Exeter
Farewell, kind lord. Fight valiantly today.
                              [*Exit* Salisbury
And yet I do thee wrong to mind thee of it,
For thou art fram'd of the firm truth of valour.
Bedford
15 He is as full of valour as of kindness,
Princely in both.

Enter the King

Westmorland
                    O that we now had here
But one ten thousand of those men in England
That do no work today.
King
                    What's he that wishes so?
My cousin Westmorland. No, my fair cousin.

20 *mark'd*: chosen, doomed.
21 *To . . . loss*: for our country to lose.

24 *Jove*: Almighty God: the Old
   Testament Jehovah, or Jupiter in
   classical mythology.
25 *feed upon my cost*: live at my
   expense.
26 *yearns*: grieves.
28 *a sin to covet*: Covetousness is
   forbidden in the tenth commandment
   of Moses.
30 *coz*: cousin, kinsman.

32 *share from me*: reduce my share of.

33 *best hope*: i.e. of spiritual salvation.

34 *host*: army.

35 *stomach to*: appetite—courage—for.

36 *passport*: letter giving right of passage
   through a foreign country.
37 *crowns for convoy*: money to pay for
   his journey.
38 *We would*: we do not want to; King
   Henry uses the royal plural pronoun—
   but he also implies that all those
   present share his opinion.
39 *fellowship*: brotherhood.
40 *Feast of Crispian*: 25 October; two
   brothers, Crispinus and Crispianus,
   were martyred together in AD 287.
44 *live old age*: live to be an old man.
45 *vigil*: eve.

50 *with advantages*: adding some
   exaggeration.

55 *flowing cups*: celebratory drinking.

57 *Crispin Crispian*: see line 40 note.

59 *remembered*: rememberèd.

20 If we are mark'd to die, we are enough
   To do our country loss. And if to live,
   The fewer men, the greater share of honour.
   God's will, I pray thee wish not one man more.
   By Jove, I am not covetous for gold,
25 Nor care I who doth feed upon my cost.
   It yearns me not if men my garments wear.
   Such outward things dwell not in my desires.
   But if it be a sin to covet honour,
   I am the most offending soul alive.
30 No, faith, my coz, wish not a man from England.
   God's peace, I would not lose so great an honour
   As one man more, methinks, would share from me,
   For the best hope I have. Oh, do not wish one more!
   Rather proclaim it, Westmorland, through my host
35 That he which hath no stomach to this fight
   Let him depart. His passport shall be made,
   And crowns for convoy put into his purse.
   We would not die in that man's company
   That fears his fellowship to die with us.
40 This day is called the Feast of Crispian.
   He that outlives this day and comes safe home
   Will stand a-tiptoe when this day is nam'd,
   And rouse him at the name of Crispian.
   He that shall see this day and live old age
45 Will yearly on the vigil feast his neighbours,
   And say 'Tomorrow is Saint Crispian.'
   Then will he strip his sleeve and show his scars,
   And say 'These wounds I had on Crispin's day.'
   Old men forget, yet all shall be forgot
50 But he'll remember, with advantages,
   What feats he did that day. Then shall our names,
   Familiar in his mouth as household words,
   Harry the king, Bedford and Exeter,
   Warwick and Talbot, Salisbury and Gloucester,
55 Be in their flowing cups freshly remember'd.
   This story shall the good man teach his son,
   And Crispin Crispian shall ne'er go by
   From this day to the ending of the world
   But we in it shall be remembered.
60 We few, we happy few, we band of brothers—

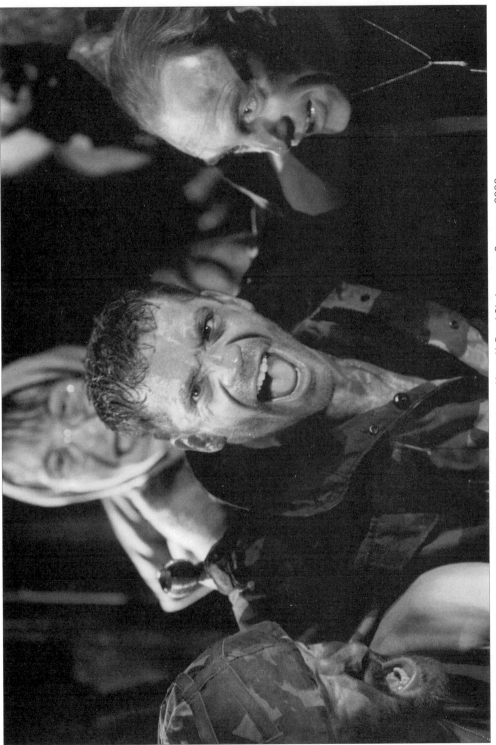

'We few, we happy few, we band of brothers', (*4*, 3, 60). William Houston as Henry V, Royal Shakespeare Company, 2000.

62 *vile*: lowly born.
63 *gentle his condition*: raise his social status to that of 'gentleman'.
64 *now abed*: On the battlefield it is only just after dawn.
66 *hold . . . cheap*: be ashamed, think themselves cowards.

68 *bestow*: prepare, arm.
69 *bravely*: boldly; *and also* flauntingly, splendidly.
   their battles: fighting positions.
70 *expedience*: expedition, convenient speed.

72 *backward*: hesitant.

74 *liege*: royal lord.
   would: I wish.

76 *unwish'd*: undone.
77 *likes me*: pleases me.

78s.d. *Tucket*: This interruption is not the trumpet call to charge, but that which sounded at *3, 7, 106* to introduce the French herald.
79 *know of*: learn from.
80 *compound*: make a bargain.
81 *assured*: assurèd.
82 *gulf*: brink, edge (of danger).
83 *englutted*: swallowed up.
84 *mind*: remind.

86 *retire*: withdrawal.

For he today that sheds his blood with me
Shall be my brother; be he ne'er so vile
This day shall gentle his condition—
And gentlemen in England, now abed,
65 Shall think themselves accurs'd they were not here,
And hold their manhoods cheap whiles any speaks
That fought with us upon Saint Crispin's Day.

Enter Salisbury

Salisbury
My sovereign lord, bestow yourself with speed.
The French are bravely in their battles set,
70 And will with all expedience charge on us.
   King
All things are ready, if our minds be so.
   Westmorland
Perish the man whose mind is backward now!
   King
Thou dost not wish more help from England, coz?
   Westmorland
God's will, my liege, would you and I alone,
75 Without more help, could fight this royal battle!
   King
Why, now thou hast unwish'd five thousand men,
Which likes me better than to wish us one.
You know your places. God be with you all.

Tucket. Enter Montjoy

Montjoy
Once more I come to know of thee, King Harry,
80 If for thy ransom thou wilt now compound
Before thy most assured overthrow.
For certainly thou art so near the gulf
Thou needs must be englutted. Besides, in mercy,
The Constable desires thee thou wilt mind
85 Thy followers of repentance, that their souls
May make a peaceful and a sweet retire
From off these fields where, wretches, their poor bodies
Must lie and fester.

King

Who hath sent thee now?

Montjoy

The Constable of France.

King

90 I pray thee bear my former answer back.
Bid them achieve me, and then sell my bones.
Good God, why should they mock poor fellows thus?
The man that once did sell the lion's skin
While the beast liv'd, was kill'd with hunting him.
95 A many of our bodies shall no doubt
Find native graves, upon the which, I trust,
Shall witness live in brass of this day's work.
And those that leave their valiant bones in France,
Dying like men, though buried in your dunghills,
100 They shall be fam'd, for there the sun shall greet them
And draw their honours reeking up to heaven,
Leaving their earthly parts to choke your clime,
The smell whereof shall breed a plague in France.
Mark then abounding valour in our English,
105 That being dead, like to the bullet's crazing
Break out into a second course of mischief
Killing in relapse of mortality.
Let me speak proudly. Tell the Constable
We are but warriors for the working day.
110 Our gayness and our gilt are all besmirch'd
With rainy marching in the painful field.
There's not a piece of feather in our host
(Good argument, I hope, we will not fly)
And time hath worn us into slovenry.
115 But by the mass, our hearts are in the trim,
And my poor soldiers tell me yet ere night
They'll be in fresher robes, or they will pluck
The gay new coats o'er the French soldiers' heads
And turn them out of service. If they do this—
120 As, if God please, they shall—my ransom then
Will soon be levied. Herald, save thou thy labour.
Come thou no more for ransom, gentle herald.
They shall have none, I swear, but these my joints,
Which if they have, as I will leave 'em them,
125 Shall yield them little. Tell the Constable.

91 *achieve*: capture.

93 *the man*: Aesop tells this fable about a man who tried to sell a bearskin before he had caught the bear; here the royal lion is the quarry.
95 *A many*: most.
96 *native*: where they were born—i.e. in England.
97 *witness live in brass*: memorial engraved in brass (e.g. on funeral monuments).
100 *fam'd*: made famous.
100–1 *the sun . . . heaven*: their honour is immortal and will rise up to heaven, just as the sun draws vapours steaming ('reeking') from the dunghill.
102 *clime*: region.
104 *abounding*: abundant.
105 *crazing*: rebounding, in ricochet.
106 *mischief*: damage.
107 *relapse of mortality*: whilst they themselves have fallen in death.
109 *for the working day*: whilst we are working.
110 *besmirch'd*: muddied.
111 *rainy marching*: marching in the rain. *painful field*: battlefield.
112 *piece of feather*: helmet-plume.
113 *Good . . . fly*: Henry offers a wry jest.
114 *slovenry*: scruffiness.
115 *in the trim*: in perfect condition.
116 *ere*: before.
117–19 *pluck . . . service*: take away their fine uniforms and dismiss the French soldiers from the battle, just as a servant was stripped of his master's livery when he was given the sack.
121 *soon*: easily (because the soldiers will have taken possession of the French treasure).

Montjoy
I shall, King Harry. And so fare thee well.
Thou never shalt hear herald any more.   [*Exit*

King
[*Aside*] I fear thou wilt once more come again for a
ransom.

Enter York

York
130 My lord, most humbly on my knee I beg
The leading of the vanguard.

King
Take it, brave York. Now soldiers, march away,
And how Thou pleasest, God, dispose the day.

[*Exeunt*

SCENE 4

France: the battlefield. Alarm. Excursions. Enter
Pistol, French Soldier, Boy

Pistol
Yield, cur!

128–9 *I fear . . . ransom*: Henry's prose
'aside' voices fears that he will not
openly admit.

129s.d. This is York's only appearance in
the play, but it prepares for the report
of his death at *4, 6*, 11–32 and
4, 8, 98; York is named by Holinshed
as asking to lead the 'vaward', being
of 'an haughty corage'.

Act 4 Scene 4
Pistol has taken a prisoner, and the Boy
acts as interpreter for the pleas, the
threats—and the ransom bargaining.

0s.d. *Alarm*: drum rolls.
Excursions: signs of action—e.g.
soldiers running over the stage—to
indicate battle in progress.

2 *Je . . . qualité*: I think you are a
gentleman of high rank.

3 *Colin . . . me*: This has been identified
as an anglicization of 'callin og o'
stor', the refrain of a popular Irish
song, 'Maiden, my treasure'. It may
have been suggested to Pistol by
similarity of sound with '*qualité*'—or
perhaps he is rejoicing at his prize.

5 *Seigneur Dieu*: Lord God.

6 *Due*: i.e. proper, just.
perpend: hearken, understand (a
mock-pompous term).

8 *fox*: broadsword.

9 *egregious*: exceptional.

10 *prenez . . . moi*: be merciful, take pity
on me.

11 *Moy*: Pistol thinks he hears 'moiety'
(= a share, half).

12 *rim*: guts, diaphragm.

14 *Est-il . . . bras*: Is it impossible to
escape the power of your arm?

15 *luxurious*: lecherous—thought to be a
particular quality of goats.

17 *pardonnez-moi*: excuse me.

18 *tun of moys*: treasure chest of half-
coins.

20 *Ecoutez . . . appelé*: Listen to me.
What's your name?

21 *le Fer*: In French the name means
'iron'.

23 *I'll . . . ferret*: I'll give him 'fer', and
clobber him, and sort him out.

26 *prepare*: i.e. for death.

French Soldier
Je pense que vous êtes le gentilhomme de bon qualité.
   Pistol
Quality? 'Colin o custure me'. Art thou a gentleman?
What is thy name? Discuss.
   French Soldier
5 *O Seigneur Dieu!*
   Pistol
O Seigneur Due should be a gentleman. Perpend my
words, O Seigneur Due, and mark: O Seigneur Due,
thou diest on point of fox, except, O Seigneur, thou do
give to me egregious ransom.
   French Soldier
10 *Oh, prenez miséricorde! Ayez pitié de moi!*
   Pistol
Moy shall not serve. I will have forty moys, or I will
fetch thy rim out at thy throat, in drops of crimson
blood.
   French Soldier
Est-il impossible d'échapper la force de ton bras?
   Pistol
15 Brass, cur? Thou damned and luxurious mountain
goat, offer'st me brass?
   French Soldier
Oh, pardonnez-moi!
   Pistol
Sayest thou me so? Is that a tun of moys? Come hither,
boy. Ask me this slave in French what is his name.
   Boy
20 *Écoutez. Comment êtes-vous appelé?*
   French Soldier
Monsieur le Fer.
   Boy
He says his name is Mr Fer.
   Pistol
Mr Fer. I'll fer him, and firk him, and ferret him.
Discuss the same in French unto him.
   Boy
25 I do not know the French for fer and ferret and firk.
   Pistol
Bid him prepare, for I will cut his throat.

27 *Que dit-il*: what is he saying.

28–30 *Il . . . gorge*: He is ordering me to
tell you that you must make yourself
ready to die, because this soldier here
is inclined to cut your throat right
now.

34–6 *Je . . . écus*: Oh, I beg you, for the
love of God, forgive me. I am a
gentleman from a good family. Save
my life and I will give you two
hundred crowns.

39 *house*: The Boy translates '*maison*'
literally.

42 *Petit . . . il*: Little gentleman, what
does he say?

43–6 *Encore . . . franchisement*: Again
that it is contrary to his oath to take
mercy on any prisoner. Nevertheless,
because of the crowns you have
promised him, he is content to give
you your liberty, your freedom.

47–50 *Sur . . . Angleterre*: On my knees I
give you a thousand thanks, and I
think myself fortunate to have fallen
into the hands of a gentleman—I
think the bravest, most valiant, and
very distinguished nobleman of
England.

French Soldier
Que dit-il, monsieur?
   Boy
*Il me commande à vous dire que vous faites-vous prêt, car
ce soldat ici est disposé tout à cette heure de couper*
30 *votre gorge.*
   Pistol
Oui, coupe la gorge, par ma foi, peasant, unless thou give
me crowns, brave crowns, or mangled shalt thou be by
this my sword.
   French Soldier
[*Kneels*] *Oh! Je vous supplie, pour l'amour de Dieu, me*
35 *pardonner! Je suis le gentilhomme de bonne maison.
Gardez ma vie, et je vous donnerai deux cents écus.*
   Pistol
What are his words?
   Boy
He prays you to save his life. He is a gentleman of a good
house, and for his ransom he will give you two hundred
40 crowns.
   Pistol
Tell him my fury shall abate, and I the crowns will take.
   French Soldier
Petit monsieur, que dit-il?
   Boy
*Encore qu'il est contre son jurement de pardonner aucun
prisonnier. Néanmoins, pour les écus que vous l'ayez*
45 *promis, il est content à vous donner la liberté, le
franchisement.*
   French Soldier
*Sur mes genoux je vous donne mille remerciements, et je
m'estime heureux que je suis tombé entre les mains d'un
chevalier—je pense le plus brave, vaillant, et très distingué*
50 *seigneur d'Angleterre.*
   Pistol
Expound unto me, boy.
   Boy
He gives you upon his knees a thousand thanks, and he
esteems himself happy that he hath fallen into the
hands of one (as he thinks) the most brave, valorous
55 and thrice-worthy seigneur of England.

56 *suck blood*: i.e. as a leech.

57 *Suivez . . . capitaine*: Follow the great captain.

58–9 *so full . . . heart*: such loud boasts from so great a coward (compare the proverb, 'Empty vessels make the most noise').

61–2 *roaring . . . dagger*: The Boy alludes to one of the regular stage routines of the Morality Plays, in which the long-clawed devil was beaten until he roared with the Vice's wooden dagger.

62 *pare*: trim.

63 *both hanged*: We heard of Bardolph's execution in *Act 3, Scene 7*, but we know nothing of Nym's fate.

65 *lackeys*: lads.
luggage: heavy baggage.

Pistol

As I suck blood, I will some mercy show. Follow me.

Boy

Suivez-vous le grand capitaine.

[*Exeunt* Pistol *and* French Soldier

I did never know so full a voice issue from so empty a heart. But the saying is true, the empty vessel makes the greatest sound. Bardolph and Nym had ten times more valour than this roaring devil i'th'old play, that everyone may pare his nails with a wooden dagger, and they are both hanged, and so would this be if he durst steal anything adventurously. I must stay with the lackeys with the luggage of our camp. The French might have a good prey of us if he knew of it, for there is none to guard it but boys. [*Exit*

Act 4 Scene 5

The French lords are appalled to see the overthrow of their vast army, but they resolve to return to the fray.

1 *O diable*: Oh hell.

2 *O . . . perdu*: Oh God! The day is lost, everything is lost.

3 *Mort de ma vie*: death of my life.

5 *plumes*: helmet plumes (which were the outward representation of the French pride).

SCENE 5

France: the battlefield. Enter Constable, Orléans, Bourbon, *and* Rambures

Constable

O diable!

Orléans

O Seigneur! Le jour est perdu, tout est perdu!

Bourbon

Mort de ma vie, all is confounded, all!
Reproach and everlasting shame
5 Sits mocking in our plumes.

A short alarm

6 *méchante fortune*: evil chance.

O méchante fortune! Do not run away.
    Constable
Why, all our ranks are broke.
    Bourbon

8 *perdurable*: everlasting.

O perdurable shame, let's stab ourselves.
Be these the wretches that we play'd at dice for?
    Orléans
10 Is this the king we sent to for his ransom?
    Bourbon
Shame, and eternal shame, nothing but shame!
Let us die! In once more, back again,
And he that will not follow Bourbon now
Let him go hence, and with his cap in hand

15 *pander*: bawd, pimp.
16 *slave*: peasant.
    no gentler: no better bred.
17 *contaminate*: polluted, violated.

15 Like a base pander hold the chamber door,
Whilst by a slave, no gentler than my dog,
His fairest daughter is contaminate.
    Constable

18 *spoil'd*: ruined.
    friend: befriend.
19 *on heaps*: in complete disorder.

Disorder, that hath spoil'd us, friend us now.
Let us on heaps go offer up our lives.
    Orléans
20 We are enough yet living in the field

21 *in our throngs*: by our numbers.

To smother up the English in our throngs,
If any order might be thought upon.
    Bourbon

24 *Let . . . long*: A variation of the
proverb, 'It is better to die with
honour than to live with shame'.

The devil take the order now, I'll to the throng.
Let life be short, else shame will be too long.
                      [Exeunt

Act 4 Scene 6
Over on the English side, King Henry (who believes that the French are undefeated) hears of the death of the noble Duke of York. When the enemy's trumpet calls to a renewed onslaught, the king orders his soldiers to kill their prisoners.

2 *keep . . . the field*: are winning.

3 *commends him*: sends his compliments.

8 *Larding*: enriching.
9 *Yoke-fellow*: equal partner.
honour-owing: honourable, honour-owning.
11 *all haggled over*: hacked all over.
12 *insteep'd*: soaked.

SCENE 6

France: the battlefield. Alarm. Enter the King *and his train, with prisoners*

King
Well have we done, thrice-valiant countrymen.
But all's not done, yet keep the French the field.

Enter Exeter *by another door*

Exeter
The Duke of York commends him to your majesty.
King
Lives he, good uncle? Thrice within this hour
5 I saw him down, thrice up again and fighting.
From helmet to the spur all blood he was.
Exeter
In which array, brave soldier, doth he lie
Larding the plain; and by his bloody side,
Yoke-fellow to his honour-owing wounds,
10 The noble Earl of Suffolk also lies.
Suffolk first died, and York, all haggled over,
Comes to him where in gore he lay insteep'd,

14 *yawn*: gape open.
15 *Tarry*: wait.

19 *kept*: lived.
   chivalry: knightly conduct.
20 *cheer'd him up*: gave him
   encouragement.
21 *raught*: reached out.
22 *grip*: grasp.

26 *espous'd*: engaged (i.e. as in
   marriage).
27 *testament*: will (which is usually
   sealed with wax, but here with blood).
28 *pretty and sweet*: gentle and patient.

30 *man*: masculine stoicism.
31 *all my mother*: all the tender feelings
   that I inherited from my mother.

33 *I must perforce*: I was forced to.
   compound: come to terms with.
34 *wilful*: i.e. because his eyes want to
   pour out ('issue') tears. Q and F both
   read 'mixt-full', which some editors
   emend to 'mistful'.
34s.d. *Alarm*: call to renew hostilities.

37 *kill his prisoners*: This was contrary to
   the strict military code of conduct.

And takes him by the beard, kisses the gashes
That bloodily did yawn upon his face.
15 He cries aloud 'Tarry, my cousin Suffolk.
My soul shall thine keep company to heaven.
Tarry, sweet soul, for mine, then fly abreast,
As in this glorious and well-foughten field
We kept together in our chivalry.'
20 Upon these words I came, and cheer'd him up.
He smil'd me in the face, raught me his hand,
And with a feeble grip says 'Dear my lord,
Commend my service to my sovereign.'
So did he turn, and over Suffolk's neck
25 He threw his wounded arm, and kiss'd his lips,
And so, espous'd to death, with blood he seal'd
A testament of noble-ending love.
The pretty and sweet manner of it forc'd
Those waters from me which I would have stopp'd,
30 But I had not so much of man in me,
And all my mother came into mine eyes
And gave me up to tears.
        King
                        I blame you not,
For hearing this I must perforce compound
With wilful eyes, or they will issue too.

    Alarm

35 But hark, what new alarm is this same?
The French have reinforc'd their scatter'd men.
Then every soldier kill his prisoners.
Give the word through.   [*Exeunt*

Act 4 Scene 7

Llewellyn and Gower discuss the progress of the battle. They are speaking the king's praises when Henry comes on to the stage, angered by the misconduct of the French and determined to fight to the last. But Montjoy declares the end of hostilities: the French are defeated. Montjoy humbly asks permission to rescue the dead bodies for burial, and leaves escorted by English heralds. King Henry, relaxing for a moment, plays one of his tricks on his followers.

1 *Kill . . . luggage*: The French have killed the boys and looted the luggage they were guarding.
expressly: specifically.

2 *law of arms*: code of military conduct.
arrant: utter.

7 *wherefore*: in consequence; but see Scene 6, line 37—and 'Commentary', p. xxviii.

10–44 Llewellyn embarks on a rhetorical 'comparison' in praise of Henry—although it is not easy for him to find points of contact.

10 *Monmouth*: A town on the border of England and Wales.

13 *Alexander the Great*: King of Macedonia (a country, not a town) 356–323 BC; he was conqueror of his whole known world—and has already in this play been compared with Henry V (*1*, 1, 46).

16 *reckonings*: all amount to the same thing; in rhetorical exercises a work is 'varied' by quoting synonyms.

19 *e'en*: indeed.

29 *come after*: follows the same pattern.
indifferent well: very closely.
figures: comparisons, parallels.

Scene 7

France: the battlefield. Enter Llewellyn *and* Gower

Llewellyn
Kill the poys and the luggage! 'Tis expressly against the law of arms. 'Tis as arrant a piece of knavery, mark you now, as can be offert, in your conscience now, is it not?

Gower
'Tis certain. There's not a boy left alive, and the
5 cowardly rascals that ran from the battle ha' done this slaughter. Besides, they have burned and carried away all that was in the king's tent, wherefore the king most worthily hath caused every soldier to cut his prisoner's throat. Oh, 'tis a gallant king!

Llewellyn
10 Ay, he was porn at Monmouth. Captain Gower, what call you the town's name where Alexander the Pig was born?

Gower
Alexander the Great.

Llewellyn
Why, I pray you, is not 'pig' great? The pig, or the great,
15 or the mighty, or the huge, or the magnanimous, are all one reckonings, save the phrase is a little variations.

Gower
I think Alexander the Great was born in Macedon. His father was called Phillip of Macedon, as I take it.

Llewellyn
I think it is e'en Macedon where Alexander is porn. I tell
20 you, captain, if you look in the maps of the world I warrant you sall find, in the comparisons between Macedon and Monmouth, that the situations, look you, is both alike. There is a river in Macedon, and there is also moreover a river at Monmouth. It is called Wye at
25 Monmouth, but it is out of my prains what is the name of the other river. But 'tis all one, 'tis alike as my fingers is to my fingers, and there is salmons in both. If you mark Alexander's life well, Harry of Monmouth's life is come after it indifferent well, for there is figures in all
30 things. Alexander, God knows, and you know, in his

34 *Cleitus*: Alexander's foster-brother,
   whom he killed in a drunken quarrel.

36 *his friends*: To Gower, Bardolph did
   not count as one of the king's friends.

43 *great belly doublet*: with his great
   belly stuffing out his doublet.
   gypes: gibes, taunts.

48s.d. *Alarm . . . Flourish*: The stage-
   direction starts with a drum-roll of
   battle and ends with a trumpet-call
   heralding the royal entrance.

50 *this instant*: Henry has apparently just
   learned of the attack on the luggage;
   see 'Commentary', p.xxix.
   trumpet: trumpeter.
51 *yon hill*: the hill referred to in
   4, 2, 30.
53 *void*: clear off.
55 *skirr*: skip.
56 *Enforced*: enforcèd.
   Assyrian slings: This seems to be an
   allusion to weapons described in the
   Book of Judith (Old Testament
   Apocrypha) 9:9.
59 *taste*: feel, experience.

rages and his furies and his wraths and his cholers and
his moods and his displeasures and his indignations,
and also being a little intoxicates in his prains, did in his
ales and his angers, look you, kill his best friend Cleitus.

Gower

35 Our king is not like him in that. He never killed any of
his friends.

Llewellyn

It is not well done, mark you now, to take the tales out
of my mouth ere it is made and finished. I speak but in
the figures and comparisons of it. As Alexander killed
40 his friend Cleitus, being in his ales and his cups, so also
Harry Monmouth, being in his right wits and his good
judgements, turned away the fat knight with the great
belly doublet. He was full of jests and gypes and
knaveries and mocks—I have forgot his name.

Gower

45 Sir John Falstaff.

Llewellyn

That is he. I'll tell you, there is good men porn at
Monmouth.

Gower

Here comes his majesty.

Alarm. Enter King Henry, Exeter, Gloucester,
Warwick, *and English* Herald, *and* Bourbon *with
prisoners. Flourish*

King

I was not angry since I came to France
50 Until this instant. Take a trumpet, herald.
Ride thou unto the horsemen on yon hill.
If they will fight with us, bid them come down,
Or void the field. They do offend our sight.
If they'll do neither, we will come to them,
55 And make them skirr away as swift as stones
Enforced from the old Assyrian slings.
Besides, we'll cut the throats of those we have,
And not a man of them that we shall take
Shall taste our mercy. Go and tell them so.

[*Exit English* Herald

Enter Montjoy

Exeter

60 Here comes the herald of the French, my liege.

Gloucester

His eyes are humbler than they used to be.

King

How now, what means this, herald? Know'st thou not

That I have fin'd these bones of mine for ransom?

Com'st thou again for ransom?

Montjoy

No, great king.

65 I come to thee for charitable licence,

That we may wander o'er this bloody field

To book our dead, and then to bury them,

To sort our nobles from our common men,

For many of our princes—woe the while—

70 Lie drown'd and soak'd in mercenary blood,

So do our vulgar drench their peasant limbs

In blood of princes, while the wounded steeds

Fret fetlock deep in gore, and with wild rage

Yerk out their armed heels at their dead masters,

75 Killing them twice. Oh, give us leave, great king,

To view the field in safety, and dispose

Of their dead bodies.

King

I tell thee truly, herald,

I know not if the day be ours or no,

For yet a-many of your horsemen peer

80 And gallop o'er the field.

Montjoy

The day is yours.

King

Praised be God, and not our strength, for it.

What is this castle call'd that stands hard by?

Montjoy

They call it Agincourt.

King

Then call we this the field of Agincourt,

85 Fought on the day of Crispin Crispianus.

---

63 *fin'd*: staked.

65 *charitable licence*: permission granted out of Christian charity.

67 *book*: put on record.

70 *mercenary blood*: the blood of soldiers fighting only for pay.
71 *vulgar*: common people.

73 *fetlock*: ankle.
74 *Yerk*: kick, lash.
   armed heels: armèd; iron-shod hooves.

79 *peer*: appear.

82 *hard by*: very near.

85 *Crispin Crispianus*: See 4, 3, 40 note.

86 *grandfather*: Edward III—actually the great-grandfather of Henry V.
an't please: if it please, if I may remind.
89 *pattle*: the battle of Crécy.

92–3 *Welshmen . . . grow*: No source other than Llewellyn is known for this account; the wearing of leeks on St David's day (1st March) is thought to commemorate a victory over the Saxons in AD 540.
94 *Monmouth caps*: round, brimless hats with high tapering crowns.

99 *I am Welsh*: Henry V was born in Monmouth.

111s.d. Although the text does not refer to his exit, Gower must go with the heralds: he is not on stage at line 142, when the king sends for him.

Llewellyn
Your grandfather of famous memory, an't please your majesty, and your great-uncle Edward the Plack Prince of Wales, as I have read in the chronicles, fought a most prave pattle here in France.
King
90 They did, Llewellyn.
Llewellyn
Your majesty says very true. If your majesties is remembered of it, the Welshmen did good service in a garden where leeks did grow, wearing leeks in their Monmouth caps, which your majesty know to this hour
95 is an honourable badge of the service. And I do believe your majesty takes no scorn to wear the leek upon St Tavy's day.
King
I wear it for a memorable honour,
For I am Welsh, you know, good countryman.
Llewellyn
100 All the water in Wye cannot wash your majesty's Welsh plood out of your pody, I can tell you that. God pless it and preserve it, as long as it pleases His Grace—and his majesty too.
King
Thanks, good my countryman.
Llewellyn
105 By Cheshu, I am your majesty's countryman! I care not who know it. I will confess it to all the worled. I need not to be ashamed of your majesty, praised be God, so long as your majesty is an honest man.
King
God keep me so.

Enter Williams

Our heralds go with him.
110 Bring me just notice of the numbers dead
On both our parts.
                    [*Exeunt* Montjoy, Gower, *and English* Heralds
                    Call yonder fellow hither.
Exeter
Soldier, you must come to the king.

114 *gage*: token.

117 *swaggered*: blustered.
118 *a*: he.
119 *take*: strike.

124 *keep his oath*: The swearing of oaths (and the fighting of duels) was prohibited to soldiers in camp.
125 *craven*: coward.

127 *great sort*: noble birth.
128 *from . . . degree*: of such a high social rank that he cannot answer a common soldier's challenge.
129 *a gentleman . . . devil*: A proverbial expression said that: 'The prince of darkness [the devil] is a gentleman'.
130 *Lucifer and Beelzebub*: the two devils ruling in hell.
133 *Jack Sauce*: rascal, saucebox.
133–4 *his black shoe trod*: walked with a devil's foot.

136 *sirrah*: my man (a 'downward' form of address, spoken to inferiors).

141 *literatured*: well read.

King
Soldier, why wear'st thou that glove in thy cap?
Williams
An't please your majesty, 'tis the gage of one that I
115 should fight withal, if he be alive.
King
An Englishman?
Williams
An't please your majesty, a rascal that swaggered
with me last night, who if a live and ever dare to
challenge this glove, I have sworn to take him a box
120 o'th'ear; or if I can see my glove in his cap, which he
swore as he was a soldier he would wear, if a live, I will
strike it out soundly.
King
What think you, Captain Llewellyn, is it fit this soldier
keep his oath?
Llewellyn
125 He is a craven and a villain else, an't please your majesty,
in my conscience.
King
It may be his enemy is a gentleman of great sort, quite
from the answer of his degree.
Llewellyn
Though he be as good a gentleman as the devil is, as
130 Lucifer and Beelzebub himself, it is necessary, look
your grace, that he keep his vow and his oath. If he be
perjured, see you now, his reputation is as arrant
a villain and a Jack Sauce as ever his black shoe
trod upon God's ground and His earth, in my
135 conscience, law.
King
Then keep thy vow, sirrah, when thou meet'st the fellow.
Williams
So I will, my liege, as I live.
King
Who serv'st thou under?
Williams
Under Captain Gower, my liege.
Llewellyn
140 Gower is a good captain, and is good knowledge and
literatured in the wars.

142 *Call him hither*: see note to line
    111s.d.

144 *favour*: token—the glove given as a
    pledge in *4*, 1, 200.
145 *Alençon*: Henry was in fact trying to
    rescue the Duke of York (see *4*, 6, 5).
146 *down together*: fighting hand-to-hand
    ('down' from their horses).

149 *apprehend*: arrest.
    an: if.

152 *would fain*: would very much like to.

158 *go seek him*: at line 142 Williams was
    sent to bring Gower 'hither'; this new
    command is issued to ensure that
    Llewellyn, now showing the glove,
    meets Williams (who has been
    authorized to challenge it).

163 *haply*: perhaps.
    o'th': on the.
164 *by bargain*: according to our
    agreement.

170 *touch'd with choler*: fired with anger—
    set off like a cannon.
171 *return*: pay back.
    injury: insult.

King
Call him hither to me, soldier.
    Williams
I will, my liege.   [*Exit*
    King
Here, Llewellyn, wear thou this favour for me, and stick
145 it in thy cap. [*Gives him* Williams's *glove*] When Alençon
and myself were down together I plucked this glove
from his helm. If any man challenge this, he is a friend
to Alençon and an enemy to our person. If thou
encounter any such, apprehend him, an thou dost me
150 love.
    Llewellyn
Your grace does me as great honours as can be desired
in the hearts of his subjects. I would fain see the man
that has but two legs that shall find himself aggrieffed at
this glove, that is all. But I would fain see it once, an't
155 please God of His grace, that I might see.
    King
Know'st thou Gower?
    Llewellyn
He is my dear friend, an't please you.
    King
Pray thee go seek him and bring him to my tent.
    Llewellyn
I will fetch him.   [*Exit*
    King
160 My lord of Warwick, and my brother Gloucester,
Follow Llewellyn closely at the heels.
The glove which I have given him for a favour
May haply purchase him a box o'th'ear.
It is the soldier's. I by bargain should
165 Wear it myself. Follow, good cousin Warwick.
If that the soldier strike him, as I judge
By his blunt bearing he will keep his word,
Some sudden mischief may arise of it,
For I do know Llewellyn valiant,
170 And, touch'd with choler, hot as gunpowder,
And quickly will return an injury.
Follow, and see there be no harm between them.
Go you with me, uncle of Exeter.   [*Exeunt*

Act 4 Scene 8
The king's practical joke on his soldiers
gives some light relief after the serious
business of the battle. Williams bravely
challenges the glove worn by Llewellyn, and
the king seems to enjoy his subjects'
embarrassment when the truth is revealed.
A herald brings a list of the dead and King
Henry assesses the losses on both sides.

1 *knight*: Knighting a captain on the
battlefield was a usual way of
honouring his company.

3 *apace*: very quickly.
toward: intended for.
4 *peradventure*: very likely, perhaps.

8 *arrant*: utter.
any's: any is.

10 *You villain*: Gower is offended by the
presumption shown by Williams, a
common soldier under his direct
command, in challenging a superior
officer.
11 *be forsworn*: break my oath.

13 *into plows*: easily—even, perhaps, 'in
two blows'.

15 *a lie . . . throat*: an outright lie.
I charge you: These words are spoken
to Gower, as Williams's captain.

SCENE 8

France: the English camp. Enter Gower *and* Williams

Williams
I warrant it is to knight you, captain.

Enter Llewellyn

Llewellyn
God's will and His pleasure, captain. I beseech you now,
come apace to the king. There is more good toward you,
peradventure, than is in your knowledge to dream of.
        Williams
5 [*To* Llewellyn] Sir, know you this glove?
        Llewellyn
Know the glove? I know the glove is a glove.
        Williams
I know this, and thus I challenge it.

Strikes him

        Llewellyn
God's blood, an arrant traitor as any's in the universal
world, or in France, or in England!
        Gower
10 [*To* Williams] How now, sir? You villain!
        Williams
Do you think I'll be forsworn?
        Llewellyn
Stand away, Captain Gower. I will give treason his
payment into plows, I warrant you.
        Williams
I am no traitor.
        Llewellyn
15 That's a lie in thy throat. I charge you in his majesty's
name apprehend him, he's a friend of the Duke of
Alençon's.

Enter Warwick *and* Gloucester

Warwick
How now, how now, what's the matter?
Llewellyn
My lord of Warwick, here is, praised be God for it, a
20 most contagious treason come to light, look you, as you
shall desire in a summer's day. Here is his majesty.

Enter King Henry *and* Exeter

King
How now, what's the matter?
Llewellyn
My liege, here is a villain and a traitor, that, look your
grace, has struck the glove which your majesty is take
25 out of the helmet of Alençon.
Williams
My liege, this was my glove—here is the fellow of it—
and he that I gave it to in change promised to wear it in
his cap. I promised to strike him if he did. I met this
man with my glove in his cap, and I have been as good
30 as my word.
Llewellyn
Your majesty, hear now, saving your majesty's
manhood, what an arrant, rascally, beggarly, lousy
knave it is! I hope your majesty is pear me testimony
and witness and will avouchment that this is the glove
35 of Alençon that your majesty is give me, in your
conscience now.

Gives glove to King

King
Give me thy glove, soldier. Look, here is the fellow of it.
Twas I indeed thou promised to strike,
And thou hast given me most bitter terms.
Llewellyn
40 An't please your majesty, let his neck answer for it, if
there is any martial law in the world.
King
How canst thou make me satisfaction?

20 *contagious*: pernicious.
20–1 *as . . . day*: A proverbial phrase: the broad daylight shows up the treachery.

27 *in change*: in exchange.

34 *avouchment*: give testimony.

38 *promised*: promisèd.
39 *most bitter terms*: i.e. in striking Llewellyn.

42 *satisfaction*: compensation.

Williams
All offences, my lord, come from the heart. Never came any from mine that might offend your majesty.
King
45 It was our self thou didst abuse.
Williams
Your majesty came not like yourself. You appeared to me but as a common man—witness the night, your garments, your lowliness. And what your highness suffered under that shape, I beseech you take it for your
50 own fault and not mine, for had you been as I took you for, I made no offence. Therefore I beseech your highness pardon me. [*Kneels*]
King
Here, uncle Exeter, fill this glove with crowns
And give it to this fellow. Keep it, fellow,
55 And wear it for an honour in thy cap
Till I do challenge it. Give him the crowns.
And captain, you must needs be friends with him.
Llewellyn
By this day and this light, the fellow has mettle enough in his belly. Hold, there is twelve pence for you, and I
60 pray you serve God and keep you out of prawls and prabbles and quarrels and dissentions, and I warrant you it is the better for you.
Williams
I will none of your money.
Llewellyn
It is with a good will. I can tell you it will serve you to
65 mend your shoes. Come, wherefore should you be so pashful? Your shoes is not so good. 'Tis a good silling, I warrant you, or I will change it.

Enter Herald

King
Now, herald, are the dead number'd?
Herald
Here is the number of the slaughter'd French.

Gives him paper

Notes:

46 *like yourself*: in your usual appearance.

48 *lowliness*: humble behaviour.

49 *shape*: disguise.

55 *for an honour*: i.e. the honour of having challenged the king himself.

57 *must needs*: will have to be.

58 *mettle*: courage (a pun with 'metal').

59 *twelve pence*: This was a large sum of money—about two days' pay—for a captain to give away.

63 *will none of*: don't want any of.

65 *mend your shoes*: By this stage in the fighting, all the soldiers' clothes were worn out (as King Henry told the French herald at *4, 3, 110–14*).

70 *good sort*: noble birth.

71–99 The list paraphrases that given by Holinshed.

74 *Full*: at least.
common: ordinary.

77 *bearing banners*: with coats of arms.

85 *blood and quality*: birth and breeding.

93 *lusty*: powerful.

100 *of name*: of high rank.
101 *five and twenty*: This is the number given by Holinshed—who adds, however, that the French estimated between one and six hundred English dead.
103 *without stratagem*: Shakespeare allows his Henry to ignore the tactics that won the battle of Agincourt; see 'The Sources of *Henry V*', p. 133.

King
70 What prisoners of good sort are taken, uncle?
   Exeter
   Charles, Duke of Orléans, nephew to the king;
   John, Duke of Bourbon, and Lord Boucicault.
   Of other lords and barons, knights and squires,
   Full fifteen hundred, besides common men.
   King
75 This note doth tell me of ten thousand French
   That in the field lie slain. Of princes in this number
   And nobles bearing banners, there lie dead
   One hundred twenty-six. Added to these,
   Of knights, esquires, and gallant gentlemen,
80 Eight thousand and four hundred, of the which
   Five hundred were but yesterday dubb'd knights.
   So that in these ten thousand they have lost
   There are but sixteen hundred mercenaries.
   The rest are princes, barons, lords, knights, squires,
85 And gentlemen of blood and quality.
   The names of those their nobles that lie dead:
   Charles Delabret, High Constable of France;
   Jacques of Châtillon, Admiral of France;
   The Master of the Crossbows, Lord Rambures;
90 Great Master of France, the brave Sir Guiscard
        Dauphin,
   John, Duke of Alençon; Antony, Duke of Brabant,
   The brother to the Duke of Burgundy;
   And Edward, Duke of Bar. Of lusty earls:
   Grandpré and Roussi, Fauconbridge and Foix,
95 Beaumont and Marle, Vaudemont and Lestrelles.
   Here was a royal fellowship of death.
   Where is the number of our English dead?

   Takes another paper

   Edward, the Duke of York, the Earl of Suffolk,
   Sir Richard Keighley, Davy Gam, esquire.
100 None else of name, and of all other men
   But five and twenty. O God, Thy arm was here!
   And not to us, but to Thy arm alone
   Ascribe we all. When, without stratagem,

104 *plain shock*: straight attack.
    even play: fair play.

108 *the village*: Maisoncelles, the nearest
    village to the castle of Agincourt.
109 *be it death*: let sentence of death.
    proclaimed: proclaimèd.
110 *To . . . God*: The Elizabethan saying
    was 'Give God thanks and make no
    boast'.

118 *Non nobis*: Psalm 115 in the Book of
    Common Prayer: 'Not unto us, O Lord,
    not unto us, but to Thy Name, give
    the praise.'
    Te Deum: The Canticle 'Te Deum
    Laudamus' from the Book of Common
    Prayer: 'We praise thee, O God, we
    acknowledge thee to be the Lord'.
119 *with charity*: with Christian rites.
    enclos'd in clay: buried.

But in plain shock and even play of battle,
105 Was ever known so great and little loss
On one part and on th'other? Take it, God,
For it is none but Thine.
     Exeter
                              'Tis wonderful.
     King
Come, go we in procession to the village,
And be it death proclaimed through our host
110 To boast of this, or take that praise from God,
Which is His only.
     Llewellyn
Is it not lawful, an't please your majesty, to tell how
many is killed?
     King
Yes, captain, but with this acknowledgement,
115 That God fought for us.
     Llewellyn
Yes, in my conscience, He did us great good.
     King
Do we all holy rites.
Let there be sung *Non nobis* and *Te Deum*,
The dead with charity enclos'd in clay,
120 And then to Calais, and to England then,
Where ne'er from France arriv'd more happy men.
                              [*Exeunt*

ACT 5

Act 5 Chorus
The Chorus accounts for the passing of time, summarizing the events that followed the battle of Agincourt (1415) until the present moment, when the audience is escorted to the signing of the Treaty of Troyes in 1420.

1 *Vouchsafe*: be kind enough.
3 *admit th'excuse*: make excuse for the treatment.
4 *due course*: correct sequence.
5 *huge . . . life*: real life size.
7 *Grant*: imagine.
 There seen: having seen him there.
8 *winged*: wingèd.
9 *Athwart*: across.
10 *Pales-in*: fences in.
11 *out-voice*: sound louder than.
12 *whiffler*: harbinger, fore-runner—the man who was employed to keep the way clear for a procession.
14 *solemnly*: in a formal procession.
15 *even now*: already.
16 *Blackheath*: a stretch of open ground, south of Greenwich, on the road from Dover to London.
17 *to have borne*: to arrange to have carried before him (in formal procession).
18 *bruised*: bruisèd.
21 *full . . . ostent*: all the emblems and displays of victory.
23 *quick . . . thought*: lively workings of your imagination.
25 *his brethren*: the aldermen of the City of London.
 in best sort: in civic array.
26 *antique*: ancient.
29 *lower . . . likelihood*: humbler but lovingly anticipated possibility.
30 *the general*: the Earl of Essex, whose expedition left England on 27 March 1599 for Ireland, and returned in September of that year; see 'Source, Date, and Text', p. xxxix.
 empress: Queen Elizabeth I.
31 *in good time*: fairly soon.

London: the Globe. Enter Chorus

Chorus
Vouchsafe to those that have not read the story
That I may prompt them, and of such as have,
I humbly pray them to admit th'excuse
Of time, of numbers, and due course of things
5 Which cannot in their huge and proper life
Be here presented. Now we bear the king
Toward Calais. Grant him there. There seen,
Heave him away upon your winged thoughts
Athwart the sea. Behold the English beach
10 Pales-in the flood with men, with wives, and boys,
Whose shouts and claps out-voice the deep-mouth'd
   sea,
Which, like a mighty whiffler 'fore the king,
Seems to prepare his way. So let him land,
And solemnly see him set on to London.
15 So swift a pace hath thought that even now
You may imagine him upon Blackheath,
Where that his lords desire him to have borne
His bruised helmet and his bended sword
Before him through the city. He forbids it,
20 Being free from vainness and self-glorious pride,
Giving full trophy, signal, and ostent
Quite from himself to God. But now behold,
In the quick forge and working-house of thought,
How London doth pour out her citizens!
25 The mayor and all his brethren in best sort,
Like to the senators of th'antique Rome,
With the plebeians swarming at their heels,
Go forth and fetch their conquering Caesar in—
As, by a lower but by loving likelihood
30 Were now the general of our gracious empress,
(As in good time he may) from Ireland coming,

32 *broached*: broachèd; spitted, impaled.

36–7 *As yet . . . home*: i.e. the grief of the French encourages the English king to remain in England.
38 *the emperor's coming*: The Holy Roman Emperor Sigismund came to England on 1 May 1416.
39 *order peace*: negotiate the terms of peace.
   omit: pass over.
42–3 *myself . . . past*: I myself have performed all the events of the intervening period by reminding you that the time has passed.
44 *brook abridgement*: tolerate the abbreviation.

Act 5 Scene 1
Although some time has elapsed since the battle of Agincourt (fought on 25 October), we are still on a battle-field in France. Llewellyn has been insulted by Pistol, and he is preparing to take revenge. At the end of the scene Pistol starts off on his return journey to England.

2 *St Davy's day*: 1 March, when the Welsh wear their national emblem.
5 *scald*: scabby.
   pragging: bragging, boasting; Llewellyn's p/b confusion is accentuated by his anger.
10 *could . . . contention*: could not start a fight.

Bringing rebellion broached on his sword,
How many would the peaceful city quit
To welcome him? Much more, and much more cause,
35 Did they this Harry. Now in London place him—
As yet the lamentation of the French
Invites the king of England's stay at home,
The emperor's coming in behalf of France
To order peace between them—and omit
40 All the occurrences, whatever chanc'd,
Till Harry's back return again to France.
There must we bring him, and myself have play'd
The interim, by remembering you 'tis past.
Then brook abridgement, and your eyes advance
45 After your thoughts, straight back again to France.
[*Exit*

SCENE 1

France: the English camp. Enter Llewellyn *and* Gower

Gower
Nay, that's right. But why wear you your leek today?
St Davy's day is past.
Llewellyn
There is occasions and causes why and wherefore in all things. I will tell you ass my friend, Captain Gower. The
5 rascally, scald, beggarly, lousy, pragging knave Pistol, which you and yourself and all the world know to be no petter than a fellow, look you now, of no merits, he is come to me, and prings me pread and salt yesterday, look you, and bid me eat my leek. It was in a place where
10 I could not breed no contention with him, but I will be so bold as to wear it in my cap till I see him once again, and then I will tell him a little piece of my desires.

Enter Pistol

Gower
Why, here he comes, swelling like a turkey-cock.
Llewellyn
'Tis no matter for his swellings, nor his turkey-cocks.

15 God pless you, Anchient Pistol, you scurvy, lousy knave,
God pless you.
Pistol
Ha, art thou bedlam? Dost thou thirst, base Trojan, to
have me fold up Parca's fatal web? Hence! I am
qualmish at the smell of leek.
Llewellyn
20 I peseech you heartily, scurvy, lousy knave, at my desires
and my requests and my petitions, to eat, look you, this
leek. Because, look you, you do not love it, nor your
affections and your appetites and your digestions does
not agree with it, I would desire you to eat it.
Pistol
25 Not for Cadwallader and all his goats.
Llewellyn
There is one goat for you.

Strikes him with cudgel

Will you be so good, scald knave, as eat it?
Pistol
Base Trojan, thou shalt die!
Llewellyn
You say very true, scald knave, when God's will is. I will
30 desire you to live in the meantime, and eat your
victuals. Come, there is sauce for it. [*Strikes him*] You
called me yesterday 'mountain-squire', but I will make
you today a squire of low degree. I pray you, fall to. If
you can mock a leek, you can eat a leek.
Gower
35 Enough, captain. You have astonished him.
Llewellyn
By Cheshu, I will make him eat some part of
my leek, or I will peat his pate four days. Bite, I pray you.
It is good for your green wound, and your bloody
coxcomb.
Pistol
40 Must I bite?
Llewellyn
Yes, certainly, and out of doubt and out of
question too, and ambiguities.

17 *bedlam*: crazy—an abbreviation of 'Bethlehem', the name of the London hospital for the insane.
Trojan: hooligan.
18 *fold up . . . web*: cut off your life; the Greek Parcae were the three goddesses of fate who spun, wove, and cut the threads of human life.
19 *qualmish at*: nauseated by.

25 *Cadwallader . . . goats*: Wales and all its creatures. Being a mountainous country, Wales was noted for its goats; Cadwallader was a legendary national hero.

32 *mountain-squire*: landlord of barren property.
33 *fall to*: enjoy your meal, get on with it.

35 *astonished*: stunned, dazed.

37 *pate*: skull.
38 *green*: raw, fresh.
39 *coxcomb*: fool's head.

42 *ambiguities*: uncertainties.

Pistol

By this leek, I will most horribly revenge—[*Llewellyn threatens him*] I eat and eat, I swear!

Llewellyn

45 Eat, I pray you. Will you have some more sauce to your leek? There is not enough leek to swear by.

Pistol

Quiet thy cudgel, thou dost see I eat.

Llewellyn

Much good do you, scald knave, heartily. Nay, pray you throw none away. The skin is good for your broken
50 coxcomb. When you take occasions to see leeks hereafter, I pray you mock at 'em, that is all.

Pistol

Good.

Llewellyn

Ay, leeks is good. Hold you, there is a groat to heal your pate.

Pistol

55 Me a groat?

Llewellyn

Yes, verily, and in truth you shall take it, or I have another leek in my pocket which you shall eat.

Pistol

I take thy groat in earnest of revenge.

Llewellyn

If I owe you anything, I will pay you in cudgels. You
60 shall be a woodmonger, and buy nothing of me but cudgels. God b'wi'you, and keep you, and heal your pate.   [*Exit*

Pistol

All hell shall stir for this!

Gower

Go, go, you are a counterfeit cowardly knave. Will you
65 mock at an ancient tradition began upon an honourable respect, and worn as a memorable trophy of predeceased valour, and dare not avouch in your deeds any of your words? I have seen you gleeking and galling at this gentleman twice or thrice. You thought because he
70 could not speak English in the native garb he could not therefore handle an English cudgel. You find it

48 *do you*: may it do you.
   scald knave: scab.

53 *groat*: a small coin, worth about
   fourpence.

58 *in earnest*: as a deposit on.

59 *cudgels*: blows and the weapons with
   which these are inflicted.
60 *woodmonger*: dealer in wood.
61 *God b'wi' you*: God be with you.

65–6 *honourable respect*: occasion
   worthy of honour.
66–7 *memorable . . . valour*: in memory
   of those who died bravely; see 4, 7,
   95.
67 *avouch*: support.
68 *gleeking and galling*: gibing and
   scoffing.
70 *garb*: accent.

73 *condition*: behaviour.
74 *hussy*: whore, strumpet.
75 *my Doll . . . Spital*: Doll Tearsheet was
    Falstaff's Doll in *Henry IV Part 2*.
    Pistol seems to think that he took
    possession of her (as well as the
    Hostess), but he knows she has died
    in the hospital for venereal diseases;
    see *2, 1, 66–7*.
    malady of France: i.e. venereal
    disease, syphilis.
76 *rendezvous*: refuge, last resort.
78 *bawd*: pimp.
    something . . . cutpurse: become
    something of a pickpocket.
80–1 *And . . . wars*: The 'Gallia wars'
    seems to allude to the *Gallic Wars* of
    Julius Caesar, so that this final
    couplet (which closes the scene) ends
    Pistol's career on a characteristic
    attempt at bravado.

Act 5 Scene 2
The year is 1420. In the French king's
palace at Troyes the peace treaty and the
marriage contracts are finally negotiated.
Whilst the lords arrange the political
business, Henry makes his proposal to
Katherine. The Duke of Burgundy
introduces a note of smutty innuendo, but
at last the contracts are agreed by all those
concerned.

1 *wherefor . . . met*: which is why we are
   met.
2 *our brother*: brother-king; the greeting
   is courteous.
3 *fair time of day*: good morning.
4 *princely*: royal.
5 *this royalty*: the royal family.
6 *contriv'd*: achieved.
7 *Duke of Burgundy*: The Duke of
   Burgundy was not himself a member
   of the royal family, and was therefore
   an impartial and effective mediator
   between the two kings.

12 *issue*: outcome.

13 *gracious*: noble, honourable; and
    achieved and blessed by God's grace.

otherwise, and henceforth let a Welsh correction teach
you a good English condition. Fare you well.   [*Exit*
    Pistol
Doth fortune play the hussy with me now? News have I
75 that my Doll is dead i'th'Spital of a malady of France,
and there my rendezvous is quite cut off. Old I do wax,
and from my weary limbs honour is cudgelled. Well,
bawd I'll turn, and something lean to cutpurse of quick
hand. To England will I steal, and there I'll steal.
80 And patches will I get unto these cudgell'd scars,
And swear I got them in the Gallia wars.   [*Exit*

Scene 2

*France: the French king's apartments at Troyes. Enter
at one door* King Henry, Exeter, Bedford,
Westmorland, *and other* Lords. *At another,* Queen
Isabel, *the* French King, *the* Princess Katherine *and*
Alice, *the* Duke of Burgundy, *and other French*

    King
Peace to this meeting, wherefor we are met.
Unto our brother France and to our sister,
Health and fair time of day. Joy and good wishes
To our most fair and princely cousin Katherine.
5 And as a branch and member of this royalty,
By whom this great assembly is contriv'd,
We do salute you, Duke of Burgundy.
And princes French, and peers, health to you all.
    French King
Right joyous are we to behold your face,
10 Most worthy brother England, fairly met.
So are you, princes English, every one.
    Queen
So happy be the issue, brother England,
Of this good day, and of this gracious meeting,
As we are now glad to behold your eyes,

15 Your eyes which hitherto have borne in them
   Against the French that met them in their bent
   The fatal balls of murdering basilisks.
   The venom of such looks we fairly hope
   Have lost their quality, and that this day
20 Shall change all griefs and quarrels into love.

16 *bent*: glance, line of fire.
17 *balls*: (1) eyeballs; (2) cannon balls.
   basilisks: (1) mythical beasts with lethal glances; (2) large cannon.
19 *quality*: power.

King
To cry amen to that, thus we appear.
   Queen
You English princes all, I do salute you.
   Burgundy
My duty to you both, on equal love,
   Great kings of France and England. That I have labour'd
25 With all my wits, my pains and strong endeavours,
   To bring your most imperial majesties
   Unto this bar and royal interview,
   Your mightiness on both parts best can witness.
   Since then my office hath so far prevail'd
30 That face to face and royal eye to eye
   You have congreeted. Let it not disgrace me
   If I demand before this royal view
   What rub or what impediment there is
   Why that the naked, poor, and mangled peace,
35 Dear nurse of arts, plenties, and joyful births,
   Should not in this best garden of the world,
   Our fertile France, put up her lovely visage?
   Alas, she hath from France too long been chas'd,
   And all her husbandry doth lie on heaps,
40 Corrupting in it own fertility.

23 *My duty*: my respect.
   on: in.

27 *bar*: court of justice, tribunal.
   royal interview: summit conference.
28 *parts*: sides.

31 *congreeted*: greeted each other.

33 *rub*: obstacle.

35 *nurse*: wet-nurse, nourisher.

37 *put up*: raise, show.
   visage: face.
39 *husbandry*: produce, harvest.
   on heaps: in disorder.
40 *it*: its.

41 *Her vine . . . heart*: The reference is to
   Psalm 104:15, 'wine that maketh
   glad the heart of man'.
42 *Unpruned*: unprunèd.
   even-pleach'd: evenly layered.
44 *fallow leas*: arable land left untilled.
45 *darnel . . . fumitory*: weeds that grow
   on uncultivated soil.
   rank: rampant.
46 *root*: take root.
   coulter: blade in front of the
   ploughshare.
47 *deracinate*: uproot.
48 *mead*: meadow.
   erst: formerly.
49 *burnet*: a herb said to be good for
   healing wounds.
50 *Wanting*: for lack of.
   rank: run riot.
51 *Conceives by idleness*: spreads by
   lying waste.
   teems: breeds.
52 *docks*: dock-leaves.
   kecksies: dry hollow stalks.
54 *fallows*: arable land lying fallow.
55 *Defective . . . natures*: creatures of the
   wilderness, wild by nature.
56 *houses*: households, families.
58 *sciences*: knowledge, learning.
   become: be appropriate for.
60 *meditate on blood*: think about
   nothing but bloodshed.
61 *diffus'd*: disorderly.
63 *reduce*: return.
   favour: appearance, approval.
65 *let*: hindrance.
66 *inconveniences*: injuries.

68 *you would*: if you desire.
69 *want*: lack.

71 *full accord*: total agreement.

Her vine, the merry cheerer of the heart,
Unpruned, dies. Her hedges, even-pleach'd,
Like prisoners wildly overgrown with hair
Put forth disorder'd twigs. Her fallow leas
45 The darnel, hemlock, and rank fumitory
Doth root upon, while that the coulter rusts
That should deracinate such savagery.
The even mead, that erst brought sweetly forth
The freckled cowslip, burnet, and green clover,
50 Wanting the scythe, all uncorrected, rank,
Conceives by idleness, and nothing teems
But hateful docks, rough thistles, kecksies, burrs,
Losing both beauty and utility.
And as our vineyards, fallows, meads and hedges,
55 Defective in their natures, grow to wildness,
Even so our houses, and ourselves, and children
Have lost, or do not learn for want of time
The sciences that should become our country,
But grow like savages, as soldiers will—
60 That nothing do but meditate on blood—
To swearing and stern looks, diffus'd attire,
And everything that seems unnatural.
Which to reduce into our former favour
You are assembled; and my speech entreats
65 That I may know the let why gentle peace
Should not expel these inconveniences
And bless us with her former qualities.
     King
If, Duke of Burgundy, you would the peace
Whose want gives growth to th'imperfections
70 Which you have cited, you must buy that peace
With full accord to all our just demands,

72 *tenors*: general aims.
    particular effects: specific details.
73 *inschedul'd briefly*: summarized.

77 *cursitory*: cursory.

78 *O'er-glanc'd*: looked over.
    Pleaseth: may it please.
79 *presently*: immediately.
80 *better heed*: further consideration.
81 *suddenly*: speedily.
82 *Pass . . . answer*: give you our final
    agreements.

85 *Huntington*: This is the only
    appearance of the character in this
    play. He was one of Henry's kinsmen
    and fought at Harfleur and Agincourt.
86 *free*: complete.

90 *consign*: subscribe.

93 *Happily*: with any luck.

94 *articles*: clauses, conditions.
    too nicely urg'd: too precisely argued
    about.
    stood upon: insisted upon.
96 *capital demand*: first article in the
    treaty; Henry has changed his original
    demands, and is now insisting only
    that his heirs should inherit the crown
    of France.
97 *forerank*: chief.
98 *good leave*: full permission.

Whose tenors and particular effects
You have, inschedul'd briefly, in your hands.
    Burgundy
The king hath heard them, to the which as yet
75 There is no answer made.
    King
                             Well then, the peace,
Which you before so urg'd, lies in his answer.
    French King
I have but with a cursitory eye
O'er-glanc'd the articles. Pleaseth your grace
To appoint some of your council presently
80 To sit with us once more, with better heed
To re-survey them. We will suddenly
Pass our accept and peremptory answer.
    King
Brother, we shall. Go, uncle Exeter,
And brother Bedford, and you brother Gloucester,
85 Westmorland, Huntington, go with the king,
And take with you free power to ratify,
Augment or alter as your wisdoms best
Shall see advantageable for our dignity,
Anything in or out of our demands,
90 And we'll consign thereto. Will you, fair sister,
Go with the princes or stay here with us?
    Queen
Our gracious brother, I will go with them.
Happily a woman's voice may do some good
When articles too nicely urg'd be stood on.
    King
95 Yet leave our cousin Katherine here with us.
She is our capital demand, compris'd
Within the forerank of our articles.
    Queen
She hath good leave.
       [*Exeunt all but* King Henry *and* Katherine *and* Alice
    King
                       Fair Katherine, and most fair,
Will you vouchsafe to teach a soldier terms
100 Such as will enter at a lady's ear
And plead his love-suit to her gentle heart?

Katherine

Your majesty shall mock at me. I cannot speak your
England.

King

O fair Katherine, if you will love me soundly with your
105 French heart I will be glad to hear you confess it
brokenly with your English tongue. Do you like me,
Kate?

Katherine

108 *vat*: what.

Pardonnez-moi, I cannot tell vat is 'like me'.

King

An angel is like you, Kate, and you are like an angel.

Katherine

110 *Que . . . anges*: What is he saying—
that I am like the angels?

110 [*To Alice*] *Que dit-il—que je suis semblable à les anges?*

Alice

111 *Oui . . . dit-il*: Yes indeed, begging
your grace's pardon, that is what he
said.

Oui, vraiment, sauf votre grâce, ainsi dit-il.

King

I said so, dear Katherine, and I must not blush to affirm
it.

Katherine

114–15 *O . . . tromperies*: The king
translates the words correctly.

O bon Dieu, les langues des hommes sont pleines de
115 *tromperies!*

King

What says she, fair one? That the tongues of men are full
of deceits?

Alice

118–19 *dat . . . princess*: Alice's rendering
of the princess's words perhaps
suggests something of her own
accent.
120 *the better Englishwoman*: i.e. because
she seems to prefer plain speaking.

Oui, dat de tongeus of de mans is be full of deceits, dat
is de princess.

King

120 The princess is the better Englishwoman. I'faith, Kate,
my wooing is fit for thy understanding. I am glad thou
canst speak no better English, for if thou couldst thou
wouldst find me such a plain king that thou wouldst

124 *sold my farm*: i.e. was no more than a
country farmer.
125 *mince it*: behave like an affected
courtier.
127 *wear out my suit*: have exhausted my
courtship.
128 *clap . . . bargain*: shake hands on the
deal.
129 *Sauf votre honneur*: saving your grace.

think I had sold my farm to buy my crown. I know no
125 ways to mince it in love, but directly to say 'I love you'.
Then if you urge me farther than to say 'Do you in
faith?', I wear out my suit. Give me your answer, i'faith
do, and so clap hands and a bargain. How say you, lady?

Katherine

Sauf votre honneur, me understand well.

King

130 Marry, if you would put me to verses, or to dance for
your sake, Kate, why, you undid me. For the one I have
neither words nor measure, and for the other I have no
strength in measure, yet a reasonable measure in
strength. If I could win a lady at leapfrog, or by vaulting
135 into my saddle with my armour on my back, under the
correction of bragging be it spoken I should quickly
leap into a wife. Or if I might buffet for my love or
bound my horse for her favours I could lay on like a
butcher and sit like a jackanapes, never off. But before
140 God, Kate, I cannot look greenly, nor gasp out my
eloquence, nor I have no cunning in protestation, only
downright oaths, which I never use till urged, nor never
break for urging. If thou canst love a fellow of this
temper, Kate, whose face is not worth sun-burning, that
145 never looks in his glass for love of anything he sees
there, let thine eye be thy cook. I speak to thee plain
soldier. If thou canst love me for this, take me. If not, to
say to thee that I shall die is true, but for thy love, by the
Lord, no. Yet I love thee too. And while thou livest, dear
150 Kate, take a fellow of plain and uncoined constancy, for

130 *Marry*: by [The Virgin Mary].
     put me to verses: ask me to write
     poetry.
131 *undid*: would destroy.
132 *measure*: metre.
133 *strength in measure*: sense of rhythm.
133–4 *measure in strength*: amount of
     physical strength.
134 *leapfrog*: i.e. by leaping over.
135–6 *under . . . spoken*: I can say
     without boasting.
137 *leap into*: achieve (with sexual
     innuendo).
     buffet: box, fist-fight.
138 *bound my horse*: make my horse leap.
     lay on: hit it out.
139 *like a jackanapes*: as tightly as a
     monkey.
140 *look greenly*: look lovesick.
141 *cunning*: skill, expertise.
     protestation: declarations of love.
142 *urged*: provoked.
143 *for urging*: if I am provoked.
144 *temper*: quality.
     not worth sun-burning: could not be
     made worse if it were sunburnt.
145 *glass*: looking-glass.
146 *thine eye . . . cook*: present me more
     attractively (as a cook garnishes a
     dish).
150 *uncoined*: not minted—and therefore
     not in current circulation (i.e. among
     women).

151 *perforce must*: must necessarily.
   do thee right: be faithful to you.
152 *to woo . . . places*: to court other
   women.
152–3 *of infinite tongue*: who talk
   endlessly.
153 *rhyme*: sweet-talk.
154 *reason*: argue.
155 *prater*: prattler.
   but a ballad: only like a popular song
   (and therefore unlikely to be
   remembered for very long).
156 *fall*: waste away.
157 *pate*: head of hair.
158 *wax*: grow.
161 *his*: its.

165 *ennemi*: The spelling may indicate
   Katherine's pronunciation.

173 *thee*: Henry's courtship now uses the
   'familiar' second-person singular,
   pronouns ('thou', 'thee', and 'thy'
   rather than 'you' and 'your') to
   address Katherine.
175–8 *Je . . . mienne*: Henry translates his
   promise of lines 170–1.
177 *Saint Denis*: patron saint of France.
   be my speed: assist me.

180 *move*: persuade.

182–3 *Sauf . . . parle*: With respect, the
   French that you speak is better than
   the English that I speak.

185 *truly falsely*: true in meaning, but
   false (= inaccurate) in grammar.

he perforce must do thee right, because he hath not the gift to woo in other places. For these fellows of infinite tongue that can rhyme themselves into ladies' favours, they do always reason themselves out again. What? A
155 speaker is but a prater, a rhyme is but a ballad, a good leg will fall, a straight back will stoop, a black beard will turn white, a curled pate will grow bald, a fair face will wither, a full eye will wax hollow—but a good heart, Kate, is the sun and the moon, or rather the sun and not
160 the moon, for it shines bright and never changes, but keeps his course truly. If thou would have such a one, take me. And take me, take a soldier. Take a soldier, take a king. And what sayest thou then to my love? Speak, my fair, and fairly, I pray thee.
   Katherine
165 Is it possible dat I sould love de *ennemi* of France?
   King
   No, it is not possible you should love the enemy of France, Kate. But in loving me you should love the friend of France, for I love France so well that I will not part with a village of it. I will have it all mine; and, Kate,
170 when France is mine and I am yours, then yours is France, and you are mine.
   Katherine
   I cannot tell vat is dat.
   King
   No, Kate? I will tell thee in French, which I am sure will hang upon my tongue like a new-married wife about
175 her husband's neck, hardly to be shook off. *Je quand sur le possession de France, et quand vous avez le possession de moi*—let me see, what then? Saint Denis be my speed!— *Donc vôtre est France, et vous êtes mienne.* It is as easy for me, Kate, to conquer the kingdom as to speak so much
180 more French. I shall never move thee in French, unless it be to laugh at me.
   Katherine
   Sauf votre honneur, le français que vous parlez, il est meilleur que l'anglais lequel je parle.
   King
   No, faith is't not, Kate. But thy speaking of my tongue
185 and I thine most truly falsely must needs be granted to

186 *at one*: the same.

189 *Can . . . tell*: i.e. does anyone else
   know.

191 *closet*: bedroom.

192 *dispraise*: disparage.

196 *saving faith*: faith that makes me
   believe.
197 *scambling*: struggling (i.e. in battle).

200 *compound a boy*: generate a son.

201 *Constantinople . . . beard*: become a
   crusader and fight against the Turks
   (for control of the Holy Land).
202 *flower de luce*: fleur-de-lis. The
   French heraldic lily became part of
   the royal coat of arms (indicating the
   English claim to the French throne) in
   the reign of Edward III.

204 *'tis . . . know*: after we are married you
   will learn—i.e. to beget a son.
205 *you*: Henry reverts to the formal mode
   of address when he makes a solemn
   proposal.
206 *moiety*: half-share.
207–8 *la plus . . . déesse*: the most
   beautiful Katherine in the world, and
   my dear, divine goddess. The French
   is not quite correct (*mon cher, divin*,
   should correctly be *ma chère,
   divine*,)—and this prompts the king's
   next comment.
209 *fausse French*: (1) inaccurate;
   (2) deceitful.
210 *sage demoiselle*: wise virgin.

be much at one. But Kate, dost thou understand thus much English? Canst thou love me?

Katherine
I cannot tell.

King
Can any of your neighbours tell, Kate? I'll ask them. 190 Come, I know thou lovest me, and at night when you come into your closet you'll question this gentlewoman about me, and I know, Kate, you will to her dispraise those parts in me that you love with your heart. But good Kate, mock me mercifully, the rather, gentle 195 princess, because I love thee cruelly. If ever thou beest mine, Kate, as I have a saving faith within me tells me thou shalt, I get thee with scambling, and thou must therefore needs prove a good soldier-breeder. Shall not thou and I, between Saint Denis and Saint George, 200 compound a boy, half French half English, that shall go to Constantinople and take the Turk by the beard? Shall we not? What sayest thou, my fair flower de luce?

Katherine
I do not know dat.

King
No, 'tis hereafter to know, but now to promise. Do but 205 now promise, Kate, you will endeavour for your French part of such a boy, and for my English moiety take the word of a king and a bachelor. How answer you, *la plus belle Katherine du monde, mon très cher et divin déesse?*

Katherine
Your majesty 'ave fausse French enough to deceive de 210 most *sage demoiselle* dat is *en France*.

211 *fie upon*: a plague upon.

213 *blood*: spirit.
flatter: persuade.
215 *untempering*: discouraging.
beshrew: curse.
216–17 *He . . . me*: It was believed that
the child's temperament was
influenced at the moment of
conception by the father's state of
mind.
218 *aspect*: appearance.

221 *layer-up*: preserver.
spoil upon: ravage to.

223 *wear*: possess and enjoy.

225 *Avouch*: give witness of.

230 *Plantagenet*: The name of the royal
family between 1154 and 1485.
231–2 *fellow with*: equal to.
232–3 *king of . . . fellows*: The king plays
with a proverbial saying: 'The king of
good fellows is appointed for the
queen of beggars'.
233 *broken music*: music in parts, part-
song.
235 *break*: break open, tell me.

237 *de roi mon père*: the king my father.

238 *it will . . . it shall*: it will certainly
please him, and it must please him;
Henry is well aware that this marriage
is the first article of the peace treaty.

242–5 *Laissez . . . seigneur*: Let go, my
lord, let go! On my word, I would
never want you to lower your dignity
by kissing the hand of your majesty's
unworthy servant. Excuse me, I beg
you, my most mighty lord.

King
Now fie upon my false French. By mine honour, in true
English, I love thee, Kate. By which honour I dare not
swear thou lovest me, yet my blood begins to flatter me
that thou dost, notwithstanding the poor and
215 untempering effect of my visage. Now beshrew my
father's ambition! He was thinking of civil wars when
he got me. Therefore was I created with a stubborn
outside, with an aspect of iron, that when I come to woo
ladies I fright them. But in faith, Kate, the elder I wax
220 the better I shall appear. My comfort is that old age, that
ill layer-up of beauty, can do no more spoil upon my
face. Thou hast me, if thou hast me, at the worst; and
thou shalt wear me, if thou wear me, better and better.
And therefore tell me, most fair Katherine, will you have
225 me? Put off your maiden blushes. Avouch the thoughts
of your heart with the looks of an empress. Take me by
the hand and say 'Harry of England, I am thine.'—
which word thou shalt no sooner bless mine ear withal
but I will tell thee aloud 'England is thine, Ireland is
230 thine, France is thine, and Henry Plantagenet is thine',
who, though I speak it before his face, if he be not fellow
with the best king thou shalt find the best king of good
fellows. Come, your answer in broken music, for thy
voice is music, and thy English broken. Therefore,
235 queen of all, Katherine, break thy mind to me in broken
English. Wilt thou have me?
Katherine
Dat is as it sall please de *roi mon père*.
King
Nay, it will please him well, Kate; it shall please him,
Kate.
Katherine
240 Den it sall also content me.
King
Upon that I kiss your hand, and I call you my queen.
Katherine
*Laissez, mon seigneur, laissez, laissez! Ma foi, je ne veux
point que vous abaissiez votre grandeur, en baisant la
main d'une de votre seigneurie indigne serviteur. Excusez-
245 moi, je vous supplie, mon très puissant seigneur.*

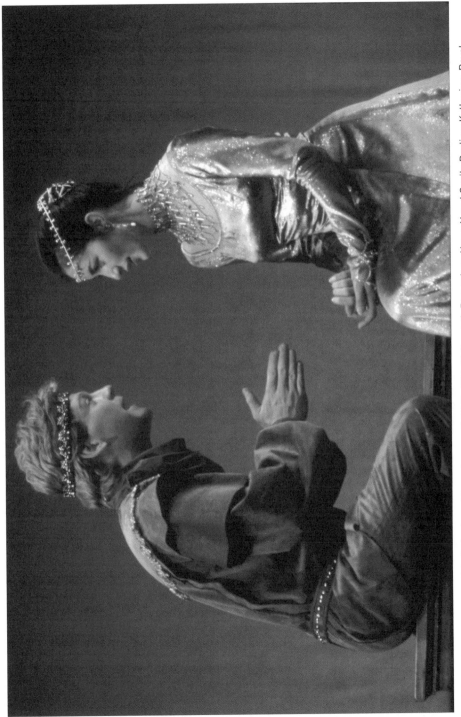

'And therefore tell me, most fair Katherine, will you have me?' (5, 2, 224–5) Kenneth Branagh as Henry V and Cecile Paoli as Katherine, Royal Shakespeare Company, 1984.

King
Then I will kiss your lips, Kate.

Katherine
Les dames et demoiselles, pour être baisées devant leurs noces, il n'est pas la coutume de France.

King
Madam, my interpreter, what says she?

Alice
250 Dat it is not be de *façon pour les* ladies of France—I cannot tell vat is *baiser en* Anglish.

King
To kiss.

Alice
Your majesty *entends* bettre *que moi.*

King
It is not a fashion for the maids in France to kiss before
255 they are married, would she say?

Alice
Oui, vraiment.

King
O Kate, nice customs curtsy to great kings. Dear Kate, you and I cannot be confined within the weak list of a country's fashion. We are the makers of manners, Kate,
260 and the liberty that follows our places stops the mouth of all find-faults, as I will do yours, for upholding the nice fashion of your country in denying me a kiss. Therefore patiently, and yielding. [*Kisses her*] You have witchcraft in your lips, Kate. There is more eloquence in
265 a sugar touch of them than in the tongues of the French Council, and they should sooner persuade Harry of England than a general petition of monarchs. Here comes your father.

Enter the French power [French King, Queen Isabel, Burgundy], *and the English lords* [Exeter, Westmorland]

Burgundy
God save your majesty. My royal cousin, teach you our
270 princess English?

247–8 *Les dames . . . France*: It is not the custom for women and maidens in France to kiss before they are married.

250 *façon . . . ladies*: fashion for the ladies.

253 *entends . . . moi*: understands better than I do.

256 *Oui, vraiment*: Yes, indeed.

257 *nice*: strict, over-precise.
curtsy: show respect for, yield to.
258 *list*: barriers (the image is from jousting).
260 *follows our places*: goes with our status.
stops the mouth: silences.
261 *as . . . yours*: as I will silence your mouth (with a kiss).

271 *would have*: want.

273 *apt*: a promising pupil.

274 *Our tongue*: the English language; see 'Background', p. 147.
condition: behaviour, temperament.
278 *Pardon . . . mirth*: excuse my unseemly laughter; Burgundy will twist the sense of Henry's words.
279–80 *conjure . . . circle*: i.e. like a magician invoking spirits.
280 *his true likeness*: as he really is; Cupid, the god of love, was usually depicted as a naked and blindfolded boy.

282 *rosed over*: blushing.
283 *deny the appearance*: refuse to admit.
285 *consign*: yield, agree to.
286 *wink*: close their eyes.
291 *wink on her*: give her the wink, indicate.
292 *know my meaning*: i.e. understand about sex.
summered: looked after.
293 *warm kept*: warm-blooded, on heat.
Bartholomew-tide: the height of summer (St Bartholomew's day is 24 August).
294–5 *endure . . . looking on*: allow themselves to be handled when before they did not wish to be seen.
296 *moral*: comparison.
ties me over: restricts me to.
297 *in the latter end*: at the end of summer; Henry also picks up the duke's innuendo.
299 *As love . . . loves*: love is blind until it really knows what it is loving.

King
I would have her learn, my fair cousin, how perfectly I love her, and that is good English.
    Burgundy
Is she not apt?
    King
Our tongue is rough, coz, and my condition is not
275 smooth, so that having neither the voice nor the heart of flattery about me I cannot so conjure up the spirit of love in her that he will appear in his true likeness.
    Burgundy
Pardon the frankness of my mirth if I answer you for that. If you would conjure in her you must make a
280 circle, if conjure up love in her in his true likeness he must appear naked and blind. Can you blame her then, being a maid yet rosed over with the virgin crimson of modesty, if she deny the appearance of a naked blind boy in her naked seeing self? It were, my lord, a hard
285 condition for a maid to consign to.
    King
Yet they do wink and yield, as love is blind and enforces.
    Burgundy
They are then excused, my lord, when they see not what they do.
    King
Then, good my lord, teach your cousin to consent
290 winking.
    Burgundy
I will wink on her to consent, my lord, if you will teach her to know my meaning; for maids well summered and warm kept are like flies at Bartholomew-tide, blind, though they have their eyes, and then they will endure
295 handling which before would not abide looking on.
    King
This moral ties me over to time, and a hot summer; and so I shall catch the fly, your cousin, in the latter end, and she must be blind too.
    Burgundy
As love is, my lord, before it loves.

300 *you may*: Henry reminds his listeners that this is a serious occasion.

303 *perspectively*: distanced and distorted, as in a 'perspective glass'.
304 *girdled*: encompassed.

307 *So please you*: if that is your will.

308–9 *so . . . on her*: as long as she brings these cities as a dowry.
309–10 *so . . . will*: thus the maiden that I wanted to have will enable me to satisfy my desire for my heir.

311 The serious business of the scene is now conducted in verse.

314 *in sequel*: following that.
315 *firm proposed natures*: proposèd; i.e. what has definitely been stipulated. The king is now asking for considerably less than he originally demanded.
316 *subscribed this*: subscribèd; signed his name in agreement.
318 *for matter of grant*: in any matter connected with grants of land or titles.
319 *name*: refer to.
    addition: title.
320–1 *Notre . . . France*: Our very dear son Henry, king of England and heir to France.
321–2 *Praeclarissimus . . . Franciae*: The Latin words should have the same meaning as the French, but Shakespeare (like the historians Hall and Holinshed) has copied 'praeclarissimus' (= most famous) for 'praecarissimus' (= most dearly beloved).

King
300 It is so. And you may, some of you, thank love for my blindness, who cannot see many a fair French city for one fair French maid that stands in my way.
French King
Yes, my lord, you see them perspectively, the cities turned into a maid, for they are all girdled with maiden
305 walls that war hath never entered.
King
Shall Kate be my wife?
French King
So please you.
King
I am content, so the maiden cities you talk of may wait on her, so the maid that stood in the way for my wish
310 shall show me the way to my will.
French King
We have consented to all terms of reason.
King
Is't so, my lords of England?
Westmorland
The king hath granted every article,
His daughter first, and then in sequel all
315 According to their firm proposed natures.
Exeter
Only he hath not yet subscribed this:
where your majesty demands that the King of France, having any occasion to write for matter of grant, shall name your highness in this form and with this addition,
320 in French: *Notre très cher fils Henri, roi d'Angleterre, héritier de France*; and thus in Latin: *Praeclarissimus filius noster Henricus, rex Angliae et heres Franciae.*
French King
Nor this I have not, brother, so denied
But your request shall make me let it pass.
King
325 I pray you then, in love and dear alliance,
Let that one article rank with the rest,
And thereupon give me your daughter.

French King
Take her, fair son, and from her blood raise up
Issue to me, that the contending kingdoms
330 Of France and England, whose very shores look pale
With envy of each other's happiness,
May cease their hatred. And this dear conjunction
Plant neighbourhood and Christian-like accord
In their sweet bosoms, that never war advance
335 His bleeding sword 'twixt England and fair France.
Lords
Amen.
King
Now welcome, Kate, and bear me witness all
That here I kiss her as my sovereign queen.

Flourish

Queen
God, the best maker of all marriages,
340 Combine your hearts in one, your realms in one.
As man and wife, being two, are one in love,
So be there 'twixt your kingdoms such a spousal
That never may ill office or fell jealousy,
Which troubles oft the bed of blessed marriage,
345 Thrust in between the paction of these kingdoms
To make divorce of their incorporate league,
That English may as French, French Englishmen,
Receive each other. God speak this 'amen'.
All
Amen.
King
350 Prepare we for our marriage; on which day,
My lord of Burgundy, we'll take your oath
And all the peers', for surety of our leagues.
Then shall I swear to Kate, and you to me,
And may our oaths well kept and prosperous be.
                              [*Sennet. Exeunt*

330 *look pale*: i.e. the white cliffs of Dover and Calais.
332 *dear conjunction*: beloved (and dearly-bought) union.
333 *neighbourhood*: neighbourliness.
334 *that*: so that.
338s.d. *Flourish*: a triumphant fanfare.
342 *spousal*: marriage.
343 *ill office*: any crooked dealing.
    fell: cruel.
345 *paction*: compact.
346 *incorporate league*: union in one body.
348 *God . . . 'amen'*: may God say 'amen [= so be it]' to this.
352 *surety of our leagues*: security of our alliance.
354s.d. *Sennet*: the trumpets signal the departure of the king and the royal procession.

Act 5 Scene 3
The Chorus has the last words, speaking a sonnet that relates Henry V to Shakespeare's earlier history plays.

1 *unable*: unequal, unskilled.

2 *bending*: bending over his writing, or taking a bow.
3 *little room*: small space.
4 *by starts*: in fits and starts.
   course: course of events, gallop.
5 *Small time*: for only a short time—Henry died in 1422 at the age of 35.
7 *best garden*: i.e. France.

9 *in infant bands*: in swaddling clothes.

11 *state*: estate.
   managing: governing.
13 *oft . . . shown*: i.e. in Shakespeare's *Henry VI* plays.
   their sake: the sake of the other plays.
14 *this*: this play.

SCENE 3

London: the Globe. Enter Chorus

Chorus
Thus far with rough and all-unable pen
Our bending author hath pursu'd the story,
In little room confining mighty men,
Mangling by starts the full course of their glory.
5 Small time, but in that small, most greatly liv'd
This star of England. Fortune made his sword
By which the world's best garden he achiev'd,
And of it left his son imperial lord.
Henry the Sixth, in infant bands crown'd king
10 Of France and England, did this king succeed,
Whose state so many had the managing
That they lost France and made his England bleed,
Which oft our stage hath shown—and for their sake,
In your fair minds let this acceptance take.   [*Exit*

The Sources of *Henry V*

The three plays presenting the career of the hero of Agincourt in Shakespeare's second tetralogy may all have been inspired initially by an anonymous play, *The Famous Victories of Henry the Fifth.* The only surviving text of this play (1598) is a debased and abbreviated version of a lost original, and it is this which Shakespeare is most likely to have known. He had recourse, also, to various semi-official histories, and especially to Holinshed's *Chronicles of England* (1587) and Hall's *Union of the Two Noble Families* (1548). A few passages from Holinshed are reprinted below to give a rough idea of Shakespeare's working, but the serious student of Shakespeare's sources should consult Kenneth Muir's book, *The Sources of Shakespeare's Plays* (London, 1977), and see the complete texts published in *The Narrative and Dramatic Sources of Shakespeare*, vol. iv, by Geoffrey Bullough (London, 1973).

Act 1, Scene 1, lines 1–19

[Early in his reign Henry summoned the high court of parliament which passed many laws, but some petitions were deferred] . . . Amongst which, one was that a bill exhibited in the parliament holden at Westminster in the eleventh year of King Henry the Fourth (which, by reason the king was then troubled with civil discord, came to none effect) might now with good deliberation be pondered and brought to some good conclusion. The effect of which supplication was: that the temporal lands devoutly given, and disordinately spent by religious and other spiritual persons, should be seized into the king's hands, sith the same might suffice to maintain, to the honour of the king and defence of the realm, fifteen earls, fifteen hundred knights, six thousand and two hundred esquires, and a hundred almshouses, for relief only of the poor, impotent, and needy persons, and the king to have clearly to his coffers twenty thousand pounds, with many other provisions and values of religious houses . . .

Act 1, Scene 2, lines 35ff.

. . . Herein did he much inveigh against the surmised and false feigned law Salic, which the Frenchmen allege ever against the kings of England in bar of their just title to the crown of France. The very words of that supposed law are these, *In terram Salicam mulieres ne succedant;* that is to say, into the Salic land let not women succeed. Which the French glossers expound to be the realm of France, and that this law was made by King Pharamound; whereas yet their own authors affirm that the land Salic is in Germany, between the rivers of Elbe and Sala; and that when Charles the Great had overcome the Saxons, he placed there certain Frenchmen, which having in disdain the dishonest manners of the German women, made a law that the females should not succeed to any inheritance within that land, which at this day is called Meissen. So that, if this be true, this law was not made for the realm of France, nor the Frenchmen possessed the land Salic till four hundred and one-and-twenty years after the death of Pharamound, the supposed maker of this Salic law; for this Pharamound deceased in the year 426, and Charles the Great subdued the Saxons, and placed the Frenchmen in those parts beyond the river of Sala, in the year 805 . . .

. . . The archbishop further alleged out of the Book of Numbers this saying: 'When a man dieth without a son, let the inheritance descend to his daughter' . . .

Act 3, Scene 7, lines 38ff.

. . . A soldier took a pix out of a church, for which he was apprehended, and the king not once removed till the box was restored and the offender strangled . . .

Act 3, Scene 7, lines 149ff.

. . . King Henry advisedly answered: Mine intent is to do as it pleaseth God, I will not seek your master at this time; but if he or his seek me, I will meet with them, God willing. If any of your nation attempt once to stop me in my journey now to Calais, at their jeopardy be it; and yet wish I not any of you so unadvised as to be the occasion that I dye your tawny ground with your red blood . . .

Act 4, Scene 3, lines 16–67

. . . It is said, that as he heard one of the host utter his wish to another thus: I would to God there were with us now, so many good soldiers as are at this hour within England! The king answered: I would not wish a man more here than I have, we are indeed in comparison to the enemies but a few, but if God of his clemency do favour us and our just cause (as I trust he will) we shall speed well enough. But let no man ascribe victory to his own strength and might, but only to God's assistance, to whom I have no doubt we shall worthily have cause to give thanks therefore. And if so be that for our offences' sake we shall be delivered into the hands of our enemies, the less number we be, the less damage shall the realm of England sustain . . .

Act 4, Scene 8, line 103

. . . He sent privily two hundred archers into a low meadow, which was near to the vanguard of his enemies, but separated with a great ditch, commanding them there to keep themselves close till they had a token to them given, to let drive at their adversaries . . . he caused stakes bound with iron sharp at both ends, of the length of five or six foot to be pitched before the archers, and of each side the footmen like a hedge, to the intent that if the barded horses ran rashly upon them, they might shortly be gored and destroyed . . . This device of fortifying an army was at this time first invented . . .

Act 5, Chorus, lines 17–22

. . . The king, like a grave and sober personage, and as one remembering from whom all victories are sent, seemed little to regard such value [of] pomp and shows as were in triumphant sort devised for his welcoming home from so prosperous a journey, insomuch that he would not suffer his helmet to be carried with him, whereby might have appeared to the people the blows and dints that were to be seen in the same . . .

What the Critics have said

Samuel Johnson   [*Act 5* Scene 1]
'The truth is, that the poet's matter failed him in the fifth act, and he was glad to fill it up with whatever he could get; and not even Shakespeare can write well without a proper subject. It is a vain endeavour for the most skilful hand to cultivate barrenness.'
The Works of Shakespeare, ed. Samuel Johnson (1765)

William Hazlitt   'Henry V it is true, was a hero, a king of England, and the conqueror of the king of France. Yet we feel little love or admiration for him. He was a hero, that is, he was ready to sacrifice his own life for the pleasure of destroying thousands of other lives: he was a king of England, but not a constitutional one, and we only like kings according to the law; lastly, he was a conqueror of the French king, and for this we dislike him less than if he had conquered the French people. How then do we like him? We like him in the play. There is he a very amiable monster, a very splendid pageant. As we like to gaze at a panther or a young lion in their cages in the Tower, and catch a pleasing horror from their glistening eyes, their velvet paws, and dreadless roar, so we take a very romantic, heroic, patriotic, and poetical delight in the boasts and feats of our younger Harry, as they appear on the stage and are confined to lines of ten syllables; where no blood follows the stroke that wounds our ears, where no harvest bends beneath horses' hoofs, no city flames, no little child is butchered, no dead men's bodies found piled on heaps and festering the next morning—in the orchestra! . . . '
from *Characters of Shakespeare's Plays* (1817)

A.W. Schlegel   'King Henry the Fifth is manifestly Shakespeare's favourite hero in English history: he paints him as endowed with every chivalrous and kingly virtue; open, sincere, affable, yet, as a sort of reminiscence of his youth, still disposed to innocent raillery, in the intervals between his perilous but glorious achievements. However, to represent on the stage his whole history subsequent to his accession to the throne, was attended with great difficulty. The conquests in France were the only distinguished event of his reign; and war is an epic rather than a dramatic object.'
from *Lectures on Dramatic Art and Literature* (1809–11)

R.G. Moulton   'In *Henry V* Shakespeare has embodied his conception of supreme heroism; and in order that the conception may be individualized, and not remain a mere poetic ideal, his choice of subject has given it the practical tinge, which of all aspects of heroism is the one most congenial to the English mind. Or rather, the hero of the poem is the English nation itself, as typified in the popular king who has caught the spirit of every class amongst his people, and concentrates them all in himself.'

from 'On Character Development in Shakespeare as illustrated by *Macbeth* and *Henry V*, in *Transactions of the New Shakespeare Society* (1880–86)

W. B. Yeats   'Shakespeare watched Henry V not indeed as he watched the greater souls in the visionary procession, but cheerfully, as one watches some handsome spirited horse, and he spoke his tale, as he spoke all tales, with tragic irony.'

from *Ideas of Good and Evil* (1903)

George Bernard Shaw   'One can hardly forgive Shakespeare quite for the worldly phase in which he tried to thrust such a Jingo hero as his Harry V down our throats. The combination of conventional propriety and brute masterfulness in his public capacity with a low-lived blackguardism in his private tastes is not a pleasant one. No doubt he is true to nature as a picture of what is by no means uncommon in English society, an able young Philistine inheriting high position and authority, which he holds on to and goes through with by keeping a tight grip on his conventional and legal advantages, but who would have been quite in his place if he had been born a gamekeeper or a farmer ... His popularity, therefore, is like that of a prizefighter: nobody feels for him as for Romeo or Hamlet.'

from *Dramatic Opinions and Essays* (1907)

J. I. M. Stewart   'Falstaff's corner of *Henry V* is extremely wonderful; the rest is a slack-water play, stirred here and there by simple patriotic feeling. For comedy now Shakespeare had so little list that he fell back upon comic Scots, Irish, and Welshmen—the recourse, I think I may say, of a professional entertainer hard pressed indeed. Moreover, that the poet of *Romeo and Juliet* should have executed the wooing of Katherine—that *ne plus ultra* of all obtuseness—must fill us with dismay until we persuade ourselves (with a school of critics romantic, no doubt) that there here glints at us from behind the mask the master's most inscrutable smile.'

from *Character and Motive in Shakespeare* (1949)

Classwork and Examinations

The works of Shakespeare are studied all over the world, and this classroom edition is being used in many different countries. Teaching methods vary from school to school, and there are many different ways of examining a student's work. Some teachers and examiners expect detailed knowledge of Shakespeare's text, others ask for imaginative involvement with his characters and their situations; and some teachers want their students to share in the theatrical experience of directing and performing a play. Most people use a variety of methods. This section of the book offers a few suggestions for approaches to *Henry V* which could be used in schools and colleges to help with students' understanding and *enjoyment* of the play.

 A Discussion of Themes and Topics
 B Character Study
 C Activities
 D Context Questions
 E Critical Appreciation
 F Essays
 G Projects

A Discussion of Themes and Topics

Talking about the play—about the issues it raises and the characters who are involved—is one of the most rewarding and pleasurable aspects of the study of Shakespeare. It is most sensible to discuss each scene as it is read, sharing impressions (and perhaps correcting misapprehensions): no two people experience any character in quite the same way, and we all have different expectations. It can be useful to compare aspects of this play with other fictions—plays, novels, films— or with modern life. A large class can divide into small groups, each with a leader, who can discuss different aspects of a single topic and then report back to the main assembly.

Suggestions

A1   What is *your* nationality? Do you have a sense of being English— or Scots, Welsh, Irish, Jewish, Muslim, African . . . ? Or are you a European? How do you determine this? Does the history of your country/nation/race mean much to you?

A2   Should rulers (either kings, presidents, or governments) have the right to confiscate private property for public use?

A3   Would you fight for your king/queen and country—or would you resist the Chorus's call to arms (Chorus 3, 22–4)?

A4   Does 'obedience to the king' (or to any individual in authority—commanding officer, employer, teacher) override personal morality?

A5   Before the battle of Agincourt, King Henry promises his followers that they will be taking part in a historic event worthy of remembrance:

> He that shall see this day and live old age
> Will yearly on the vigil feast his neighbours,
> And say 'Tomorrow is Saint Crispian.'
> Then will he strip his sleeve and show his scars,
> And say 'These wounds I had on Crispin's day.'   (4, 3, 44–8)

How would you choose to commemorate/celebrate such an occasion?

B   Character Study   Shakespeare's characters can be studied in many different ways, either from the *outside*, where the detached, critical student (or group of students) can see the function of every character within the whole scheme and pattern of the play; or from the *inside*, where the sympathetic student (like an actor) can identify with a single character and can look at the action and the other characters from his/her point of view.

Suggestions

a)   from 'outside' the character

B1   'The king has two faces': contrast the character that Henry presents in public with what you can see of his private self.

B2   Is the Archbishop of Canterbury more a man of the world than a man of God?

B3   Do King Henry's practical jokes indicate a sense of humour, or are they cruelly manipulative?

B4   Describe the characters and dramatic functions of

a)   Exeter
b)   The Dauphin
c)   Burgundy

B5 'Apart from the king himself, Llewellyn is the only character worth the name in *Henry V*—and his personality seems excessive for his part in the action.' How far would you agree with this statement?

    b) from 'inside' the character

B6 Record King Henry's thoughts in a 'stream-of-consciousness' narrative as he listens to the archbishop's exposition of the 'law Salic that they have in France'.

B7 As one of the French ambassadors, describe your feelings before, during, and after the audience with the English king.

B8 'Confessions of a Conspirator': write—or ghost-write—the musings of one of the three traitors (Cambridge, Scroop, and Gray) before the execution day.

B9 Deliver the *Act 3* soliloquy of the Boy, formerly Falstaff's page, in a modern idiom.

B10 'The Seige and Surrender of Harfleur': the Governor writes an official communiqué, or a personal letter, to explain (or excuse) his action.

B11 Emulate Bourbon's rhapsodies on his horse: expatiate on the wonders of your own favourite—bike/car/footballer/pop star/pet animal.

B12 In the character of Pistol (and remembering Gower's observations in *Act 3*, Scene 7)

    a) write a letter to the Hostess describing your conquest of the Frenchman
    b) devise a ballad recounting your exploits in the 'Gallia wars'.

B13 Tell the story of the night before Agincourt from the viewpoint of one of the soldiers, Bates, Court, or Williams.

B14 Send despatches from the Agincourt front to the French king, giving the account of Bourbon, Constable, or Grandpré describing

    a) the English army before the battle
    b) the state of the French morale
    c) the defeat of the French forces.

B15 'A winning match!' As the Princess Katherine, confide your thoughts and emotions to your diary before and after your encounter with the English king.

B16 'She told me everything': a series of letters/articles for the press from Alice, describing the progress of the courtship you have witnessed and the part you played in it.

B17 The French royal family speak their minds at last! The story of the engagement which has been fought, won (or lost), and arranged between Henry V and the French princess told in the character of

    a) The French king
    b) The French queen
    c) The Dauphin

C   Activities   These can involve two or more students, preferably working *away from* the desk or study-table. They can help students to develop a sense of drama and the dramatic aspects of Shakespeare's play—which, after all, was written to be spoken and performed, not read silently.

C1   Traditionally the Chorus's speeches have always been delivered by a single actor; in the workshop divide them between several speakers or groups of speakers. Which method do you prefer?

C2   Hold a 'round-table' discussion after the declaration of war on France, making sure that all interests are represented (the churchman, the politician, the agnostic philosopher, the 'statutory' woman, the member of an ethnic minority).

C3   In small groups, devise models—like the archbishop's beehive— for the harmonious state; present these for criticism to the entire class.

C4   War has been declared, and men are enlisting for service: interview as many as you can for radio/TV news, questioning them about their motives, hopes, and fears.

C5   The usual war correspondents are gathered at Harfleur, preparing copy for their different media. Write their reports, bearing in mind the intended audience (radio/TV) or readership (newspapers). Compare the different 'angles'.

C6   Find out all you can about Prince Hal and Falstaff, then devise a scene in which the Hostess, Pistol, Nym, Bardolph, and the Boy (Falstaff's page) reminisce about 'the good old days'.

C7   Improvise a scene between four officers about the proper conduct of a modern-day battle, using stereotypes such as Gower, Llewellyn, Jamy, and Macmorris. These could be representatives of different ethnic groups, or even of different services (army, navy, air-force ...).

C8 The Battle of Agincourt—a television documentary looking back on the first (or any subsequent) anniversary. How the land lay: the deployment of troops on either side. 'I was there': interviews with survivors. 'The right and wrong': debate by politicians. 'Oh God, Thy hand was here': discussion by churchmen.

C9 Organize media coverage at Troyes—what are the hopes and fears of the two parties? Interview Burgundy before and after the summit conference and peace talks.

D Context Questions

Questions like these, which are sometimes used in written examinations, can also be helpful as a class revision quiz, testing knowledge of the play and some understanding of its words.

D1 Fortune is —'s foe, and frowns on him. For he hath stolen a pax, and hanged must a be.

  (i)   Who is the person speaking, and to whom ('—') does he refer?
  (ii) To whom is he speaking, and what does he want?
  (iii) What do we know of '—'; what happens to him?

D2 The offer likes not, and the nimble gunner
With linstock now the devilish cannon touches.
        Alarm, and chambers go off.

  (i)   Who delivers these lines, and to whom are they addressed?
  (ii) What was the 'offer', and to whom was it made?
  (iii) What follows the *Alarm*?

D3 Alas, she hath from France too long been chas'd,
And all her husbandry doth lie on heaps,
Corrupting in it own fertility.

  (i)   Who is 'she' and why has she been chased from France?
  (ii) Who has been chasing her?
  (iii) Who is the speaker of these lines, and what is the occasion?

E Critical Appreciation

These present passages from the play and ask questions about them. Some examination boards allow candidates to take their copies of the play into the examination room, asking them to re-read specified sections of the play (such as the ones printed here) and answer questions on them.

E1   *Act 3*: Chorus, lines 1–17

Thus with imagin'd wing our swift scene flies
In motion of no less celerity
Than that of thought. Suppose that you have seen,
The well-appointed king at Hampton Pier
Embark his royalty, and his brave fleet   5
With silken streamers the young Phoebus feigning.
Play with your fancies, and in them behold
Upon the hempen tackle ship-boys climbing.
Hear the shrill whistle, which doth order give
To sounds confus'd. Behold the threaden sails,   10
Borne with the invisible and creeping wind,
Draw the huge bottoms through the furrow'd sea,
Breasting the lofty surge. O do but think
You stand upon the rivage, and behold
A city on th'inconstant billows dancing,   15
For so appears this fleet majestical,
Holding due course to Harfleur. Follow, follow!

Use this speech to discuss the functions of the Chorus in *Henry V*. Why is imagination especially important in this play?

E2   *Act 4, Scene 4*, lines 58–67: the Boy speaks—

I did never know so full a voice issue from so empty a heart. But the saying is true, the empty vessel makes the greatest sound. Bardolph and Nym had ten times more valour than this roaring devil i'th'old play, that everyone may pare his nails with a wooden dagger, and they are both hanged, and so would this be if he durst steal anything adventurously. I must stay with the lackeys with the luggage of our camp. The French might have a good prey of us if he knew of it, for there is none to guard it but boys.

Comment on the dramatic importance of this speech.

E3   *Act 3, Scene 1*, lines 15–34: King Henry speaks—

Now set the teeth and stretch the nostril wide,
Hold hard the breath, and bend up every spirit
To his full height. On, on, you noble English,
Whose blood is fet from fathers of war-proof,
Fathers that like so many Alexanders   5
Have in these parts from morn till even fought,
And sheath'd their swords for lack of argument.
Dishonour not your mothers. Now attest
That those whom you call'd fathers did beget you.

Be copy now to men of grosser blood, 10
And teach them how to war. And you, good yeomen,
Whose limbs were made in England, show us here
The mettle of your pasture. Let us swear
That you are worth your breeding, which I doubt not,
For there is none of you so mean and base 15
That hath not noble lustre in your eyes.
I see you stand like greyhounds in the slips,
Straining upon the start. The game's afoot.
Follow your spirit, and upon this charge
Cry 'God for Harry, England, and Saint George!' 20

Describe King Henry's attempts to appeal to the common soldiers. Do you think he is successful?

F   Essays   These will usually give you a specific topic to discuss, or perhaps a question that must be answered, in writing, *with a reasoned argument*. They *never* want you to tell the story of the play—so don't! Your examiner—or teacher—has read the play, and does not need to be reminded of it. Relevant quotations will always help you to make your points more strongly.

F1   'There is only a single character in *Henry V*': how far is this true?

F2   'As well as writing history, Shakespeare also criticizes its events and heroes.' Discuss.

F3   'For King Henry, doing the will of God is only an excuse for doing what is politically expedient.' Do you agree?

F4   *Henry V* is a very long play, and often needs to be cut for stage (or film) presentation; what scenes or episodes would you be willing to discard?

F5   Give your reasons for disputing or sharing these comments made by previous critics (see p.137).

- a) 'The truth is, that the poet's matter failed him in the fifth act' (Dr Johnson).
- b) Shakespeare 'spoke his tale, as he spoke all his tales, with tragic irony' (W. B. Yeats).
- c) 'His [Henry's] popularity . . . is like that of a prizefighter: nobody feels for him as for Romeo or Hamlet' (G. B. Shaw).
- d) 'the hero of the poem is the English nation itself' (R. G. Moulton).

F6   Arbitrate between Hazlitt—'We feel little love or admiration for [Henry V]'—and Schlegel—'King Henry the Fifth is manifestly Shakespeare's favourite hero'.

G   Projects   In some schools, students are asked to do more 'free-ranging' work, which takes them outside the text—but which should always be relevant to the play. Such Projects may demand skills other than reading and writing: design and artwork, for instance, may be involved. Sometimes a 'portfolio' of work is assembled over a considerable period of time; and this can be presented to the examiner as part of the student's work for assessment.

The availability of resources will, obviously, do much to determine the nature of the projects; but this is something that only the local teachers will understand. However, there is always help to be found in libraries, museums, and art galleries.

G1   The historical Agincourt.

G2   Shakespeare's sources for *Henry V*.

G3   Great performances by great actors.

G4   Weaponry at the time of *Henry V*.

G5   'The wooden O': Shakespeare's theatre.

G6   Research the origins and symbolism of
'. . . the balm, the sceptre, and the ball,
The sword, the mace, the crown imperial . . .'— 4, 1, 248–9.

Background

England c. 1599

When Shakespeare was writing *Henry V*, most people believed that the sun went round the earth. They were taught that this was a divinely ordered scheme of things, and that—in England—God had instituted a Church and ordained a Monarchy for the right government of the land and the populace.

'The past is a foreign country; they do things differently there.'

L. P. Hartley

Government For most of Shakespeare's life, the reigning monarch of England was Queen Elizabeth I. With her counsellors and ministers, she governed the nation (population about five million) from London, although not more than half a million people inhabited the capital city. In the rest of the country, law and order were maintained by the land-owners and enforced by their deputies. The average man had no vote—and his wife had no rights at all.

Religion At this time, England was a Christian country. All children were baptized, soon after they were born, into the Church of England; they were taught the essentials of the Christian faith, and instructed in their duty to God and to humankind. Marriages were performed, and funerals conducted, only by the licensed clergy and in accordance with the Church's rites and ceremonies. Attendance at divine service was compulsory; absences (without good—medical—reason) could be punished by fines. By such means, the authorities were able to keep some check on the populace—recording births, marriages, and deaths; being alert to any religious nonconformity, which could be politically dangerous; and ensuring a minimum of orthodox instruction through the official 'Homilies' which were regularly preached from the pulpits of all parish churches throughout the realm. Following Henry VIII's break away from the Church of Rome, all people in England were able to hear the church services *in their own language*. The Book of Common Prayer was used in every church, and an English translation of the Bible was read aloud in public. Shakespeare would be most familiar with the Bishops' Bible, which he would hear in church, and with the Geneva version of the New Testament which, being a small volume, he probably possessed. The Christian religion had never been so well taught before!

Education   School education reinforced the Church's teaching. From the age of four, boys might attend the 'petty school' (French '*petite école*') to learn the rudiments of reading and writing along with a few prayers; some schools also included work with numbers. At the age of seven, the boy was ready for the grammar school (if his father was willing and able to pay the fees).

A thorough grounding in Latin grammar was followed by translation work and the study of Roman authors, paying attention as much to style as to matter. The arts of fine writing were thus inculcated from early youth. A very few students proceeded to university; these were either clever scholarship boys, or else the sons of noblemen. Girls stayed at home, and acquired domestic and social skills—cooking, sewing, perhaps even music. The lucky ones might learn to read and write.

Language   At the start of the sixteenth century the English had a very poor opinion of their own language: there was little serious writing in English, and hardly any literature. Latin was the language of international scholarship, and Englishmen admired the eloquence of the Romans. They made many translations, and in this way they extended the resources of their own language, increasing its vocabulary and stretching its grammatical structures. French, Italian, and Spanish works were also translated, and for the first time there were English versions of the Bible. By the end of the century, English was a language to be proud of: it was rich in synonyms, capable of infinite variety and subtlety, and ready for all kinds of word-play—especially the *puns*, for which Shakespeare's English is renowned.

Drama   The great art-form of the Elizabethan and Jacobean age was its drama. The Elizabethans inherited a tradition of play-acting from the Middle Ages, and they reinforced this by reading and translating the Roman playwrights. At the beginning of the sixteenth century plays were performed by groups of actors, all-male companies (boys acted the female roles) who travelled from town to town, setting up their stages in open places (such as inn-yards) or, with the permission of the owner, in the hall of some noble house. The touring companies continued, in the provinces, into the seventeenth century; but in London, in 1576, a new building was erected for the performance of plays. This was the Theatre, the first purpose-built playhouse in England. Other playhouses followed, including Shakespeare's own theatre, The Globe, which was completed in 1599. The English drama reached new heights of eloquence.

There were those who disapproved, of course. The theatres, which brought large crowds together, could encourage the spread of disease— and dangerous ideas. During the summer, when the plague was at its worst, the playhouses were closed. A constant censorship was imposed, more or less severe at different times. The Puritan faction tried to close down the theatres, but—partly because there was royal favour for the drama, and partly because the buildings were outside the city limits— they did not succeed until 1642.

Theatre   From contemporary comments and sketches—most particularly a drawing by a Dutch visitor, Johannes de Witt—it is possible to form some idea of the typical Elizabethan playhouse for which most of Shakespeare's plays were written. Hexagonal in shape, it had three roofed galleries encircling an open courtyard. The plain, high stage projected into the yard, where it was surrounded by the audience of standing 'groundlings'. At the back were two doors for the actors' entrances and exits, and between these doors was a curtained 'discovery space' (sometimes called an 'inner stage'). Above this was a balcony, used as a musicians' gallery or for the performance of scenes 'above', and projecting over the stage was a thatched roof, supported on two pillars, forming a canopy—which seems to have been painted with the sun, moon, and stars for the 'heavens'.

Underneath was space (concealed by curtaining) which could be used by characters ascending and descending through a trap-door in the stage. Costumes and properties were kept backstage, in the 'tiring house'. The actors dressed lavishly, often wearing the secondhand clothes bestowed by rich patrons. Stage properties were important for defining a location, but the dramatist's own words were needed to explain the time of day, since all performances took place in the early afternoon.

A replica of Shakespeare's own theatre, the Globe, has been built in London, and stands in Southwark, almost exactly on the Bankside site of the original.

Shakespeare's Globe, Southwark, London, England. Photograph by Richard Kalina.

Suggested Further Reading

Critical Works: Bate, J., 'Hal and the Regent', *Shakespeare Survey 38* (1985), 69–76.

Brown, J.R., *Shakespeare's Plays in Performance*, (London, 1966; Penguin Shakespeare Library, Harmondsworth, 1969).

Edwards, P., *Threshold of a Nation*, (Cambridge, 1979).

Gurr, A., '*Henry V* and the Bees' Commonwealth', *Shakespeare Survey 30* (1977), 61–72.

Holderness, G. (ed.), *Shakespeare's History Plays: 'Richard II' to 'Henry V'*, New Casebooks, (Macmillan, 1992).

Jones, G.P., '*Henry V*: The Chorus and the Audience', *Shakespeare Survey 31* (1978), 93–104.

Quinn, Michael (ed.), *Shakespeare: 'Henry V'*, Casebook Series, (Macmillan, 1969).

Reese, M.M., *The Cease of Majesty*, (London, 1961).

Ribner, Irving, *The English History Play in the Age of Shakespeare*, (Princeton, NJ, 1957; rev. edn., 1965).

Tillyard, E.M.W., *Shakespeare's History Plays*, (London, 1944).

Traversi, Derek A., *Shakespeare: From 'Richard II' to 'Henry V'*, (Stanford, Calif., 1957).

Sources: Muir, Kenneth, *The Sources of Shakespeare's Plays* (London, 1977).

Additional Background Reading: Bate, Jonathan, *The Genius of Shakespeare* (Picador [Macmillan], 1997).

Blake, N.F., *Shakespeare's Language: an Introduction* (London, 1983).

Gibson, Rex, *Shakespeare's Language* (Cambridge, 1997).

Honan, Park, *Shakespeare: A Life* (Oxford, 1998).

Langley, Andrew, *Shakespeare's Theatre* (Oxford, 1999).

Muir, K., and Schoenbaum, S., *A New Companion to Shakespeare Studies* (Cambridge, 1971).

Thomson, Peter, *Shakespeare's Theatre* (London, 1983).

William Shakespeare, 1564–1616

Elizabeth I was Queen of England when Shakespeare was born in 1564. He was the son of a tradesman who made and sold gloves in the small town of Stratford-upon-Avon, and he was educated at the grammar school in that town. Shakespeare did not go to university when he left school, but worked, perhaps, in his father's business. When he was eighteen he married Anne Hathaway, who became the mother of his daughter, Susanna, in 1583, and of twins in 1585.

There is nothing exciting, or even unusual, in this story; and from 1585 until 1592 there are no documents that can tell us anything at all about Shakespeare. But we have learned that in 1592 he was known in London, and that he had become both an actor and a playwright.

We do not know when Shakespeare wrote his first play, and indeed we are not sure of the order in which he wrote his works. If you look on page 155 at the list of his writings and their approximate dates, you will see how he started by writing plays on subjects taken from the history of England. No doubt this was partly because he was always an intensely patriotic man—but he was also a very shrewd business-man. He could see that the theatre audiences enjoyed being shown their own history, and it was certain that he would make a profit from this kind of drama.

The plays in the next group are mainly comedies, with romantic love-stories of young people who fall in love with one another, and at the end of the play marry and live happily ever after.

At the end of the sixteenth century the happiness disappears, and Shakespeare's plays become melancholy, bitter, and tragic. This change may have been caused by some sadness in the writer's life (one of his twins died in 1596). Shakespeare, however, was not the only writer whose works at this time were very serious. The whole of England was facing a crisis. Queen Elizabeth I was growing old. She was greatly loved, and the people were sad to think she must soon die; they were also afraid, for the Queen had never married, and so there was no child to succeed her.

When James I came to the throne in 1603, Shakespeare continued to write serious drama—the great tragedies and the plays based on Roman history (such as *Julius Caesar*) for which he is most famous. Finally, before he retired from the theatre, he wrote another set of comedies. These all have the same theme: they tell of happiness which is lost, and then found again.

Shakespeare returned from London to Stratford, his home town. He was rich and successful, and he owned one of the biggest houses in the town. He died in 1616.

Shakespeare also wrote two long poems, and a collection of sonnets. The sonnets describe two love-affairs, but we do not know who the lovers were. Although there are many public documents concerned with his career as a writer and a business-man, Shakespeare has hidden his personal life from us. A nineteenth-century poet, Matthew Arnold, addressed Shakespeare in a poem, and wrote 'We ask and ask—Thou smilest, and art still'.

There is not even a trustworthy portrait of the world's greatest dramatist.

Approximate order of composition of Shakespeare's works

Period	Comedies	History plays	Tragedies	Poems
I	Comedy of Errors	Henry VI, part 1	Titus Andronicus	
	Taming of the Shrew	Henry VI, part 2		
1594	Two Gentlemen of Verona	Henry VI, part 3		Venus and Adonis
		Richard III		Rape of Lucrece
	Love's Labour's Lost	King John		
II	Midsummer Night's Dream	Richard II	Romeo and Juliet	Sonnets
	Merchant of Venice	Henry IV, part 1		
1599	Merry Wives of Windsor	Henry IV, part 2		
	Much Ado About Nothing			
	As You Like It	Henry V		
III	Twelfth Night		Julius Caesar	
	Troilus and Cressida		Hamlet	
1608	Measure for Measure		Othello	
	All's Well That Ends Well		Timon of Athens	
			King Lear	
			Macbeth	
			Antony and Cleopatra	
			Coriolanus	
IV	Pericles			
	Cymbeline			
1613	The Winter's Tale	Henry VIII		
	The Tempest			